Managing Complex Change in School

Leading and managing change in schools is a complex topic. In this timely book the authors take the reader through a journey of how to lead and manage multidimensional change in order to create engaged learners, teachers, leaders and managers. They provide a readable and straightforward account of a major, high-profile innovation in one school and draw from it key lessons for leaders and managers of change in schools.

Managing Complex Change in School synthesizes a wealth of literature and research on managing change, and shows how the emerging field of complexity theory can inform the effective management of multidimensional change.

Arising from an in-depth, mixed methods evaluation of the key school, this book is practice-focused and is an invaluable companion for practitioners handling positive change in schools.

Alejandro Salcedo Garcia is Principal of Escola São Paulo, Macau.

Keith Morrison is Director of Institutional Development at Macau University of Science and Technology.

Ah Chung Tsoi is Dean of the Faculty of Information Technology at Macau University of Science and Technology.

Jinming He was Research Assistant at Macau University of Science and Technology.

Managing Complex Change in School

Engaging pedagogy, technology, learning and leadership

Alejandro Salcedo Garcia,
Keith Morrison, Ah Chung
Tsoi and Jinming He

LONDON AND NEW YORK

First published 2014
by Routledge
2 Park Square, Milton Park, Abingdon, Oxfordshire OX14 4RN

and by Routledge
711 Third Avenue, New York, NY 10017

First issued in paperback 2016

Routledge is an imprint of the Taylor & Francis Group, an informa business

© 2014 Alejandro Salcedo Garcia, Keith Morrison, Ah Chung Tsoi and Jinming He

The right of Alejandro Salcedo Garcia, Keith Morrison, Ah Chung Tsoi and Jinming He to be identified as authors of this work has been asserted by them in accordance with sections 77 and 78 of the Copyright, Designs and Patents Act 1988.

All rights reserved. No part of this book may be reprinted or reproduced or utilised in any form or by any electronic, mechanical or other means, now known or hereafter invented, including photocopying and recording, or in any information storage or retrieval system, without permission in writing from the publishers.

Trademark notice: Product or corporate names may be trademarks or registered trademarks, and are used only for identification and explanation without intent to infringe.

British Library Cataloguing in Publication Data
A catalogue record for this book is available from the British Library

Library of Congress Cataloging in Publication Data
Garcia, Alejandro Salcedo.
  Managing complex change in school : engaging pedagogy, technology, learning and leadership / Alejandro Salcedo Garcia, Keith Morrison, Ah Chung Tsoi and Jinming He
  pages cm
  Includes bibliographical references and index.
  1. Educational leadership. 2. Educational change. 3. Educational technology. I. Morrison, Keith (Keith R. B.) II. Title.
  LB2801.A1G37 2014
  371.2–dc23
                              2013050549

ISBN 13: 978-0-415-78732-1 (pbk)
ISBN 13: 978-0-415-72878-2 (hbk)

Typeset in Galliard
by Sunrise Setting Ltd, Paignton, UK

Contents

List of illustrations vi
Acknowledgements vii
Introduction viii

1 Multidimensional innovation 1

2 ICT and learning: challenge and change 35

3 The background to the case study 64

4 Starting points and rules of engagement 97

5 The project in mid-stream: the U-curve of innovation 136

6 Turning the corner 169

7 Postscript and lessons learned 210

References 234
Index 251

Illustrations

Figures

1.1	'Stages of Concern' from Hall and Hord (1987, 2011)	20
1.2	'Levels of Use' from Hall and Hord (1987, 2011)	21
3.1	The 'true' experiment	88
5.1	The U-Curve of innovation	136
5.2	The web of engaged learning	139
5.3	Levels of use and degrees of commitment to an area of an innovation	146
6.1	Managing complex change	194
6.2	Nodes and connectors in the innovation	197
6.3	Levels of organizational culture	205
6.4	Stake's countenance model of evaluation	207
7.1	Facilitating and inhibiting factors in the school innovation	225
7.2	Embedded and non embedded pilot innovations	231
7.3	Key features in managing multidimensional innovation for engaged learning	232

Tables

1.1	Dimensions of innovation	6
1.2	Leadership qualities and behaviours for innovation	12
2.1	Different uses of ICT in education	36
2.2	Four features of learning from Vygotsky	39
2.3	Old and new pedagogies with ICT	57
2.4	Key features of e-learning and collaborative learning	58
2.5	Traditional and newer teacher roles with ICT	58
3.1	Students in schools in Macau, 2008	66
3.2	Schools and students in Macau, 2011–12	67
3.3	Students and teachers in Macau Catholic schools in 1999	69
3.4	Data collection, instrumentation and reporting	91
6.1	Statistically significant regressions onto dependent variables	190

Acknowledgements

The authors are very grateful to all members of Escola São Paulo for their willingness to allow the evaluators into the school and classrooms, and their immense cooperation with, and commitment to, this evaluation and innovation project. Without their cooperation it would not have happened. The authors and the school are grateful to the Macau Special Administrative Region government's Direcção dos Serviços de Estatística e Juventude (DSEJ) for its visible and significant support for this project in a multitude of ways. The authors and the school are grateful to the following for their support for the project in the school: Automated, DyKnow, H3C, HP, Lenovo, Mediasite, Microsoft and Macau University of Science and Technology. The authors are grateful to the following for permission to reproduce material in this volume: Connecticut State Department of Education, for Figure 6.1; the European Union for the report of the European Students' Union, funded by the European Commission, by Attard, A., Lorio, E. D., Geven, K. and Santa, R. (2010) *Student-Centered Learning SCL Toolkit*; the European Union for details of the Scientific and Policy Report by the Joint Research Centre of the European Commission by Kampylis, P. G., Bocconi, S. and Punie, Y. (2012) *Towards a Mapping Framework of ICT-enabled Innovation for Learning*; the National College for School Leadership, UK, for material from Leithwood, K., Day, C., Sammons, P., Harris, A. and Hopkins, D. (2006) *Seven Strong Claims about Successful School Leadership*.

Introduction

All change is multidimensional. We delude ourselves if we think otherwise. Effective innovation involves engaging and engaged learners, teachers, leaders and managers. Engaging technologies has a triple meaning: the need to engage – 'take on board' – the exponential rise of information and communication technologies (ICT) in education; the need to recognize that effective innovators must not only be learners but engaged learners and users; and the need to engage the key participants in an innovation as agents in, rather than recipients of, the innovation. Change changes people and people change change.

This book arose from an in-depth, mixed methods evaluation of a high-profile, multidimensional innovation in a school in Macau, China. As part of its 'Empowering Students for an Open School' (ESOS) project, the school introduced a major innovation across the entire school, starting with a one-year pilot project. This book reports on that pilot project and on the earliest stages of the subsequent introduction of the innovation across the school. The innovation was multidimensional; the school moved towards according a key role for advanced and extensive ICT in the curriculum, pedagogy and assessment. Radical changes in teaching and learning moved from didacticism and transmission teaching to collaborative, interactive, engaged and real-world learning. This was part of a programme to raise student motivation, attitude, interest, achievement and performance, and to promote student-centred learning. Part of the innovation was aimed at promoting higher-order thinking and problem-solving in students, changing assessment strategies to provide formative feedback to students and teachers, developing extended parental involvement and communication, and enhancing staff development for sustainable change. A feature of the innovation was its aim to improve the under-achieving, poorly motivated and low-performing students, and to ensure that learning was facilitated through advanced instructional technologies. The school had already been restructuring its curriculum and the innovation reported here took that into new territory.

Unlike many other parts of the world, this change was not externally mandated; it was an internal decision, taken by a self-organizing school in the decentralized schooling system in Macau in which very great autonomy over decision-making resided in the school. The study here reports the successes, setbacks and challenges facing the case-study school as the innovation was implemented, and how the lessons from that school can transfer into wider innovation theory and practice.

This is not only the story of one school. Rather, the book takes the school as a 'critical case study', as its experiences of leading and managing innovation embodied many features of complex innovation experienced very sharply and clearly, and the book provides lessons for managing complex change in schools more widely. Many lessons are drawn for leading and managing change and innovation, and these are rooted in a wealth of relevant literature throughout the book. As we move towards increased ICT in schools, their potential to facilitate wholesale pedagogical improvements in engaged learning is massive. ICT on its own will not automatically bring change; rather it is the teachers, the pedagogy, the culture of the school and a host of other factors addressed in this book, which have to change and develop. We engage pedagogy, technology, learning and leadership to bring about engaged students, engaged teachers, engaged parents, engaged learning, engaged leadership and engaged innovation.

The book is arranged into seven chapters. Chapter 1 sets the foundations of innovation and change in relevant research and literature. Chapter 2 roots the innovation in a literature review of ICT and engaged learning. Chapter 3 sets the context of the school within the territory of Macau, China, which has a schooling system in which schools have very great autonomy. The chapter also sets out the key features of the innovation in the school and the needs which it was designed to meet.

The evaluation of the innovation project was staged over one year, with three rounds of reporting. Chapter 4 reports on the key issues at the very early stage of the innovation implementation, and it draws lessons to be learned for leading and managing change more widely. Chapter 5 reports the innovation six months on, and comments on the 'U-curve' of implementation and the lessons that can be drawn from it for leading and managing change. Chapter 6 presents the results of the evaluation of the innovation conducted at the end of the school year, and it, too, draws lessons for leading and managing change and innovation at later stages of implementation. Chapter 7 pulls together the many strands entwined in leading and managing multidimensional innovation and change in schools, and it makes many recommendations for ensuring effective innovation. Throughout the book the significance of tenacious leadership is affirmed repeatedly, together with an enduring emphasis on the people dimension of change. People make change, but not always in the ways initially intended, and attention to the 'people factor' is central to making change work.

A major feature of this book is its concern with multidimensional change, how it can be planned, what its dimensions are, how it can be led and managed effectively and what considerations have to be addressed at different stages and levels of the innovation. The book is replete with practical advice. To complement the practical lessons from this book, not only are its messages reinforced by in-depth literature reviews, but the book argues for the powerful role of complexity theory, not only in understanding multidimensional change, but also in assisting the concrete practice of implementing change in schools. Innovation is multidimensional, nonlinear, people-focused and a creative, human act. This argues against mechanistic, predictable models of change and, indeed, the thrust of the book is to show how the success of the innovation reported was predicated on the people involved and how the change evolved as the people evolved. Successful innovation has to engage all parties; they are all engaged learners.

This book presents an honest and unsparing portrait of change and innovation in one school, and what lessons can be learned from it that apply more widely to schools and institutions undertaking multidimensional innovation. One of our authors – Dr Alejandro Salcedo Garcia – is the school Principal; the other three authors were the evaluators of the innovation of the one-year pilot project in the school, and all three came from Macau University of Science and Technology. Professor Keith Morrison is Director of Institutional Development and of the university's Educational Development Centre; Professor Ah Chung Tsoi is Dean of the Faculty of Information Technology; and Mr Jinming He is a PhD student in the university, acting as the Research Assistant to the evaluation project. We earnestly hope that this volume will inspire, inform and support effective, engaged innovation and change in schools.

1 Multidimensional innovation

Writing in 2010, Crossan and Apaydin identify over 10,000 papers on innovation over the previous 27 years, and a Google Scholar search of the word 'innovation' yields over half a million 'hits' since 2009, whilst a similar search of the words 'education innovation' yields just under half a million in the same period. It is not so much that 'change is in the air' as change is in our DNA. We can almost touch it and taste it. We are fascinated by it and seem unable to live without it.

Stand on any street corner for more than a few minutes or go to any restaurant, bus, train or public place and what will you see? Young people – the 'heads down generation' – almost obsessively fixated on their mobile electronic devices, largely oblivious to the people around them. Walk down any street and you will see young people talking apparently to themselves like persons possessed until you see their mobile phone or electronic gadgetry. Whilst parents spend hours in front of the television, their children are glued to their computer or smartphone screens, searching, endlessly searching.

For many, the virtual world has become less than a virtuous world, both connecting people and disconnecting them from each other, with friends rather than real friendships, a world that sacrifices deep concentration to superficially connected hyperlinks and unrequited searching on the internet. It is a world of the immediate, instantly gratified, non-linear, eternal present rather than the in-depth pursuit of rich, thought-through knowledge and reflection.

Why, then, have yet another publication to feed our gluttony and putative human frailty? Education, or, rather, schooling, for so long the dormouse of innovation, over the last two decades has been slowly stirring and waking up to the power of information and communication technologies (ICT) not only to revolutionalize access to knowledge, but to change pedagogy beyond recognition. The coupling of ICT with a basic human need for social contact awakens an inestimable power to further collaborative, active, interactive and engaged learning. Look at the massive impact of online gaming that keeps youngsters hooked to their screens into the early hours of the morning, then contrast this to the tame, anaesthetized world of the school textbook and the schoolroom; it is not difficult to see the gulf that obtains between the possible and the actual in learning.

The coupling of ICT, engaging pedagogies and engaged learning can be realized through effective change and innovation in schools. Nothing new in that, you may say, until you walk into many classrooms and witness a sight that would be familiar to Victorian educators: rows or grouped tables of children listening to the pearls of wisdom from the teacher and then repeating them. As Hattie (2009: 252) remarks, an important question is why we are so reluctant to change, even in the face of evidence that our strongly held beliefs do not work. His answer is that change disturbs our comfort zone and we may have a range of reasons for, and interests in, preserving the status quo. Indeed, he reports that the nearer an innovation comes to the core of schooling, the less likely it is to influence learning and teaching (2009: 253), leading to disengaged learners. He comments that teaching methods have barely changed over the last 200 years (2009: 254).

Moving away from ineffective traditionalism, *really* moving away from this, constitutes a *massive* innovation in schools. And why do we use such a potentially inflammatory adjective? Because moving away from this means little short of re-culturing schools, and, as any elementary foray into organizational culture will tell you, culture is deep-seated and difficult to change. Not only that, but innovation is inherently multidimensional and that brings its own challenges for leadership and management.

This book tells a story. It reports an innovation in a single school that catches the tide of fundamental change in school brought about by the ICT revolution, addressing several areas of innovation in a single project: a key role for advanced and extensive ICT; wholesale pedagogic change from didacticism and transmission teaching to collaborative, interactive, engaged, student-centred and real-world learning; improved student motivation and positive attitudes; improved student achievement and performance; an increase in the amount and quality of higher-order thinking and problem-solving in students; a changing assessment from solely assessment of learning to assessment for and as learning, with inbuilt feedback; improvement of parental involvement and communication; reframing and restructuring of the curriculum and resources; and capacity building for sustainable change.

In the school instanced here are the essential ingredients of a multidimensional innovation, from leadership to ICT, reculturation, staff development, student empowerment, engaged learning, radical pedagogical change, resourcing, assessment, change management and a legion of other concerns. The innovation in this school exemplifies key issues in managing and leading change and innovation; it is a critical case study in that it is the vehicle for major elements of school development caught sharply in a single example. Before we turn to the substance of the innovation itself, we identify the roots of innovation theory and practice in both traditional and emergent literatures and perspectives.

Defining innovation

'Innovation' is a catch-all word that defies simple definition. Crossan and Apaydin's (2010: 1155) major systematic review of over 1,000 rigorously selected papers on innovation, listed in the Social Science Citation Index, define it as the creation, adoption assimilation and use of something new, being both a process and an outcome. Innovation is a deliberate, intentional intervention to bring in something different for current practice, and Hattie (2009: 251) indicates that teachers' effects on student outcomes 'increase markedly' from their normal effect sizes (defined later) of 0.15 to 0.35 when there is an innovation, particularly regarding teaching as a form of experimentation.

Kampylis *et al.* (2012) provide a wide range of definitions of innovation, arguing that whilst 'there is no generally accepted single definition of innovation', there is a common core of key components:

- Innovation is an *intentional activity*; the innovator does something (deliberately) rather than merely thinking about it.
- This intentional activity is designed to address unsolved problems and *benefit* in some way the *innovator(s)* (individual, team or organization) through the development or improvement of a product, process or method.
- Innovation – whether incremental, radical or disruptive – is about *change* and implies a degree of *novelty*; innovative product, process or method must be novel to some extent, at least for the innovator(s).
- Innovation is a *dynamic* and *unpredictable social process* involving *complex interactions* between various actors who 'actively seek to learn from one another'.
- Innovation occurs in a specific social, economic, technological, organizational and cultural *context* that influences its development, diffusion and use (Kampylis *et al.* 2012: 6).

Innovation is a dynamic, new or original idea, process or practice that is intentionally designed to solve problems, meet needs and *improve* lives and which involves often complex social and interpersonal change (e.g. Cairney 2000: 18; Robinson 2001: 25; Smits 2002: 866; Renzulli 2003: 79; the OECD and Eurostat 2005: 46; Mulgan *et al.* 2006).

This chapter sets out key theoretical foundations underpinning the leadership and management of multidimensional innovation in schools, which, in turn, underpin the mixed methods research into innovation in one school which is reported in the later chapters. The chapter argues that innovation is inherently multidimensional, and it indicates what some of the dimensions might be. Given these many dimensions, the chapter argues that a central place is accorded to effective leadership, and it indicates key features of leadership here. One of the several tasks of leadership of innovation, it is argued,

4 Multidimensional innovation

is to establish the environment and conditions for innovation to flourish, and the chapter indicates what those conditions might include. A key feature here is the need to attend to participants' concerns in an innovation, and how these might change over the duration of the innovation, including facilitation and resistance. In setting all of these issues into an appropriate theoretical context, the chapter argues that complexity theory, as a theory of change, evolution, innovation and adaptation, offers a fitting theoretical underpinning to the book and to the innovation itself, and the chapter sets out the view of complexity theory that is espoused here. The chapter, therefore, has several key areas of focus, including:

- Dimensions of innovation;
- The importance of leadership;
- Organizational health and climate;
- Attending to staff concerns (people and innovation, including 'Stages of Concern' and 'Levels of Use' of an innovation, resistance and facilitation (Hall and Hord 2011));
- Complexity theory and innovation.

Within each of these sections are contained overviews of key sub-elements of innovation (e.g. multiple definitions of 'dimensions'; facilitation and resistance; setting the conditions and environment for innovation; communication; person-centred innovation; feedback and support, etc.).

Dimensions of innovation

Innovation is intrinsically multidimensional. Cooper (1998) identifies three major dimensions: *product-process*, *radical-incremental*, and *technological-administrative*, but these are only starting points. For example, in ICT alone Law *et al.* (2011) identified six dimensions of innovation: learning objectives; roles of teachers and learners; new pedagogies; how ICT is used; connectedness (with outside parties); and multiplicity of learning outcomes. Kampylis *et al.* (2012: 9–10) suggest that innovations, particularly in respect of ICT and learning, hinge on:

1. The *nature of innovation* (incremental, radical, disruptive).
2. The *implementation phase* (pilot, scale, mainstreaming).
3. The *access level* (local, regional/national, cross-border).
4. The *impact area* (process, service, organization).
5. The *target* (single actors, multiple actors, a wide range of actors).

In this book, the term 'dimension' has been deliberately chosen as it has many meanings; for example: (a) an element, its length, size, weight, mass, height and width; (b) the overall size or magnitude of something (we say that a large person has ample dimensions); (c) an aspect, property or feature of something (e.g. the cultural dimension of schooling); (d) the number of measures or minimum number of coordinates needed to identify something or a point on that something (e.g. length, breadth, height) and time (the fourth dimension), so an object or event may exist in four dimensions, which includes space-time; (e) that which can be measured (the original meaning of dimension); (f) that which includes as yet unknown matters – the 'fifth dimension'. We do not wish to stretch the term needlessly, but to use it to make the point that any innovation has many different contributing elements and, therefore, needs many measures or means to understand it.

If we take the notion of 'dimension' in a scientific sense, then we can suggest that there are five dimensions: height, width, depth, time and the fifth dimension of the unknown. This is a neat metaphor for the dimensions of the innovation reported in the subsequent chapters. In respect of 'height', one can suggest that the innovation reported touched all levels of the school hierarchy of participants, from school principal to senior managers, middle managers, teachers, parents and students (not necessarily in that order of hierarchy). In respect of 'width', the reported innovation had a very wide scope, encompassing many different elements of the school, curriculum, pedagogy and assessment. In respect of 'depth', it was clear that this innovation did not deal in superficial, technical matters, but in terms of deep-seated, fundamental changes of values and practices. In respect of 'time', the innovation had a significant time dimension, as it was designed to unfold over time rather than being a 'once and for all' event. In respect of the fifth dimension – the 'unknown' – the reported innovation encountered many unanticipated challenges in its opening stages, and these had a bearing on what transpired as the innovation rolled out over time; the fifth dimension is significant, and it reminds innovators that they do not have perfect knowledge, and to expect the unexpected – as Egan (1993) indicates, change involves identifying our blind spots, developing new perspectives, establishing priorities and searching for points of leverage.

Innovation has many dimensions; it is an input, a process and an outcome. It includes people, groups, practices, resources, leadership, learning, knowledge and expertise, managing, organizing, development, implementation, performance, behaviour, values, levels of analysis, stages, decision making and many others. 'Dimensions' implies not only elements but also the magnitude of each element and, indeed, of the innovation itself (e.g. radical to incremental, fundamental to superficial) (Crossan and Apaydin 2010). Despite the diversity of meanings and elements of 'innovation', these authors identify 10 major dimensions of innovation:

- *Innovation as process*: including (1) the driver of innovation; (2) source (invention and adoption); (3) locus (organization and its networks); (4) level (leadership, managerial, individual, group, entire organization); (5) direction (top-down, bottom-up).

6 Multidimensional innovation

- *Innovation as an outcome*: including, (6) the form (service, product, process); (7) magnitude (incremental, radical); (8) referent (organization, clients, area of work); (9) type (administrative, technical); (10) nature (explicit, tacit).

They set these in the context of 'determinants of innovation': leadership (individual and group levels), managerial (organizational level) and processes (process level), and they identify several contributing dimensions of innovation (see Table 1.1). This book takes as its subject a case study of an innovation in one school, and Table 1.1 interprets the 'determinants of innovation' in relation to the school in question.

Table 1.1 Dimensions of innovation

Dimension of innovation	Dimension of innovation as addressed in the school in question
Size/magnitude	Very great
Incremental	Commencing with a pilot in three classes in two subjects, and extending to most subjects and all classes from Primary 4 upwards. Levels of Use over time (Hall and Hord 1987, 2011): 'non-use' to 'orientation' to 'preparation' to 'mechanical use' to 'routine use' to 'refinement' to 'integration' to 'renewal'
Radical	Fundamental changes to pedagogy, ICT usage, teacher collaboration, engaged learning
Scale	Large
Process	Many and substantial, led by the school principal. collaborative learning, active and interactive pedagogy, ICT usage, pedagogy, student motivation, student attitude and interest, engaged learning, parental involvement, teacher collaboration, assessment, curriculum
Product	Multiple changes in many areas: collaborative learning, active and interactive pedagogy, ICT usage, pedagogy, student motivation, student attitude and interest, engaged learning, parental involvement, teacher collaboration, assessment, curriculum
Administrative	Securing copyright agreements for resources
Technical	ICT tablets for all students, extended ICT hardware and software across the school
Generation of innovation (from idea generation initiation to design to implementation to diffusion to adoption to routinization)	Stages of Concern (Hall *et al.* 1986), from 'awareness' to 'informational' to 'personal' to 'management' to 'consequential'(impact on students) to 'collaboration' to refocusing'
Timing	One school year for the pilot, thereafter taking up to three years for the entire project to unfold

(Continued)

Table 1.1 (Continued)

Dimension of innovation	Dimension of innovation as addressed in the school in question
Participants and participant groups (internal)	School principal and senior officers, head of subjects, subject teachers, ICT manager and staff, curriculum manager, students, school counselling staff
Participants and participant groups (external)	Parents, local school authority (governmental), hardware and software designers and providers (Automated, DyKnow, H3C, HP, Lenovo, Mediasite and Microsoft)
Organizational structure and sub-units	Curriculum and subject teams, section heads units/ (primary and secondary), ICT department, senior management team
Primary characteristics (non-perception-based)	Logged data on ICT usage, students' assessment results
Secondary characteristics (perception-based)	Self-reporting for questionnaires, diaries of the innovation, interviews with many different individuals and groups
Networks (internal)	Subject teachers, pilot group teachers, senior and middle school managers and subject heads
Networks (external)	Parents
Environmental determinants	Local school authority (governmental), hardware and software designers and providers (Automated, DyKnow, H3C, HP, Lenovo, Mediasite and Microsoft)
Organizational climate/health	Remaining to be convinced of efficacy of innovation in practice, work overload, limited experience of innovation, positive interpersonal relations, limited collaborative practice, hierarchical organizational structure, accepting of senior managers' instructions
Organizational culture	Hierarchical with staff working as instructed. Little voicing out of concerns by junior staff. Strong leadership. Experience of innovation in some areas of the school, e.g. student empowerment and curriculum development, and strongly directed by the principal and senior staff. Some self-protection and avoidance of conflict present. Cooperative staff who carry out instructions
Organizational determinants: functional specialization, differentiation, professionalism, formalization, centralization, managerial attitude and tenure, technical knowledge, administrative intensity, resources,	Clear organizational hierarchy in the school: principal, deputy principals, section heads (kindergarten, primary, secondary), curriculum and ICT heads, subject heads (in primary and secondary sections), teachers. Very limited knowledge or experience of the innovatory practices, ICT aspects. Initial total unfamiliarity with the hardware and software involved. Vertical communication more extended than horizontal communication. Very limited staff development in the field of the innovation

(Continued)

8 Multidimensional innovation

Table 1.1 (Continued)

Dimension of innovation	Dimension of innovation as addressed in the school in question
internal and external communications, vertical differentiation, structural complexity, organizational structure and size, strategy, organizational learning	
Learning orientation	Staff willing to learn, but feel that their learning and preparation time is far too telescoped
Management and leadership	Strong, committed leadership, with a strong senior team of relevant managers
Resources: financial, human, material, temporal, locational, administrative	Financial resources in place for the purchase of equipment at the start of the pilot, and subsequently in place for the entire project. School wired for wi-fi internet, server hardware and software in place. Few teachers involved in the pilot, and immense pressure on them. Considerable time taken to secure copyright arrangements from publishers. Insufficient initial development time for resources or hardware and software familiarization. Insufficient staff expertise in the innovation elements before being put into practice with students
Individual factors (personality, motivation, cognitive ability, work characteristics, mood)	A range of perceptions and reactions from staff and parents; from enthusiasm to acceptance to hesitancy to resistance
Group characteristics (team structure, climate, processes, leadership style, member characteristics)	Very determined leadership from the principal in spite of setbacks. The principal's word stands. Staff are members of several teams simultaneously (e.g. senior management, curriculum, subjects, sections)
Internal sources (professional background of managers, workforce skills and expertise, internal efforts)	Managers deployed very well according to their strengths. Subject teachers inexperienced in the requirements of the innovation, and having to launch the project from a very limited starting basis of knowledge, experience and expertise
Embodied and embedded social practices and tacit knowledge	Practices to date had been traditional didacticism, with teachers working largely in isolation, with a very open attitude to parental involvement in the school
Innovation capability	Strong in the school principal, treasurer and ICT manager, limited in scope elsewhere but willingness to try

The list is formidable. Multidimensional innovation is often only as strong as its weakest link; there are many elements and dimensions of a complex reality when an innovation is set in motion, e.g. people, tasks, contents and elements of change, purposes and processes of change. Given the multidimensional nature of innovation, the much-vaunted call for 'alignment' of all parties, elements and dimensions in undertaking an innovation is perhaps wishful thinking. How can an innovation or innovators move forward with an intervention given the enormous potential for misalignment, disagreement or discord between and within the elements and agents? Each party will have its own opinions, views and perspectives on the innovation and on whether, where or how much it is or is not working. These will differ; one person's view of success is another's person's view of failure.

Nor is the problem of alignment simply one of gathering sufficient evidence in evidence-based judgments of effective innovation. In the intervention reported in this book, 'hard' data were reported (e.g. students' marks and automatically logged data on computer usage) along with 'soft' data (self-reported views and opinions from many parties), but in some instances and on some topics these did not agree with, even contradicted, each other, both within and between different elements. Which data are 'telling the truth'? Is there a single truth or are there multiple truths? Whose opinion carries most weight? (For example, in the innovation reported here, students' questionnaire data indicated that their motivation towards learning had not really increased as a consequence of the innovation, whereas all the other parties indicated that the students' motivation had improved markedly.) In a multidimensional innovation it is to be expected that there will be differences of view across and between, even within, different participants on different dimensions.

The multidimensionality of an innovation also renders it difficult to know how, where and when to start. When is the right time to start an innovation; which parts of an innovation; what counts as the starting moment? What precedes the implementation in practice, and when can the preceding preparations and innovation really be said to start? The adoption of an innovation may be a piecemeal process over time, the initiation of which may be unclear but the consequence of an accumulated set of factors over time. Whilst the research, development and dissemination/diffusion (RD&D) model of innovation may be suitable for a specific product – a new car, a new washing machine – it may be less applicable to an educational innovation. Even an apparently clearly discernible educational innovation (e.g. No Child Left Behind) does not arise out of the blue; it has antecedents and is located in a specific spatial-socio-cultural-temporal context and conditions. All of this points to the need to survey and understand the initial conditions and contexts in which innovations are planned and implemented (a situational analysis or needs analysis). From here the innovation can see which parts of the proposal constitute a genuine innovation, which parts can be grafted onto existing conditions, which parts might present more challenges to existing practices, which parts require more or less staff and student development, and so on. The point here is that an innovation may not simply be something that is entirely new, to be dropped on an institution. Rather, some parts strike a chord with existing practices and some do not. Finding out which parts are consonant with existing practices and which parts are not is an important starting point, and it is essential to plan a concrete intervention to start the innovation (Hall and Hord 2011).

Let us say that we have done this initial mapping of the relationship between the existing and the proposed situation/intervention, how then do we proceed? Many years ago, the psycholinguist Frank Smith (1971) indicated that the way to learn to read was by reading, and the way to learn to write was by writing (Smith 1982). By analogy, the same applies to innovation: we learn how to innovate by innovating. For example, Fullan (2013) notes that leadership is learned by doing it, and that innovating effectively is learned by innovating (Fullan 2013). Innovation is essentially a practical activity that can be planned and prepared for, but which seldom unfolds as planned. We learn on-the-job, rehearing the adage of 'learning by doing'. Innovation is about what happens rather than what is planned. Innovation is the start, the process, the medium and the outcome of innovation.

For example, I may plan to install extended ICT usage for changing pedagogies in a school, from traditional lectures to problem-based learning, so I might provide hardware, software, copious resources, staff development and extensive training in the new hardware and software. But then the innovation might founder, because insufficient attention has been given to addressing real needs such as student and staff expertise, motivation and incentives, or the leadership of the school may exercise insufficient leadership in providing support to staff when parents complain, or the innovation might be so removed from existing practice that the new ICT is used simply as a more attractive presentational device which underlines transmission teaching, i.e. lectures with added entertainment. In this instance, what I had planned to be the innovation and what actually turned out to be the innovation are different, and, whilst I might have been able to anticipate some of this, in all likelihood I could not have predicted everything. However, that should not prevent the innovation from getting under way; rather it is to alert innovators to the point that different dimensions of an innovation will have different outcomes. To start an intervention is like putting a toe in the water, but before we put our toe into the water we have already changed into our swimming costume, gauged the ambient temperature, assessed our swimming ability, taken safety precautions, and so on. In other words, the first step in the implementation is not the first step of the innovation. Then we take our first step and respond to what happens – so it is with innovation. Innovation is an iterative, proactive and reactive process within an overall plan.

Further, deep change takes time, and innovation can be a tricky customer, as it is deceptive. We may believe that an innovation is straightforward and comparatively superficial, i.e. its dimensions of size and scale are limited, only to find that it unleashes deep-seated issues, and that, actually, the innovation strikes to the heart of an organization. As Dalin *et al.* (1993) remarked, changing the culture of the school is the real agenda, though it may not present itself as such.

For example, I may wish to increase collaborative learning in classrooms, allotting time in several lessons for this to complement a more didactic stage of the lesson, apparently a simple matter of devising a group activity to process learning. However, it becomes unclear if and how this will be monitored and assessed, what the teacher's role will be in this and what the intended learning outcomes are. It becomes not only difficult to assess each group member's contribution but the teacher loses some of his or her traditional control of the learning and the students. Further, to bring in this apparently innocuous and straightforward innovation requires different kinds of learning, different kinds of resources, and teachers planning together and coordinating what they do in order to ensure necessary consistency, and this challenges their widely claimed and widely respected autonomy. So, what starts out as a matter of a few minutes of change in each classroom goes to the heart of several aspects of the culture of the school – its values, ways of working and, significantly, the people in the school. The magnitude and scale of the dimensionality is a key element to be assessed, and, as Senge (1990) remarks, we eat an elephant one bite at a time.

Whilst an innovation will be inherently multidimensional, the trick is to ensure that, as far as possible, not only do the different dimensions 'hang together' and mutually support each other (tightly coupled), but that they are sufficiently independent (loosely coupled) such that if one part of the innovation is not working as fully as another part, then the entire innovation does not founder.

The importance of leadership

Fullan (2001) remarks that behaviour changes before beliefs and values, so we change behaviour first and handle the values changes as they arise; these two dimensions (behaviour and values) may be discordant with each other, and handling them is a key task for effective leadership. Leadership is a crucial ingredient of effective innovation. An OECD report on school leadership (Pont *et al.* 2011: 5) noted that it has a significant role in improving school outcomes in respect of influencing teachers' motivations and capabilities together with the school climate and context text. Hence leaders have to address personal factors, capacity building, conditions for innovation to flourish and organizational climate (discussed below).

With regard to leadership, Crossan and Apaydin (2010: 1170 ff.) identify a vast range of leadership qualities and behaviours, together with the senior management contributions to innovation, which are summarized in Table 1.2.

Effective leadership is a significant contributor to effective innovation, if not the pre-eminent contributor. Holmes *et al.* (2013) indicate that the effective leadership of change requires 'alignment of administrative processes with learning outcomes' (2013: 271), problem-solving skills, and interpersonal skills with the building of trust, including emotional and social intelligence, all within the cultivation of a positive culture and person- and social-centred climate in the school. Indeed, the authors comment on the need for a clear, consistent and continuous focus on teaching and learning by school leaders.

Table 1.2 Leadership qualities and behaviours for innovation

Overall	Individual level	Group level (top management team)
Technical and professional expertise	Tolerance of ambiguity	Education and age
Creative skills	Self-confidence	Tenure
Ability to process complex information	Openness to experience	Diversity of background and experience
Ability to take multiple roles	Unconventionality	External ties
Provide support and guidance	Originality	Exploiting existing resources
Create conditions for innovation implementation	Rule governd-ness	Exploration of new opportunities
Motivation for innovation	Authoritarianism	Development of new resources and capabilities
Ability to identify environmental threats and opportunities	Independence	Management lever (1): mission/goals/structures
Provision for experimentation	Proactivity	Management lever (2): structures and systems
Toleration of failure	Intrinsic (versus extrinsic) attribution bias	Management lever (3): resource allocation
Supporting learning and employee development	Determination to succeed	Management lever (4): organizational learning and knowledge management
Acceptance of group diversity	Personal initiative	Management lever (5): culture
Ability in knowledge management and ideas generation	Managerial tolerance of change	
Linkages with higher education institutions		
Formal information gathering		

Hattie (2009: 85) notes that the influence on student outcomes from the leader's goal setting and team building have effect sizes of 0.22 and 0.30, respectively. (Effect size is a measure of the difference that an intervention or factor can make on a dependent variable. Many effect sizes are calculated using the statistic Cohen's *d*, which scales effect sizes thus: 0 to 0.20 = weak effect; 0.21 to 0.50 = modest effect; 0.51 to 1.00 = moderate effect; >1.00 = strong effect.) Leithwood and Seashore-Louis (2011) and Leithwood *et al.* (2010) indicate that leaders' influence on student outcomes can account for up to 43 per cent of the variation in student achievement, echoing Leithwood and Riehl (2003: 4) in their observation that leadership's effects are second only in the size of their effects on student learning to those of the curriculum and teachers' instructional practices. Leithwood *et al.* (2004) report that the leadership practices which are most closely associated with enhanced levels of student outcomes are:

- *Setting direction*: for every learner to reach his/her potential, inserting this into the whole school curriculum together with high consistency and high expectations.
- *Managing teaching and learning*: ensuring a high degree of consistency and innovation in teaching practices together with personalized learning for every student.
- *Developing people*: to promote schools as professional learning communities for teachers and enable students to become active learners.
- *Developing the organization*: developing evidence-based practice in schools, with collaborative networks and communities.

Leithwood *et al.* (2006) make 'seven strong claims about successful school leadership':

1. School leadership is second only to classroom teaching as an influence on pupil learning.
2. Almost all successful leaders draw on the same repertoire of basic leadership practices.
3. The ways in which leaders apply these basic leadership practices – not the practices themselves – demonstrate responsiveness to, rather than dictation by, the contexts in which they work.
4. School leaders improve teaching and learning indirectly and most powerfully through their influence on staff motivation, commitment and working conditions.
5. School leadership has a greater influence on schools and students when it is widely distributed.
6. Some patterns of distribution are more effective than others.
7. A small handful of personal traits explains a high proportion of the variation in leadership effectiveness (Leithwood *et al.* 2006: 3).

Robinson *et al.* (2009) indicate that having leaders who promote and participate in teachers' professional development can have twice as much effect size, or even more, on student outcomes in comparison to any other aspect of leadership (see also Leithwood *et al.* 2006; Day *et al.* 2010; Hallinger 2010; Pont *et al.* 2011). The case is overwhelming for leadership to have a major impact on innovations and on student outcomes. Hall and Hord (2011: 130) report significant gains in maths and writing with leaders who adopted 'initiator' and 'manager' change facilitation roles in comparison to leaders who adopted 'responder' (reactive) styles of leadership. Indeed, in the school in question in this book, the principal was both a change initiator and change manager, 'developing, articulating and communicating a shared vision of the intended change', 'planning and providing resources', 'investing in professional learning', 'checking on progress', 'providing continuous assessment' and 'creating a context supportive of change' (Hall and Hord 2011: 148–51).

Organizational health and climate

Whilst effective leadership is a critical element of innovation, the task of leaders is not only to lead an innovation but also to set the *conditions* and *environment* for leadership (Morrison 2002a). Here attention is paid to organizational climate and organizational health. The effective school has robust organizational health (cf. Miles 1975), comprising:

- Clear goals;
- Excellent communication channels;
- Democratic power, sharing decision-making;
- Effective use of human resources;
- Collaboration and a sense of belonging;
- High morale;
- Innovativeness;
- Autonomy from the environment;
- Adaptability to changing demands;
- Problem-solving adequacy.

Hoyle (1975) suggests that the health of an organization must be robust if innovation is to be effective, and he makes the point that, without it, 'tissue rejection' is likely to occur. One can liken this to organ transplantation – for example, not only would one not use a defective heart in a heart transplant operation, but one would also prepare the recipient's body (e.g. with immuno-suppressants) to receive the new heart in order for it not to reject the new organ.

The partner to organizational health is organizational climate. The concept of organizational climate is not new (e.g. Halpin 1966). Gilmer (1966), Litwin and Stringer (1968), and Tagiuri (1968) suggest that organizational climate refers to the particular characteristics of an organization, its social systems and structures, its working practices, its defining qualities, its distinguishing features (from other organizations) and the perceptions that employees have of the organization, all of which combine to impact on work and achievement.

Halpin (1966) uses the concept of organizational climate to identify those types of organization where change is more or less likely to occur. He suggests that if the climate is not propitious for change then change is unlikely to be successful, and he argues that the climate which is most conducive to change is the open climate. Here, the distinguishing features are high morale, openness, cooperation, the minimum of bureaucracy and records, high job satisfaction and motivation, mutual respect for all employees and a feeling of genuineness. The leader is a model of appropriate behaviour and runs a loose-tight organization. Collegiality abounds (cf. Hargreaves and Shirley 2009). Indeed, social relationships extend outside the organization.

Hoy *et al.* (1991) apply Halpin's work to the educational context and identify climates in education that are conducive to change. They identify eight components of organizational climate (1991: 14, 133). Four of these refer to the teachers' behaviour:

- *Disengagement* (where teachers are out of touch with that which is happening in the school);
- *Hindrance* (where the teachers feel that the principal is burdening them with routine, bureaucratic and unnecessary work);
- *Esprit* (morale, which develops with successful task accomplishment and social-needs satisfaction);
- *Intimacy* (the extent to which teachers enjoy good social relations with each other).

Signalling the importance of principal behaviour in the promotion of a positive school climate, the remaining four are:

- *Aloofness* (where the principal is distant and relies on procedures);
- *Production emphasis* (where the principal is directive and reluctant to act on feedback);
- *Thrust* (where the principal strives to move the organization forward through personal example);
- *Consideration* (where the principal demonstrates warmth and humanity).

Using these terms, Hoy *et al.* (1991: 16) indicate that the conditions – the climate – for effective innovation are:

- Low disengagement;
- Low hindrance;
- High esprit;
- Average intimacy;
- Low aloofness;
- Low production emphasis;
- High thrust;
- High consideration.

They report a high correlation (0.58) between 'initiating structure' and 'principal influence', signalling clearly the importance of leadership to support innovation. Similarly, the high correlations between 'trust in principal' and 'supportive behaviour' (0.56) and between 'trust in principal' and 'commitment' (0.66) indicate the significance of these in terms of the leadership setting, the most suitable conditions in which innovation operates. This is reinforced by the high correlation between 'trust in colleagues' and 'commitment' (0.65). The high correlation (0.64) between 'supportive behaviour' and 'consideration' and 'trust' (0.56 and 0.24, respectively) emphasizes the importance of interpersonal matters in leadership of innovation.

In a study which builds on the work of Halpin and Hoy et al., Tam and Cheng (1996) identify primary schools with different degrees of positive organizational climate. The authors use several of the terms from Hoy et al.; for example, esprit, intimacy, disengagement and hindrance.

In the 'synergistic school', they report a low level of organizational formalization and hierarchical authority, high esprit, low disengagement and low hindrance, and a high level of participative decision making. There is high morale, high cooperation, participation and cohesiveness, and all of this within a climate of support from a visionary and charismatic principal who encourages professional development (1996: 243–4). The 'synergetic school' possesses the most positive climate and is characterized by strong principal leadership. The results indicate the benefits of strong leadership and synergy, participation and person-centredness in developing a positive school climate. The synergistic school is characterized by an absence of bureaucracy and the presence of a positive social climate. The results reaffirm the need to promote the positive school climate, and leadership is a critical factor here. This is echoed in the work of Sergiovanni (1998), who argues that leadership should also move beyond being bureaucratic, visionary and entrepreneurial, and towards being pedagogical, i.e. by enabling schools to become human and humane communities which emphasize both social contracts and capacity building in teachers.

If responsibility is to be shared then it requires trust to be placed in all participants. As Fairholm and Fairholm (2000: 102) suggest, leadership is a collective and relation-based rather than individual activity, and it requires a climate of mutuality, coordinated action and, chiefly, trust (see also Bennis 1993: 166). A major task of leadership, then, is to build a *culture of trust* (Goldstein and Hazy 2006: v; Lichtenstein et al. 2006: 10; Surie and Hazy 2006: 17; Parellada, 2007: 159). Tschannen-Moran (2000) found a series of statistically significant links between:

- Collaboration with the principal and trust in the principal ($r = 0.32$, $\rho<0.05$);
- Collaboration between teachers and trust between them ($r = 0.30$, $\rho<0.05$);
- Collaboration with parents and trust in them ($r = 0.79$, $\rho<0.01$).

Collaboration and trust, she affirms (2000: 314), are reciprocal. Building trust requires attention to several important factors (cf. Fairholm and Fairholm

2000; Luke 1998; Tschannen-Moran 2000) including: positive and genuine interpersonal communication; involvement rather than alienation; putting others before oneself (echoing notions of servant leadership); leaders being sensitive to followers' needs; having flat organizational structures rather than complicated hierarchies; honesty with people; freedom for participants to control their work within a shared vision; and trust that teachers have the expertise and will to make decisions in the interests of the school. Trust, suggests Tschannen-Moran (2000: 314), requires people to be benevolent, reliable, competent, honest and open. Clearly, trust also requires people in whom trust can be placed, e.g. their expertise and moral sense, it would be senseless to place trust in the hands of ignorance or innocence; the corollary of this is that trust requires the development of expertise in all staff. Together, these authors aver that trust is a central condition for effective leadership.

Putting together the elements of these studies, Watkin (2000) reports an important study of headteachers (principals) of schools. Highly effective headteachers, he found:

1 Were driven strongly by a set of personal values which supported students' achievement (which included respect for others and balancing challenge with support);
2 Created a vision for the school and planned the realization of that in practice (which included strategic thinking and the drive for improvement);
3 Built commitment and support (which included impact, influence and holding people accountable);
4 Regarded situations (e.g. lack of resources) as opportunities rather than problems;
5 Cultivated and valued feedback and used it formatively (gathering information and gaining understanding, including social awareness and scanning the environment);
6 Drew on networks within and outside the school in order to achieve their goals;
7 Set clear expectations and clear limits of acceptability;
8 Demanded 'delivery', i.e. set performance standards, and planned for such 'delivery', including analytical thinking, taking the initiative, transformational leadership, teamworking, developing potential and understanding others;
9 Challenged poor performance.

He reported that headteachers of high achieving schools possessed all the key characteristics (1)–(9) above, particularly in holding people accountable together with developing their potential (i.e. challenge and support).

Taken together, these studies suggest that paying attention to the *conditions* and *environment* for innovation are essential dimensions of effective innovation, and that, in turn, these feature highly amongst the tasks of effective leaders of innovation. As will be shown in this book, the leadership of the principal in the school in question provides a clear example of these in practice.

Innovation capability

A key, critical component of successful innovation is capability. Put simply, participants need the competencies, skills, knowledge, confidence and ability to be able to implement the innovation. Based on shared characteristics of institutions that have successfully instituted innovations, Barnes and Soken (2012) note that innovation capability engages 'focusing leadership', 'deep competency', a 'facilitative culture', 'active learning', 'enabling structures' and 'intelligent decision making'. Their comments resonate well with the preceding discussion of the importance of leadership, organizational health and climate. Indeed, Hall and Hord (2011) note that support for innovation is a key principle for successful change, and they underline the central importance of providing training, professional development and education on an ongoing basis.

With regard to innovations in ICT, Hargreaves and Shirley (2009) and O'Mahony (2003) identified professional development of teachers – both internally and externally provided – as a key factor in effective change, arguing that this builds teacher confidence and commitment as well as ability and competence. They underline the need for such professional development to be ongoing rather than simply at the start of an innovation.

Mumtaz (2000) identifies conditions for effective innovation with ICT, including the experience of initial, immediate success with ICT (with hands-on experience of user-friendly software and hardware), and formal and informal support for ICT development and usage. She notes that teachers' positive attitudes towards ICT are not always matched by their abilities to use it or their confidence in using it, and it is here that they need support and development. In turn, she notes, this requires time to be set by for the development of ICT usage by teachers.

Further, the ICT Cluster of the European Commission Education & Training 2010 programme (ICT Cluster 2010: 11) noted that effective innovation in ICT included, amongst other themes:

- Leadership and institutional change for a renewed strategy on learning;
- Digital competencies and new transversal skills;
- A learner-centred paradigm;
- Professional development, with the teacher as learner.

The cluster drew attention to the key significance of leadership (2010: 15), not least to promote new pedagogies with ICT and to promote staff development and capability (2010: 14), so that teachers can catch the potential of ICT as an effective tool for teaching and learning, together with an infrastructure of technology and support (2010: 15).

The report notes the importance of leadership for ICT in improving student outcomes, motivation, achievement and attainment (2010: 16), and it repeatedly underlines the need for professional development of teachers to work with ICT and pedagogy, right across the student age ranges.

The Education, Audiovisual and Culture Executive Agency of the European Commission (2011) placed the ongoing professional development of teachers in ICT and its associated pedagogical implications as a critical feature of effective teaching and learning (2011: 67–8). These several major sources underline the inescapable point that, without ongoing and sufficient professional development and support, innovation capability will be seriously hampered, if not impossible.

Attending to staff concerns

Hall *et al.* (1986) and Hall and Hord (2011) suggest that participants in school innovation have different concerns during the process and unfolding of an innovation, and that it is important both to understand and to address them. Here, Hall (2010: 245) notes that the leadership of the school plays a pre-eminent, critical role in affecting the success of teachers' implementation of an innovation. In the example of the school in this book, this was eminently the case. Attention has to be given to the affective side of participants, with empathy and support, i.e. not only being concerned with what teachers are doing with an innovation. They argue that failure to attend to personal aspects of innovation, particularly if they seem to be taking precedence over other concerns, is problematic and must be attended to if the innovation is to proceed smoothly (Hall 2010: 249–50). Hall (2010: 243) and Hall and Hord (2011: 73) identify four basic areas of concern:

1 *Impact*: how the innovation is affecting students and what can be done to increase outcomes.
2 *Task*: time, logistics, schedules and fitting everything in that must be done are of concern.
3 *Self*: personal feelings of uncertainty, whether one can succeed with this innovation and whether the supervisor will support the efforts are central in thought.
4 *Unconcerned*: other things are of more concern at this time than the innovation.

These are further subdivided into *unconcerned, informational, personal, management, consequence, collaboration* and *refocusing*. 'Unconcerned' relates to unawareness of the innovation; 'self' relates to 'informational' and 'personal' issues; 'task' relates to 'management' issues; and 'impact' relates to 'consequence', 'collaboration' and 'refocusing' issues (Hall and Hord 2011: 73). Hall *et al.* (1986) and Hall and Hord (2011) place these concerns into a

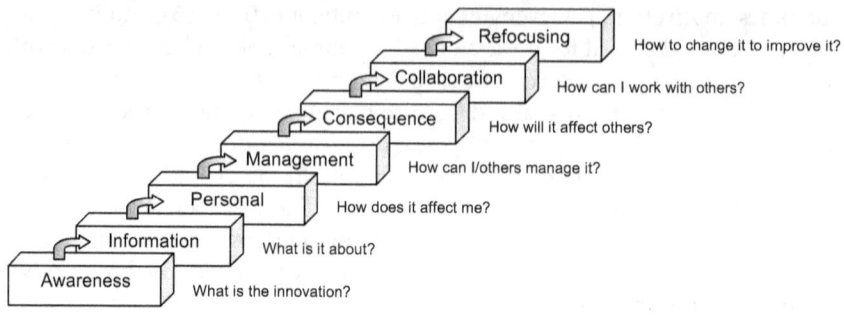

Figure 1.1 'Stages of Concern' from Hall and Hord (1987, 2011)

temporal sequence of different 'Stages of Concern' in their Concerns Based Action Model (CBAM) of innovation, noting that predominant concerns change during the course of an innovation – from its inception to the later stages of its implementation (see Figure 1.1).

The movement is from unconcerned, to concerns about self, thence to task and finally to impact. Hall (2010) argues that, from a vast range of evidence spanning over four decades, this process can take from three to five years.

In the early stages of an innovation, the participants' main concerns are to acquire *information* about it (e.g. its general characteristics, effects and requirements for using it), and they may have anxieties and concerns about how the innovation will affect them *personally* (e.g. what demands will be placed on them by the innovation, where they might be inadequate in meeting the demands of the innovation, what will be their tasks and role in the innovation, what decision making will occur and what will be their personal commitment to the innovation). Slightly later in the innovation their predominant concerns will focus on how the innovation will actually operate (what will happen) and how it will be *managed*. Still later in the innovation their main concerns will be with the *consequences* of the innovation (e.g. on students, on themselves) and how they will be able to collaborate with other colleagues in implementing the innovation. Later still in the innovation, their main concerns might be with *refocusing*, i.e. how to modify the original conception of the innovation once it has bedded down to some extent in the institution.

Coupled with Stages of Concern, Hall and Hord (1987, 2011) indicate that 'Levels of Use' will change over time, moving from non-use to fully-fledged use (levels 0 to II being essentially different kinds of non-use, whilst levels III to VI being different kinds of use) (see Figure 1.2):

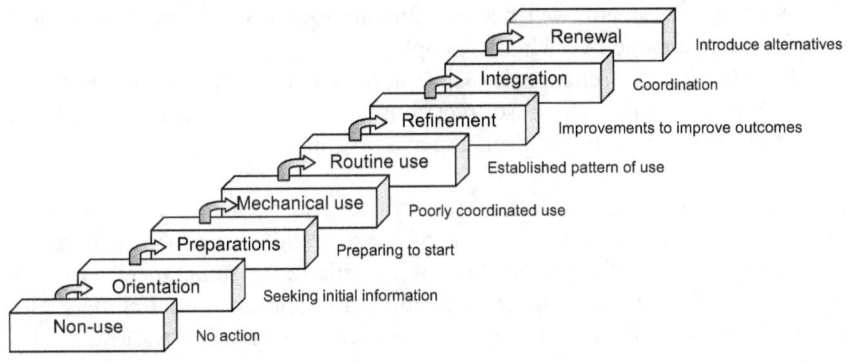

Figure 1.2 'Levels of Use' from Hall and Hord (1987, 2011)

Level 0: *Non-use* (no action is being taken with regard to the innovation).
Level I: *Orientation* (participants seek initial information about the innovation).
Level II: *Preparations* (preparations made for the first foray into using the innovation).
Level III: *Mechanical use* (the user works with the innovation but in a poorly coordinated way and not necessarily as intended).
Level IVa: *Routine use* (the user makes few changes to the innovation and has an established pattern of use).
Level IVb: *Refinement* (the user makes some refinements in order to produce better outcomes).
Level V: *Integration* (the user makes a deliberate effort to coordinate his/her use with others' use).
Level VI: *Renewal* (the user seeks to introduce alternatives to the existing use of the innovation).

Progressing through the levels marks a progress from non-use to a much more sophisticated use of the innovation. In the school in question in this book, data were deliberately collected to ascertain where the participants were in their use of the innovation, so that appropriate support, facilitation, consolidation and development could be provided appropriately.

Coupled with Stages of Concern and Levels of Use is the more general issue of impeding and facilitative factors in change and innovation. Dalin *et al.* (1993) identify four main barriers to change:

1 *Value barriers* (where the proposed innovation challenges one's values or where one disagrees with the proposed values in the innovation).
2 *Power barriers* (where people may accept an innovation if it gives them more power or may resist it if it gives them less).

3 *Psychological barriers* (innovations threaten people's self-confidence, security, self-esteem, well-being, vulnerability, stress levels and emotional make-up; change overwhelms people).
4 *Practical barriers* (change de-skills and re-skills people, workload increases and there is a need for resources: human, material, financial, temporal, administrative, technological, expertise, support).

Morrison (1998) adds to these sources of resistance: fear of the unknown, of failure, of looking stupid, of loss of control and status, of letting go of the present, of loss of expertise; lack of information; a reluctance to experiment; lack of trust from the leaders and poor organizational climate and health in the school; lack of clarity in the benefits of the innovation; uncertainty and ambiguity.

With regard to ICT, Mumtaz (2000) identified several 'inhibitors' of teachers' use of ICT:

- Lack of teaching experience with ICT;
- Lack of on-site support for teachers using ICT;
- Lack of supervisory help for students using ICT;
- Lack of ICT hardware;
- Lack of time to integrate ICT into the curriculum;
- Lack of financial support;
- Resistance to organizational change;
- Time management problems;
- Lack of support from the administration;
- Teachers' perceptions;
- Personal and psychological factors.

As can be seen, several of these ICT-related inhibitors are similar to the resistances noted by Dalin *et al.* (1993), Hall and Hord (2011) and Morrison (1998). Indeed, Fullan (1991) noted that people might resist change if they do not have a coherent or clear sense of reasons for the innovation and how to proceed in it, and he argues that teachers might not actually be rejecting or resisting a change but might be behaving entirely rationally in requesting further information and development in connection with it so that they can understand and make sense of the innovation. Similarly, the ICT Cluster (2010) of the European Commission Education & Training 2010 programme notes that lack of understanding of ICT and its associated pedagogical changes (e.g. from teacher-centredness to learner-centredness, and from passive to active and interactive learning) are important sources of resistance (2010:27). The report notes that changing teaching style is significantly more difficult than simply providing equipment and infrastructures for innovation (2010: 27).

By contrast, Morrison (1998) identifies facilitating factors which can be harnessed in promoting innovation, including: communication; involvement and participation; principal support; clarity of purpose and focus; support for risk-taking; celebration of small achievements; tolerance of failure; identification of problems and of ways of addressing them; a trusting environment; positive organizational health and climate; sensitivity to people; building trust; addressing the timing of different stages of the innovation (preparation for implementation); provision of training and development; working with different motivations; providing positive feedback; working collegially and collaboratively; offering incentives; meeting psychological and physical needs; empowering and respecting people as participants; celebrating achievement; and enabling success to be experienced.

At the heart of the issue here is the recognition that innovations are not only about content and management, but about people, their emotions, cognitions, perceptions, abilities, motivations and concerns. As Mumtaz (2000) noted, teachers' beliefs (about what and how to teach) and skills (e.g. competencies in pedagogy and ICT) both contributed to their acceptance of change. Decisive factors in effective change with regard to their use of ICT were their motivation and commitment to student learning, the support provided by the school and their access to ICT. Indeed, she remarked on the importance of situated learning, collaborative reflection and collegial interaction in sustaining innovations.

Mumtaz (2000) and O'Mahony (2003) noted that staff concerns about ICT included:

- Quantity and quality of classroom and staff ICT resources, training and support;
- Willingness to be involved;
- Incentives to change;
- Support and collegiality in the school;
- Commitment to professional learning.

Hargreaves and Shirley (2009) argue powerfully for the use of ICT in promoting learning, whilst Webb and Cox (2004) note that innovation for developing ICT and pedagogy requires 'a significant investment of time by teachers' (2004: 247); this becomes an organizational and leadership matter, not solely an individual teacher's concern. Webb and Cox note the need for extensive support and development of teachers' time, capability and competence in using ICT with active and interactive pedagogies, to both understand and make use of the affordances of ICT in both primary and secondary schools (2004: 253, 258).

Complexity theory and innovation

One of the theoretical underpinnings of innovation in this book derives from complexity theory (Morrison 2002a, 2010), with its emphasis on emergent order rather than control, emergence through self-organization, interconnectedness, unpredictable change, non-linear change in dynamical systems, holism and its derivates in (a) holistic leadership and management; (b) promoting effective environments and conditions for change; and (c) the importance of communication and feedback. Complexity theory has been included for three main reasons. First, it accords closely with what took place in the school; the theory and the practice fit closely. Second, it facilitates the identification of key features of the leadership and management of the innovation. Third, as more of a side issue, it provides a counter to those theories of complexity and its leadership which argue against the role or value of hierarchy in the leadership of change, and, instead, indicates how central tenets of complexity theory can sit comfortably within both hierarchical and distributed leadership (which was the case in the school) (cf. Stacey 2001). Here, the principal's organizational structure for the innovation was both hierarchical and distributed, including senior members of the school in management and leadership positions (e.g. of curriculum, of ICT, of pedagogy).

In very many cases the agendas for school development and improvement are externally generated and externally driven. However, what if there is no external mandate or impetus to change or innovate? In this case, the moral imperative of schooling, as evidenced (e.g. in the work of Fullan (2001, 2003, 2011a, 2011b), Fullan and Hargreaves (2008) and Hargreaves and Fullan (2012)) suggests that self-organized, emergent change and development is often more effective than externally imposed change, and that the self-identified need for change and how it will be managed often brings more sustained development and greater commitment to change and innovations. (On the other hand, of course, advocates of externally imposed change might argue that, without external pressure, many schools may simply stagnate.) In the context of the present example, complexity theory offers a powerful way of theorizing innovation, as several of complexity theory's central elements fit closely with the self-imposed, self-generated and self-organized innovation as it unfolded in the school. Indeed, complexity theory is *per se* a theory of change, innovation, evolution and development, which, when applied to schools, possesses several characteristic elements:

- Regarding the school as a dynamical, open, complex adaptive system (i.e. one which exhibits emergent, self-organizing behaviours (Mitchell 2009: 13));
- Self-organization;
- Emergence through self-organized, creative, proactive and reactive interaction within and between environments (cf. Gell-Mann 1994: 17);
- Non-linear and unpredictable change;
- Development and promotion of the conditions for innovation;
- Holism as greater than the sum of the parts (e.g. cultural change rather than superficial innovations);
- Collaboration, connection, communication and feedback;
- Learning and change through feedback;
- Cooperation and co-evolution;

- Emergent order replacing control;
- Intelligent and informed adaptation to emergent factors and internal and external environments (Battram 1999: 33).

Complexity theory has *self-organization* as one of its key principles, and this was instanced in the school in question here. Here, self-organization was a purpose, process and outcome of the innovation.

Stacey (2000: 333–4) cautions against equating self-organization with individualism, complete democracy, anarchy, the empowerment of all the junior members of staff and the disempowerment of the senior staff. Rather, he suggests that self-organization is not a 'constraint-free form of behaviour' (2000: 334) but has to take account of differentials of power, influence, constraint, competition, limited consensus, differential capabilities and capacities to respond. Hence, senior managers can still enable and constrain actions and behaviour (2000: 335–6). This was the situation which obtained in the school in question here, where the innovation took place in an organizational structure which was both hierarchical and distributed. Indeed, it was the interaction of these factors that produced self-organization. Stacey *et al.* (2000: 124) expressly indicate the limits to individual choice within power structures and argue that conflicting constraints ('power relations' (2000: 155)) are essential for genuine novelty to emerge. Power is a central issue, and one cannot behave as though it is not present (see also Stacey 1992: 189). Complexity theory is not license; it operates within boundaries and organizational structures.

Complexity theory holds many attractions for school leadership, management and organizational behaviour. For example, it provides a lens for examining, managing and leading change and schools. This touches many aspects of such leadership and management, particularly the view of change that is facilitated in open, non-linear, far-from-stable environments (Falconer 2007). Complexity theory suggests that school leaders and managers may enable, generate and facilitate *conditions* for self-organized emergence and change – organizational learning – rather than (or as well as) mandating specific behaviours. In practice this takes many hues, as leadership and management are complex activities, defying simple solutions, recipes and keys (Guastello *et al.* 2005; Siggelkow and Rivkin 2005, 2006; Lichtenstein *et al.* 2006: 3; Surie and Hazy 2006; Majchrzak *et al.* 2006; Espinosa *et al.* 2007). Indeed, complexity theory suggests that emergent, self-organized order may supersede command and control in many situations (Stacey 1992, 1995, 1996, 2000, 2001; Brown and Eisenhardt 1998; Tetenbaum 1998; Kelly and Allison 1999; Marion and Uhl-Bien 2001; Andriani and Passiante 2004; Majchrzak *et al.* 2006; Falconer 2007) though not in other situations (e.g. Carley and Hill 2001; Solow and Szmerekovsky 2006).

Complexity theory suggests that leadership emerges through interactions, networking, connectivity and relationships, as these enhance operational effectiveness (Goldstein and Hazy 2006: v; Lichtenstein *et al.* 2006: 10; Surie and Hazy 2006:

17; Parellada 2007: 159). Leadership and management, from the perspective of complexity theory, is adaptive, participative and enabling (Schreiber and Carley 2006). On the one hand this advocates distributed leadership that operates in ever-changing and unpredictable environments (e.g. Gronn 2000, 2002, 2003; Lakomski 2000; Gunter 2003; Harris 2003; Falconer 2007), and, on the other hand, it suggests that employee empowerment, voice, creativity and diversity have considerable significance (Stacey 2000; Parellada 2007: 164; Capra 2007: 16; Capra *et al.* 2007: xv).

A key element of complexity theory here is *connection*: how to connect not only the different elements of the innovation and to identify how they mutually potentiate each other – the benefits of synergy – but how to work on, with and for connection between people and task, people and each other, leaders and followers, internal and external environments. Connection and building connectedness are fundamental properties of complexity theory, spawning feedback, synergy and responsiveness (Morrison 2002a).

Connectedness benefits from a distributed knowledge system, distributed leadership, knowledge management and devolved decision making (e.g. McElroy 2000: 202; Marion and Uhl-Bien 2001; Gronn 2002, 2003; Brodbeck 2002; Gunter 2003; Harris 2003; Schreiber and Carley 2006). Knowledge and decision making are not necessarily centrally located in a command and control centre (e.g. the principal's office). Rather, they circulate throughout the system, rendering communication and collaboration vital (Cilliers 1998; McElroy 2000; Aronson *et al.* 2002; Hübler 2007). Self-organization emerges and is internally generated (Sawyer 2005; Falconer 2007). As Kauffman (1995) avers, 'order comes for free' rather than being the product of external control. Order is not imposed; it emerges spontaneously, of itself, willed or not, unlike mandated control (Bak 1996: 31; Battram 1999). Connectedness implies relationships, for example, between individuals and teams, between teams, between subsystems, between the institution and its environment (Lewin and Regine 2000: 19). Further, these relationships are mutual, not one-way. On an interpersonal level, this suggests an increased need for trust between equal partners – a collaborative rather than a competitive mentality.

Complexity theory connects people with others and with both cognitive and affective aspects of the individual persona. The natural consequence of this view of innovation is an emphasis on the *conditions* to promote emergence, including motivation, enjoyment, passion and cooperative and collaborative activity. Here, knowledge is perpetually being constructed and reconstructed (the mind and the brain being complex adaptive systems) through the assimilation and accommodation of new knowledge to existing knowledge (connectionist models – 'joined-up thinking'), thereby changing both the existing and new emergent situation, rather than either being fixed and finite.

The version of complexity theory here (and there are several other versions (Miller and Page 2007; Mitchell 2009; Morrison 2008, 2010)) is as a theory of change, evolution and adaptation through a combination of cooperation, competition and co-evolution of the organism with its environment (e.g. Battram 1999; MacIntosh and MacLean 1999; Stewart 2001; Morrison 2002a; Chu *et al.* 2003; Andriani and Passiante 2004; Burnes 2005; Surie and Hazy 2006: 14). Leaders and managers face continuous and ubiquitous change and innovation in education, in which closer links within and between, and responsiveness to, the external and internal environments of schools are constantly being required.

Complexity theory breaks with stable, simple successionist, cause-and-effect models of change, linear predictability, and a reductionist, analytically-atomistic approach to understanding phenomena and management. Rather, complexity theory replaces them with organic, far-from-equilibrium, dynamical, non-linear and holistic approaches to leadership and management (Santonus 1998: 3), working with anticipated and unanticipated changes and challenges. A non-linear system is characterized by the whole being greater – and different – from the sum of its parts (Mitchell 2009: 23), and the behaviour of the whole being different from the sum of the behaviour of the parts (2009: 27). Here relations and interactions within interconnected networks are important in times of turbulence and change (e.g. Stacey 1995, 1996; Youngblood 1997: 27; Cilliers 1998; Wheatley 1999; Marion and Bacon 2000; Marion and Uhl-Bien 2001: 391; McKelvey 2004; Smith and Humphries 2004; Houchin and MacLean 2005; Amis *et al.* 2004; Sundarasaradula *et al.* 2005; Falconer 2007).

In this view of complexity theory, an organism (Waldrop 1992: 294–9), however defined, senses and responds to its environment, thereby changing that environment, which then changes the organism (Prigogine and Stengers 1985; Battram 1999; Lichtenstein 2000; Stewart 2001; Schreiber and Carley 2006). As a member of a web of life, with interrelated connections and networks (Capra 1996), one cannot consider the organism without considering its environment; the emphasis is on collective, relational behaviour and holism rather than on isolationism, individualism and solipsism (Parellada 2007). In the school situation reported in this book, not only did the school principal sense the external environment, but also took active steps to engage that external environment and to connect it with the internal environment of the school. Further, the principal worked on connecting the elements of the internal environment of the school, establishing and developing the conditions for innovation, and linking the several strands of the innovation into a coherent whole, and the later chapters of the book address this.

Cohen and Stewart (1995: 348) argue that the organism deliberately seeks out information from the environment (internal and external) in order to learn (see also Bailey 2000: 202), suggesting that school leaders need to develop:

- Communication, as it is vital for sensing the environment;
- Sensors, as they are necessary for working with the environment;

- Internal structures and systems, which give, receive and act on messages;
- Internal coordination, distributed leadership and information at all levels (Swieringa and Wierdsma 1992; Gronn 2002, 2003; Gunter 2003; Harris 2003).

For example, in the school in question here, one feature of the innovation was the increased active participation of the parents, and the intention to promote greater collaboration between staff.

Changes in the organism involve emergent *self-organization* and *autocatalysis* (Waldrop 1992: 16–17, 86; Lewin 1993: 38; Kauffman 1995: 27; Marion and Uhl-Bien 2001: 396). The collectivity of the organism and its environment evolves itself, from within (e.g. Battram 1999; Marion 1999; Lichtenstein 2000). In effective self-organization, the organism is characterized by *adaptability, open systems, learning, feedback, communication* and *emergence* (e.g. Prigogine and Stengers 1985; Cohen and Stewart 1995; MacIntosh and MacLean 1999; Fullan 2001; Smith and Humphries 2004; Houchin and MacLean 2005; Sawyer 2005; Majchrzak *et al.* 2006).

A key feature of complex adaptive systems is that order emerges through self-organization of interacting elements and constant self-readjustment of the system (Coveney and Highfield 1995: 85). From a management perspective, Stacey (1992: 183–4) suggests that self-organization is a process in which teams and groups form themselves spontaneously around issues, with the participants themselves deciding what their boundaries will be. Self-organization, argues Marsick (2000: 10), occurs through feedback and communication.

Order is not imposed from without or by external constraint; it emerges from within – it is autocatalytic, emerging spontaneously of its own accord (Cohen and Stewart 1995: 265). Autocatalysis describes the ability of elements to catalyse each other and, thereby, to generate new forms from within. Order and freedom are, thus, partners rather than competitors (Wheatley 1999: 87); control and order are conceptually separate.

Complex adaptive systems possess a capability for self-organization which enables them to develop, extend, replace, adapt, reconstruct or change their internal structure or *modus operandi* so that they can respond to, and influence, their environment. A school that is responsive to its environment (internal and external) may reorganize its activities: it may become a community resource; it may involve parents in a far more extended way than heretofore, for example in policy decision making; it may set up student councils; it may move towards student-centred learning through a massive injection of ICT hardware.

The interaction of individuals feeds into the wider environment which, in turn, influences the individual units of the network. They co-evolve, shaping each other (Stewart 2001); and co-evolution requires connection, cooperation and competition: competition to force development and cooperation for mutual survival. The behaviour of a complex system as a whole, formed from its several elements, is greater than the sum of the parts (Bar-Yam 1997; Goodwin 2000; Mitchell 2009).

Feedback must occur between the interacting elements of the system. Mitchell (2009: 14) argues that complex adaptive systems both use and produce information from their external and internal environment; in other words, feed-forward and feedback. Negative feedback is regulatory (Marion 1999: 75), for example learning that one has failed in a test. Positive feedback brings increasing returns and uses information to change, grow and develop (Wheatley 1999: 78); it amplifies small changes (Stacey 1992: 53; Youngblood 1997: 54). A baby eats voraciously, and the more he eats, the faster he grows; his rate of growth accelerates. Once a child has begun to read she is gripped by reading, she reads more and learns at an exponential rate.

If learning and development through feedback are to take place (and Fullan (1991) argues that change equals learning), if connectedness is to work successfully and if knowledge is to be collected from a distributed, dispersed system, then an essential requirement will be an effective communication system. Communication in schools is a key variable in their success and their person-centredness (cf. Peters 1989; Cilliers 1998). The amount of feedback and communication is frequently inversely proportional to its capability for predictability. The greater the amount of feedback is given, be it as data, information or knowledge, the less it is possible to predict what the results of that high information content might be. The balance has to be struck between selective (and inadequate) information for predictability and control, and a necessarily high amount of information for self-organization to occur.

Communication is central to complexity theory and to organizational and leadership theory that draws inspiration from complexity theory. Significant, open-ended and lateral communication must replace vertical or bilateral forms of communication, in which directions, decisions and instructions descend from on high in a hierarchical bureaucracy, and information ascends to the top of the hierarchy, i.e. in which the nature or contents of the communication are different. Complexity theory suggests that, in a networked structure for self-organization, communication must take multiple forms, must be through multiple channels and must be open.

Emergence is the partner of *self-organization*, and self-organization was a feature of the innovation in the school in question here, the innovation being internally rather than externally generated. Self-organization emerges, it is internally generated; it is the antithesis of external control. The self-organized order emerges of itself as the result of the interaction between the organism and its environment.

Emergent systems are unpredictable and non-linear. Emergence is a process of constant creativity. Organisms and systems propel themselves through 'self-organized criticality' (the movement towards a level of disequilibrium such that a small event may trigger a huge change) (Bak 1996) towards the 'edge of chaos' (Kauffman 1995). The edge of chaos is that point between linear predictability and complete chaos at which a system is at its most creative, imaginative and adaptable, whilst still being ordered. Creative emergence is characterized by increasing connectivity, networking and feedback (e.g. Stacey *et al.* 2000: 146; Parellada 2007). The closer one moves towards the edge of chaos, the more creative, open-ended, imaginative, diverse, and rich are the behaviours, ideas and practices of individuals and systems, and the greater is the connectivity, networking and information sharing (content and rate of flow) between participants (Stacey *et al.* 2000: 146). Innovation requires creativity and imagination.

In handling multidimensionality, we can learn from 'simplexity' theory (Kluger 2007) – the combination of simplicity and complexity – which argues that behind complex and complicated phenomena often lie simple rules, a bounded group of interacting elements and a core, unified set of purposes.

Waldrop (1992: 241–2) provides an example of this in Reynolds's computer program, Boids, where just three initial conditions are built into a mathematical formula that reproduces the flight of a flock of birds. These are: (a) the boids (birds) strive to keep a minimum distance from other objects (including other boids); (b) the boids strive to keep to the same speed as other boids; (c) each boid strives to move towards the centre of the flock (see www.youtube.com/watch?v=IRa1SWdJouM). The example of boids is very fitting: there is no cosmological or teleological 'ghost in the machine' that is determining how the birds should fly; the flock of birds/boids is self-organizing. The complex emerges from the simple (Hartwell 1995: 8); complexity and order are not imposed from without (Marion 1999: 29). There is no single leader or central control; rather there is *distributed control* (Lewin and Regine 2000: 30). In the school in question, it will be shown that, for example, a few key tenets guided much of the innovation: promote interactivity and engagement in teaching and learning; promote collaboration and participation (e.g. in teaching and learning, with parents); promote motivation and positive attitudes; enhance all of these through ICT; pursue the goals of the project in the face of challenges and setbacks.

The term 'simplexity' has been adopted by Fullan (2013) in respect of educational change, arguing for the identification of core purposes and holding fast to them: the simple elements are the contents of the innovation; the complex parts are the people involved. The management company, Tabar (2013: 1), remarks that simplexity involves identifying the simple rules that drive or underpin the operations of complex systems or conditions. This book uses elements of simplexity theory to underline the need for leaders and managers of complex change to identify the key purposes and values of an innovation, to hold to them firmly, to identify the glue which holds together the dimensions of the multidimensional innovation and to indicate how to connect the different elements of a multidimensional change. Indeed, dynamical systems (Peak and Frame 1994: 122) are a product of initial conditions and often simple rules for change – the dynamics of change. General laws for emergent order can govern adaptive, dynamical processes (Kauffman

1995: 27). The basic rules and components can be simple, and give rise to emergent complexity through their interaction (Waldrop 1992: 86).

Further, *learning* is a critical factor within an ever-changing environment of innovation. Systems or organisms which cannot learn from their environment (internal and external), and environments which cannot learn from constituent elements, wither, stagnate or, indeed, perish. It is unsurprising, perhaps, that the current orthodoxies for education in an ever-changing environment stress the learning society, the learning organization, lifelong learning, learning networks and learner-centred education. As mentioned earlier, Fullan (1991) and Dalin *et al.* (1993) remark that change *equals* learning (cf. Hall and Hord 2011). If self-organization is to lead to, or be an effective consequence of, innovation then the self-organizing system must be constantly learning (Morrison 1998; Dumont *et al.* 2010; Groff 2012).

At an organizational level, McMaster (1996: 10) suggests that organizational learning involves: an ability (within the organizational structures) to receive, understand and interpret, in various ways, signals from the environment; an ability to respond in various ways to those signals, including creating new internal structures and organizational features; and an ability to influence the environment both proactively and reactively. A school needs, itself, to become a learning organization as well as to develop the learning potential of its students.

Complexity theory has much to offer the leadership and management of school innovation as, at heart, it is a theory of emergent change and evolution through self-organization. As such, it fits very comfortably with the self-organized, self-decided and self-determined change that took place in the school in question in this book.

The view of complexity theory adopted in this book is of organizations operating in conditions of change in unpredictable and emergent situations, and of the need to consider the nature of evolution, self-organization, feedback, connectivity, emergence, networking, adaptability, open systems, learning and communication. Indeed, schools exhibit many features of complex adaptive systems, being dynamical and unpredictable, non-linear organizations operating in unpredictable and changing external environments. Further, schools both shape and adapt to macro- and micro-societal change, organizing themselves, responding to, and shaping their communities and society (i.e. all parties co-evolve).

Taking stock

This chapter has set out a vast range of dimensions to change and innovation:

- All levels of the school hierarchy;
- The scope of innovation;
- Fundamental, deep-seated innovation;

- Participants values and practices;
- Timing and time factors in innovation;
- Unanticipated challenges in innovation;
- Innovation as input, process and outcome;
- Participants in innovation: individuals and groups;
- Tasks and roles in innovation;
- Resources;
- Leadership and management;
- Innovation as learning and capacity building;
- Knowledge and expertise in innovation;
- Stages of innovation from non-use to preparation to implementation to modification;
- Performance, achievements and outcomes of innovation;
- Decision making;
- Dimensions as the number and magnitude of elements;
- Organizational climate and organizational health;
- Changes in cognitive, behavioural and affective aspects of people;
- Collaboration and cooperation;
- Stages of Concern and Levels of Use;
- Resistance and facilitation.

To this list must be added the several dimensions of the content of the innovation in the school in question:

- A key role for advanced and extensive ICT;
- Radical changes in teaching and learning from didacticism and transmission teaching to collaborative, interactive and real-world learning;
- Raising student motivation, attitude, interest and behaviour;
- Raising student achievement and performance;
- Promoting engaged, student-centred learning;
- Promoting higher-order thinking and problem-solving in students;
- Changing assessment strategies to provide formative feedback to students and teachers;
- Developing parental involvement, communication and enhancement of parental participation in the education of their child(ren);
- Restructuring the curriculum and its development;
- Promoting staff development for sustainable change, active and interactive learning;
- Promoting distributed leadership and management in the school.

The combination of all of these elements renders the leadership and management of innovation not only a multidimensional task but, in many respects, a Herculean task. This task places on the leader an enormous responsibility, and the leader must not only have broad shoulders but strength of personality to lead and carry through innovation.

This chapter has set out key theoretical foundations underpinning the leadership and management of multidimensional innovation in schools, which, in turn, underpin the mixed methods research on innovation in one school which is reported in the later chapters. It has argued that innovation is inherently multidimensional, and it has indicated what some of the pertinent dimensions might be in the case studied through this book. The chapter has argued that, given these many dimensions, a central place is occupied by effective leadership, and it indicates what key features of leadership are relevant. Principal amongst these is the ability to handle several dimensions simultaneously and without weakening, and to establish the environment and conditions for innovation to flourish, including the need to attend to not only the contents of the innovation itself (and this had many dimensions in itself) but also participants' concerns in an innovation, recognizing that these change over the duration of the innovation. The chapter argued that resistances and facilitating factors can be identified, and that one of the tasks of leadership is to address resistances and to harness the power of facilitating factors.

In setting all of these issues into an appropriate theoretical context, the chapter has argued that complexity theory, as a theory of change, evolution, innovation and adaptation, offers a fitting theoretical underpinning to the book and to the innovation itself, and it sets out the central tenets of the view of complexity theory espoused in the book and in the innovation itself. In this it recognized that complexity theory can embrace hierarchy as well as distributed leadership, and that is an important feature of the school in question.

Together these several elements set the agenda for this book, which address many areas in a single volume:

- The leadership and management of multidimensional, complex change and innovation in schools and school level;
- Multi-levelled change in school;
- The combination of ICT, pedagogic change and engaged learning from a leadership and management view in the context of innovation in school;
- Mixed methods research to evaluate a multiple and multidimensional change and innovation in a school;
- A rooting of the analysis of the leadership in leadership and complexity theory taken together;
- The handling of unanticipated and emergent issues in self-organized change in school;
- The changing nature of the innovation as it unfolded over time;
- Implications of ICT for interactive and collaborative, student-centred learning, curriculum and assessment development;
- School development in tandem with parental involvement.

In other words, this book draws together material from several fields, applies it to the topic of leading and managing multidimensional innovation in school at a process level and indicates how to conduct rigorous evaluations of such changes and how this is rooted in theories of effective leadership and complexity theory.

As much of the innovation reported here concerned learning, it is essential to provide an appropriate theoretical foundation to the learning, linking it to material in this chapter, not least as the essence of innovation is, itself, learning, and it is to this that the next chapter turns.

2 ICT and learning
Challenge and change

Introduction

In the school in question, a major element of its innovatory programme was the use of ICT as a lever of change, including (but not limited to) to pedagogy, student motivation and assessment. This chapter addresses contemporary changes to teaching and learning that have been brought about with ICT in classrooms. It roots the discussion in principles of social and cognitive constructivism, student-centred and engaged learning, collaborative learning, active and interactive learning, student motivation and involvement in learning, communication and participation. All of these areas are related to ICT, and are the central substance of the actual innovation in the school reported in this book. Further, the chapter indicates the roles of leaders and leadership in developing ICT for pedagogy, student learning and achievement, teachers and parents.

The chapter proceeds in several stages. First, it sets out a range of uses of ICT in learning in schools. Second, it sets key principles of effective learning with ICT in the context of constructivism, particularly social constructivism, as this provides a firm theoretical foundation for important teaching and learning discussed in the chapter. Third, developing further these key principles, the chapter defines key terms – engaged, student-centred, active, interactive and collaborative learning – and indicates that there is no single definition of these terms but that they cover a spectrum of issues, all of which were predominant features of the innovation in the school in question. Fourth, the chapter sets out the many claims that are made for ICT in promoting effective learning and education, but it notes that using ICT to enhance learning is not automatic or a guarantee of raising student achievement, but is conditional on the presence of several other features of education, and the chapter identifies what these are. These include teacher capability and professional development, school cultures that are open to innovation and developments in pedagogy, formative assessment and an emphasis on ongoing feedback for learning, and effective leadership. Fifth, the chapter argues that a key to unlocking successful innovation in bringing about these elements of effective teaching and learning is leadership, and the chapter discusses what that leadership might comprise.

The key points addressed in this chapter were all key elements of the innovation in the school in question, which was concerned with:

- Collaborative, interactive, engaged, student-centred, real-world learning;
- A focus on raising student motivation, attitude, interest and behaviour;
- A focus on raising student achievement and performance;
- The promotion of higher-order thinking and problem-solving in students;
- Changing assessment strategies to provide formative feedback to students and teachers;
- Developing parental involvement, communication and enhancement of parental participation in the education of their child(ren);
- Restructuring the curriculum and its development;
- Promoting staff development for sustainable change, active and interactive learning;
- Promoting distributed leadership and management in the school.

There is a strong resonance between the key features of effective learning as set out in this chapter and the key features of the innovation that were introduced in the case study school.

Connecting ICT and learning

There is a multiplicity of kinds and uses of ICT in learning (see Table 2.1), and, given the scope of these, this suggests that teachers and students have to acquire a very considerable range of skills in using ICT to maximum benefit.

Table 2.1 Different uses of ICT in education

Animations	Music composers
Applications (Apps)	Notice boards
Assessment programmes	Online information sources
Blended learning	Personal distance tutoring
Bulletin boards and forums	Personal web pages
Chatlines	Presentation packages (e.g. Word, PowerPoint, Photoshop)
Communication	
Conferencing	Programming
Database entry programmes and spreadsheets	Reference hypermedia
Database packages (including remote databases)	Simulations
	SMS text messaging
Desktop publishing	Smartphones

(Continued)

Table 2.1 (Continued)

Digital cameras and digital scanners	Social networking (e.g. Facebook, Twitter)
Drill and practice	Software CD-ROMs and virtual libraries
E-learning programmes and materials	Spreadsheets
Email,	Talking books
Games	Transferring data/files
Graphics packages	Videoing and video creation
Handling information	Virtual learning communities and study centres
Ideas processors	Web authoring
Instructional hypertexts	Whiteboards
Internet and the World Wide Web	Wikis
LOGO	Word processing
Measurement and control	
Modelling packages	
Multimedia	

The impact of ICT and new technologies is to shift the emphasis from teaching to learning and from the product to both the process and product of learning. Students need to focus on how and where to acquire, store and utilize knowledge rather than to remember it all (Loveless and Ellis 2001). Effective teachers will be those who can scaffold learning for students, and support them in the navigation of their own learning. This has major implications for the structure and contents of learning.

Learning and technology are intimately connected. The laws of commutativity indicate that Fullan's (1991) equation, that change equals learning, also means that learning equals change. We cannot learn without changing, be these changes to ourselves, knowledge, our methods of learning, and so on, and, as technologies change (e.g. from the book to the ICT) so our centres of learning – schools – must change their methods. It is a truism to aver that schools are moving from teacher-centred teaching to engaged, learner-centred learning, from an emphasis on transmission to an emphasis on interaction, collaborative, active learning and higher-order thinking. Further, didactic, one-way teaching and learning gives way to collaborative and interactive learning. This chapter concerns pedagogy, learning, technology and change, and the 'elective affinity' between them; they are intertwined. It is no accident that the previous chapter introduced complexity theory (one definition of complexity is 'intertwined').

Fullan's (2013) volume, *Stratosphere*, offers a powerful advocacy and practice of the integration of ICT, pedagogy and change knowledge. These impact on the leadership and management of change, requiring capacity building in both teachers and students (2013: 68). As he notes elsewhere (Fullan 2011a: 14), effective innovation is accomplished through capacity building and ownership, themselves contingent on ongoing commitment and cumulative learning.

Echoing the discussion of simplicity in the previous chapter, Fullan (2011b, 2013) comments that complex innovations can be frequently addressed through comparatively few levers of change and a few 'core priorities' (Fullan 2011b: 20), i.e. simplicity. Indeed, he notes that simplicity can deliver 'salvation' in a complex situation (2011b: 149); here, the leader has to identify and remain focused on a few ambitious goals (the simple part of simplicity) and then ensure a positive interaction between the people involved in the innovation and the content of the innovation itself (the complex part) (Fullan 2013: 57). In the school in question, the few levers were the coupling of ICT with the areas set out at the start of this chapter, to bring about pedagogical change.

Fullan (2013: 15) notes that the solution to pedagogical change and ICT lie in the integration of pedagogical advances with technology, student engagement and change knowledge, to render learning exciting for both teachers and students. The links between ICT and collaborative, interactive, engaged and higher-order learning and thinking are already well established (see Fullan 2013). Further, he argues that the criteria for the integration of pedagogy and ICT are that such integration must be so highly attractive that participants cannot resist it, that the innovation is straightforward to use (even if initially challenging), and that it must address real-life problems (2013: 33), be relevant to the situation, and engage people working together creatively (2013: 43).

The roots of learning and ICT in constructivism

The ICT Cluster (2010) from Europe reports the close association between socio-constructivist and collaborative learning approaches with ICT (2010: 27). Key features of changes in pedagogy, facilitated by ICT, are rooted in constructivism (Cohen *et al.* 2010) – social constructivism (e.g. the work of Vygotsky 1978, 1981) and cognitive constructivism (the work of Piaget on thinking and learning) – which emphasize:

- Situated learning (i.e. context- and individual-specific, placing emphasis on social interaction and active learning);
- Metacognition;
- Higher-order thinking and the social nature of learning;
- A move away from didactic approaches to teaching;
- An emphasis on the process of learning, not simply on the product;
- The breaking of subject boundaries and the development of project-based, real-world ('authentic') learning and authentic assessment;
- Student-centred learning;
- The significance of intrinsic motivation.

The social nature of ICT cannot be underestimated. It promotes higher-order cognition, collaborative learning, authentic tasks and rich feedback. However, it has to be learned, practised and developed. Vygotsky (1981: 163) encapsulates the significance of the social basis of learning when he writes that all higher-order functions and their interrelationships are socially mediated, transmitted and constructed. Indeed, he regards this position as a fundamental principle. Table 2.2 sets out four key features of learning from a Vygotskyan social constructivist perspective.

Table 2.2 Four features of learning from Vygotsky

Principles of situated cognition and Vygotskyan thought	Design considerations for e-learning
Situatedness: learning is embedded in rich cultural and social contexts; learning is reflective and metacognitive, internalizing from the social to the individual	e-learning environments should be Internet or web based; e-learning environments should be as portable as possible; e-learning environments can focus on tasks and projects, enabling learning through doing and reflection; e-learning environments can focus on depth over breadth
Commonality: learning is an identity formation or act of membership; learning is a social act/ construction mediated between social beings through language, signs, genres and tools	e-learning environments should create a situation where there is continual interest and interest and interaction through the tools embedded in the environment; e-learning environments should capitalize the social communicative and collaborative dimensions allowing mediated discourse; e-learning environments should have scaffolding structures;
Interdependency: learning is socially distributed between persons and tools; learning is demand driven – dependent on engagement in practice	e-learning environments should create interdependence between individuals, where novices need more capable peers, capitalizing on the Zone of Proximal Development (ZPD); e-learning environments should be designed to capitalize on the diverse expertise in the community; e-learning environments should be personalized to the learner with tasks and projects embedded in the meaningful activity context; e-learning environments can track the learner's history, profile, and progress and tailor personalized strategies and content;
Infrastructure: learning is facilitated by an activity – driven by appropriate mechanisms and accountability structures	e-learning environments should have structures and mechanisms to facilitate the activity (project) processes in which the learners are engaged; e-learning environments have the potential to radically alter traditional rules and processes that were constrained by locality and time.

Papert (1989) notes that constructivism is premised on the view that, in order to learn effectively, learners must construct, reconstruct and manipulate knowledge rather than knowledge being a matter of simple transmission, and that having the learner as the active constructor of knowledge creates meaningful and powerful learning.

With regard to constructivism and ICT, Grabe and Grabe (2001) suggest that the important point is not the use of computers but what they are being used for and how they are being used. Castro (1999) claims that using ICT in classrooms, particularly in a constructivist approach, has great potential to develop students' higher-order cognitive skills (see also Wishart 1990). Mumtaz (2000) notes that the more that teachers are involved in professional development, coupled with support from the school for experimenting with ICT, the more likely they are to hold philosophies of teaching that are compatible with constructivism and advances in pedagogy. Sang *et al.* (2011) note that teachers' beliefs about constructivist teaching interact with their attitudes towards ICT usage in school and that the development of their use of ICT is contingent to a significant degree on the support for their professional ICT-related development by the school.

Engaged, student-centred, active, interactive and collaborative learning with ICT

Key features of effective learning

In a synthesis and reflection on international developments in learning, Hopkins *et al.* (2011) note that effective learning is characterized by being learner-centred, structured, well-designed, personalized, social and inclusive, with students at the centre of everything that teachers do (2011: 10–13). This, they aver (2011: 13), requires ongoing professional development of teachers, high expectations from the leaders, challenging teaching and learning tasks, and an unyielding focus on the quality of teaching and learning (2011: 13). This resonates with the work of Dumont *et al.* (2010) and Groff (2012), who identify seven key principles for learning:

1. Learners at the centre (with cooperative learning).
2. The social nature of learning (with cooperative learning).
3. Emotions are integral to learning.
4. Recognizing individual differences.
5. Stretching all students.
6. Assessment for learning.
7. Building horizontal connections.

The school in the present book placed significant emphasis, in its innovation, on cooperative learning, the raising of student motivation, and changes to assessment, with greater emphasis placed on formative assessment and the inclusion of class participation in student assessment, all facilitated by ICT. As Groff writes, learning is premised on social constructivism, it is collaborative and is informed by, and informs the social context of, learning (2012: 3) (cf. Hannon 2009).

Louis *et al.* (2010) locate key drivers of effective learning in schools in three areas. First, leadership (second only to classroom instruction), which provides direction and influence, comprises both the leadership of the principal and distributed and shared leadership amongst stakeholders and key players (2010: 6–7). Where leadership is shared, creating a professional community and supportive school climate (echoing the reference to organizational climate in Chapter 1), not only does this strengthen working relationships, but it raises student achievement (2010: 10). Second, collaborative cultures are important features of effective teaching and learning, and the leaders have a key role in establishing these (2010: 11). Third, leaders set directions, develop people, redesign the organization and manage the instructional programme (2010: 14).

Kampylis *et al.* argue for 'a new culture of learning' (2012: 7) which can be brought about by ICT, placing learners at the heart of the learning process and involving hitherto impossible pedagogies including per group interaction to an unprecedented extent (2012: 7) and linking their learning to real-life experiences. Echoing the work of Craft (2005) and Loveless (2007, 2008, 2011), Kampylis *et al.* cite plentiful research to show how digital technologies have very considerable potential to potentiate creative learning processes. Importantly, the authors recognize the importance of preparing teachers for these new pedagogies, as such major changes transform teaching and learning, disrupt traditional pedagogy, and require changes to values, practices, behaviour, assessment and institutional infrastructure (2012: 8) (cf. Law *et al.* 2011).

'Engaged learning' has many meanings and dimensions, e.g. cognitive, affective, social, interactive, behavioural and personality-related. Whilst some views regard it as 'hands-on' learning, others add to this 'minds-on', i.e. cognitively engaged in meaningful learning, and not just 'busy'. For some it means a reduction in didacticism, teacher talk and lecturing; for others it means cognitive engagement with a lecture. Engaged learning is where the student actively participates in his or her own learning (in terms of both content and process), concentrates, is attentive and 'on-task', is thinking about his or her learning and is intrinsically motivated. It connotes student interaction with peers and the teacher, collaborative learning, students taking responsibility for their own learning, self-regulated learning, problem-solving and higher-order thinking and peer-group learning.

Just as 'engaged learning' has many definitions, so too does 'collaborative learning' – from simply two or more people learning together to complete a task to the co-construction of knowledge, planning together, learning from each other, contributing to a shared or individual outcome, working towards single shared goals and outcomes, explaining to each other, challenging each other, regulating each other, negotiating with each other (in contrast to 'instructing'), a social contract, a cognitive contract, a division of labour and ways of interacting.

Roschelle and Teasley (1995: 70) define collaboration as an activity that is both coordinated and synchronous, in which the participants strive for a shared view of a problem and its solution. Dillenbourg (1999: 7) notes that an activity or situation is collaborative where participants have a common goal and work together interactively to achieve it without much division of labour, i.e. they all work on the same activity. He distinguishes between collaborative and cooperative work: in the former, the division of labour is low (everyone works together on the same activity), whereas in the latter it is much higher (the work is divided and then the whole is assembled from the separate parts) (1999: 8).

Just as with 'engaged learning' and 'collaborative learning', the term 'student-centred' has a range of definitions. Napoli (2004: 2–3) suggests that it has several key characteristics:

- A recognition that students learn in many different ways and that learning is an active, dynamic process marked by constant change and new linkages between knowledge, as students construct their own meanings.
- An emphasis on the processes and experiences of learning rather than solely on content.
- Importance accorded to dialogue, collaboration and a view of learning as a social enterprise.
- High value placed on formative assessment, constructive feedback and self-assessment.
- Concern for student outcomes rather than teacher input.
- Encouragement of higher-order thinking, problem-solving and communication.
- Increased significance of student autonomy and empowerment.

Here, prominence is given to the student taking responsibility for her/his learning, with a premium placed on student involvement and participation in which the student comes to regard herself/himself differently as a result of the learning experience. For the teacher, there is a marked shift in role from being a transmitter of information to being a facilitator of learning.

Writing for the European Commission, Attard *et al.* (2010) regard student-centred learning as 'both a mindset and a culture' (2010: 4) and as:

> a learning approach which is broadly related to and supported by constructivist theories of learning. It is characterised by innovative methods of teaching which aim to promote learning in communication with teachers and other learners and take students seriously as active participants in their own learning, fostering transferable skills such as problem-solving, critical thinking and reflective thinking.
>
> (Attard *et al.* 2010: 4)

Lea *et al.* (2003: 322) indicate that student-centred learning relies on active rather than passive learning and emphasizes deep learning and understanding rather than superficial learning and simple memorization and repetition, that it enables students to practise autonomy in and take responsibility for their own learning, and that it fosters an interdependence and mutual respect between learner and teacher and a reflexive approach to learning by both learner and teacher.

O'Neill and McMahon (2005: 2) identify three main features of student-centred learning: increasing student choice in learning; an emphasis on active learning; and an emphasis on the shift in power relationships from asymmetrical to equal relationships between teacher and student (see also Gibbs's (1995: 1) view that student-centred learning changes power relationships in respect of what, when and how material is learned, for what purposes and intended outcomes, how these are judged and evaluated, and by whom, with the student and teacher together deciding these. This echoes the earlier work of Brandes and Ginnis (1986) who suggest that student-centred learning embraces several key tenets:

- The student taking full responsibility for her/his learning;
- The importance of student involvement and participation for learning;
- Equal relations between teacher and learner;
- The teacher as facilitator and resource person;
- The confluence of cognitive and affective aspects of the learner;
- The outcomes of learning being manifested in changes in the learner.

As the authors note, the individual is entirely and completely responsible for his own behaviour, learning and participation (1986: 12).

The combination of the elements set out in this section – collaboration, interaction, communication, engagement, student-centredness, increased student responsibility and empowerment, the intention to harness and raise student motivation for learning and achievement, and, indeed, motivation particularly of lower-achieving students – was a feature of the school in question in this book.

Whilst here is not the place to go into the several theories of motivation (e.g. psychoanalytic, ethological, socio-biological, drive, gestalt theories and their derivatives, expectancy theories, achievement motivations, social learning theories, attribution theories) (see e.g. Weiner 1992), suffice it to say that it is not a unitary concept (Leo and Galloway 1996) or a single theory of why people behave as they do, why they seek certain goals, what the determinants of behaviour are, and why they are willing to do some things and not others.

In the context of this chapter, the innovation retains the early distinction between intrinsic and extrinsic motivation (even though it has been questioned as being conceptually naïve, an artificial, invalid and false separation or dichotomy, e.g. Lepper *et al.* 1997; Covington and Mueller 2001). It is retained because it clarifies a matter of *emphasis*, and the preceding analysis suggests that the kind of motivation required in the innovation here was more intrinsic – for its own sake and for personal development – than extrinsic (achievement of an external end, or reward for, accomplishment and achievement). In discussing collaboration, engaged learning, student-centredness and increasing student responsibility, the emphasis here is placed on raising students' motivation – willingness, drive, enthusiasm, commitment interest, raised self-esteem and experience of success, lowered failure – to learn and to achieve in school for its own sake and for personal satisfaction rather than, for example, for marks, grades and external markers of achievement. (In the school in question, set in the East Asian context in which marks and grades reign supreme, how this was addressed is discussed in subsequent chapters, e.g. enabling students to gain marks for class participation.)

The link between collaborative, active learning, interactive learning, student-centredness, and engaged, effective learning is well established through the authors cited above (see also Lumpkin 2007: 159). Olson notes that:

- Successful, engaged learners are responsible for their own learning. These students are self-regulated and able to define their own learning goals and evaluate their own achievement.
- In order to have engaged learning, tasks need to be challenging, authentic, and multidisciplinary. Such tasks are typically complex and involve sustained amounts of time.
- Assessment of engaged learning involves presenting students with an authentic task, project, or investigation, and then observing, interviewing, and examining their presentations and artifacts to assess what they actually know and can do.
- The most powerful models of instruction are interactive. Instruction actively engages the learner, and is generative. Instruction encourages the learner to construct and produce knowledge in meaningful ways. Students teach others interactively and interact generatively with their teacher and peers.
- For engaged learning to happen, the classroom must be conceived of as a knowledge-building learning community. Such communities not only develop shared understandings collaboratively but also create empathetic learning environments that value diversity and multiple perspectives.
- Collaborative work that is learning-centered often involves small groups or teams of two or more students within a classroom or across classroom boundaries.
- The role of the teacher in the classroom has shifted from the primary role of information giver to that of facilitator, guide, and learner. As a facilitator, the teacher provides the rich environments and learning experiences needed for collaborative study.

- One important student role is that of explorer. Interaction with the physical world and with other people allows students to discover concepts and apply skills. Students are then encouraged to reflect upon their discoveries.

(2008: 7–8)

Moeller and Reitzes (2011: 17) comment that student-centred learning to develop engaged learning implies major changes to the roles of both students and teachers. Here, students, with teachers as their facilitators (rather than, for example, didacts or lecturers), explore their own areas of interest and development, producing evidence of their own learning. Teachers provide opportunities for their students to take control of their own learning pathways and outcomes. The authors indicate that there is much to be done in developing teachers' capabilities in working with new technologies, changing their pedagogies, values and school cultures, and that professional development has a key role to play in this (2011: 14). These are key features of the innovation in the school in question. Moeller and Reitzes (2011) add a note of caution, indicating that, whilst technology can support student-centred learning, without changes to pedagogy and teacher behaviour, technology on its own is unlikely to transform traditional lecture-based learning environments suddenly into student-centred environments (2011: 44).

In furthering collaborative learning, Perifanou (2010) reports the importance of positive interdependence, individual accountability, fruitful interaction, the development of social skills, and group processing. She comments (2010: 10) that collaborative learning promotes high achievement (socially, personally and cognitively), motivation, independent learning, critical thinking and higher-order thinking.

Kearsley and Shneiderman (1999) link engaged learning strongly to technology-based learning and constructivism. They define engaged learning as those student activities which require higher-order cognitive processes such as reasoning, problem-solving, judgements, and decision-making. Engaged learning rests on, and develops, the intrinsic motivation of students to learn because the tasks and the learning environments are meaningful to them. Collaboration, they aver, increases student motivation and engagement, and engagement is concerned with real-world learning.

Effective learning with ICT

Two major reviews of ICT and pedagogy in Europe drew similar conclusions. The ICT Cluster (2010) notes that active and interactive teaching which uses ICT should offer all students the chance to learn by doing (2010: 22), with innovations in pedagogy bringing about individualized learning (2010: 23). Here, it recognizes that ongoing teacher education and training are key factors to the success of this enterprise (2010: 25). The Education, Audiovisual and Culture Executive Agency of the European Commission (2011) highlighted the significance of ICT in promoting active, innovative and experiential learning (2011: 43), with project-based learning, and engaged learning high on the agenda. The bundle of terms such as collaborative learning, interactive learning, problem-based learning, project-based learning, self-directed learning and engaged learning are often used together and, indeed, synonymously (Olson 2008: 1).

Sringam and Geer (2000: 8) note that collaborative learning through electronic means embraces planning, sharing and contributing, agreeing and disagreeing, negotiating, testing ideas, and coming to a final consensus in statements and applications of the knowledge that has been co-constructed.

Webb and Cox (2004) note that ICT-related pedagogies include students conducting investigations, conjecture, exploration, explanation of relationships, with the teacher probing and challenging students both individually and in small groups and, importantly, handing over control and regulation of the learning much more to students (2004: 274); in short, higher-order thinking. Significantly, they note the need for a major change in teachers' knowledge and philosophy of the nature and potential of ICT in order to enable students to benefit from the ICT curriculum (2004: 263). From this, teachers can understand the affordances provided by ICT and from this develop their pedagogical practices (2004: 264), creating a student-centred environment with the full integration of ICT into the curriculum (2004: 266).

Mumtaz (2000) notes the importance of teachers' pedagogical knowledge (combining content and pedagogy), where that pedagogy includes: a positive attitude towards ICT; student choice rather than teacher direction; and student empowerment as (individual) learners rather than recipients of teacher instruction. In promoting these, she notes that this involves the development of teachers' ICT competencies, the integration of ICT into the curriculum (and with changes made to the curriculum where relevant) and changes to teachers' roles.

Zandvliet and Fraser (2004) note that suitable learning environments (widely interpreted, e.g. physical, emotional, cognitive) to promote engaged learning with ICT include student cohesiveness, involvement, autonomy and independence, task orientation and cooperation. These involve small-group project work, a student-centred approach to teaching and an emphasis on problem-solving, with teachers acting as facilitators. This echoes a substantial review of pedagogy related to ICT by Webb and Cox (2004) in which they show that teachers' roles include setting joint tasks, promoting students, self-management, 'fostering multiple perspectives' (2004: 240) and scaffolding learning, making the complex simple and understandable, motivating students to learn independently and harnessing the power of collaborative learning with ICT to promote student decision-making.

Blended learning constitutes a 'fundamental paradigm shift' (Dziuban *et al.* 2004), as it moves pedagogy away from teacher-centredness to learner-centredness, from passive learners to active and interactive learners (student-instructor, student-student, student-content, student-outside resources) and it integrates formative and summative assessment into learning, i.e. assessment *for* learning and *as* learning. Long and Jennings (2005) found that students using blended learning outperformed those using face-to-face learning (see also Sun *et al.* 2008), whilst Englert *et al.* (2007) note that students with disabilities outperformed their peers when using blended learning. Strobel and van Barneveld (2009) found that project-based learning, facilitated by ICT, promoted long-term retention, skill development and enhanced student and teacher satisfaction, whereas traditional approaches were more effective for short-term retention and passing standardized tests. Further, Barbour and Reeves (2009: 402) report that online learning can benefit students who have their own particular, independent ways of, and interests in, learning orientations and who are effective in managing their own time and learning.

Problem-solving, a higher-order thinking skill, involves the recognition and clarification of the problem, evaluating strategies to solve it, selecting a solution, implementing the strategy and evaluating its effectiveness. With regard to ICT, Ager (1998, 2000) suggests that ICT develops several problem-solving skills: understanding and representing the problem and the situation, gathering, selecting and organizing relevant information, planning strategies for intervention and hypothesis formulation and testing. Wood *et al.* (1999) argue that problem-solving is not a matter of accumulating facts, but applying higher-order thinking skills. With regard to Internet use, Ager (1998) suggests that higher-order skills involve judgements of the accuracy, validity, reliability, plausibility and bias of information, prediction, pattern recognition and hypothesizing.

Cohen *et al.* (2010: 67) note that effective use of ICT requires teachers to be able to operate in different learning situations; e.g. one-to-one learning; whole-class teaching and learning; group work; independent/individual work. They note that teachers will need to develop their expertise in promoting interaction, e.g. when to intervene and when to stand back; how to help students to search for information; how to help students to define the task and use information-seeking strategies to locate and access information; how to evaluate and synthesize information; and how to help students to search, edit, draft, format, collate, connect, model, summarize and present information for a particular purpose and a real audience. The authors suggest that ICT has very considerable potential to change teaching and learning styles and behaviour, but that this is conditional upon a range of factors, at the heart of which lie both teachers and students, and that this engages the need to focus on student motivation; explicit identification of the desired outcomes of learning; modelling, demonstrating and supporting students towards the outcomes; active learning; formative assessment and summative assessment linked to intended learning outcomes; opportunities to practise new skills and to learn and create new knowledge; collaborative learning; and real-world/authentic learning.

The effective use of ICT depends on a range of factors:

- Teacher competence, expertise and preparedness to change (Moseley et al. 1999);
- Teachers are needed to mediate ICT (Higgins 2001);
- Teachers will be continually and actively assessing students' understanding of the meaning that they have derived from the activities and how they can choose the directions for development (Higgins 2001);
- Increased, rich and unambiguous feedback to students concerning progress (Herron 1996);
- Teachers must recognize that the task is to engage students cognitively, not as a classroom control device (Davis et al. 1997);
- The learning objectives must be clear (Scardamalia and Bereiter 1994), and the pedagogical use of ICT must match the learning objectives of the lesson (Higgins 2001);
- The focus of the technology use must not be too diffuse (Higgins 2001);
- 'Ground rules' for collaboration between students must be set, e.g. listening with respect, responding to challenges with reasons, encouraging partners to give their views and trying to reach agreement (Higgins 2001);
- The potential of multi-sensory ICT must be used to enhance learning (Paivio 1986; Pankuch 2000);
- Cooperative learning must be extended (Underwood and Brown 1997);
- Opportunities must be provided for prolonged ICT contact (Grabe and Grabe 2001);
- Teachers must be vigilant to balance the exploration of software with the possible student frustration if it is too complex (Cox 1997);
- Teachers must set appropriate tasks for students to maximize the benefits of ICT usage (Cox 1997);
- Teachers must recognize that different degrees of support will be required for different kinds of software and application, and for students with different degrees of confidence and expertise in using ICT (Cox 1997).

It is as if the provision of ICT is a useful but not sufficient condition for effective development, and that *teachers* are the critical factor, rather than hardware or software (Valdez et al. 2000).

In an early work, Cradler (1994) indicates a number of other conditions that appear to need to be met if the potential of ICT is to be realized and effective learning ensured:

1 Technology development factors:
    o The opportunity to provide immediate feedback to students and to adjust task difficulty in response to student performance, i.e. to improve matching and individualization;
    o Ease of use by both teachers and students;

- Sustained student motivation, interest and use;
- Increased student control of the rate and pacing of learning;
- Increased individualization of learning;
- The opportunity of ICT to provide students with simulations not available in the classroom or from books;
- The opportunity to use multiple technologies;
- Teacher and student involvement in the development and use of the technologies;
- The degree to which the developments are aligned to existing practices, curricula and resources.

2 Technology application factors:
- The development of instruction that relies on – i.e. it cannot operate without – the new technologies;
- The provision of guidelines on how to use and integrate the technology into the classroom;
- Access to the technology and educational programmes;
- Enhancement and expansion of the curriculum (i.e. so that the technology is not only used to reinforce an existing curriculum, but also that it is, in part, compatible with it);
- The ease with which the technology can be used and adapted for, and into, a range of learning environments (including the home);
- The appropriate adult resources (expertise, availability);
- The applicability of the technology for a diverse range of students.

Osberg (1997) suggests that, in the context of higher-order thinking and ICT, it is important for teachers to develop creative and critical skills through ICT, and to apply learning through ICT to relevant and real-life situations. In turn, this requires a move away from a didactic approach towards a role for teachers as enablers of learning (Davis *et al.* 1997; Noss and Pachler 1999).

The content of curricula has increased potential to provide authentic, real-world learning and materials (Kramarski and Feldman 2000). For example, Chaika (1999) found that mathematics students who used multimedia not only reduced their anxiety but also saw greater relevance of their mathematics for the real world. Clear connections must be made in the minds of the learners, together with the ability to transfer knowledge. This, suggest Roschelle *et al.* (2000), places a premium on learning and applying underlying concepts rather than simply the memorization of facts and simple solutions.

What is being suggested here is the need for engaged and meaningful learning, with real-life tasks, which will be multidisciplinary, project-based, participative ('minds-on' as well as 'hands-on') and collaborative (Jones *et al.* 1995). Collaborative work will require fluid and *ad hoc* grouping of students, with active pedagogies.

Hawkins (2002) found that collaboration through ICT was learned through:

- Listening to and repeating what students had said;
- Talking by referring to what the previous person had said;
- Thinking of ways or phrases to encourage other members of the group;
- Explaining something to someone without doing it for them;
- Setting up some group rules to be agreed by all group members;
- Asking each other for help when they need it;
- Helping someone when they ask for it;
- Encouraging each other;
- Sharing ideas;
- Discussing things together that they did not like;
- Being able to chat whilst working;
- Being loyal to each other.

Grabe and Grabe (2001) note that in cooperative learning with and through ICT, the teacher's task is to make it clear that learners have to critique ideas rather than people, and that cooperation takes time to develop. They suggest that, in this process, cooperative activities should be rewarded, for example the rewarding of interdependence, individual accountability and each person's contribution to the overall group project. Similarly, Roschelle *et al.* (2000) argue that students can learn the skills of supportive criticism through questioning of each other, diagrams, statements, sharing databases, opinions and information.

Dykes (2001) reported important cognitive benefits of peer interaction with ICT, in that students were compelled to face each others' ideas, could provide each other with mutual support and guidance, could provide scaffolding for each other, could take complementary roles in the group, gave and received meaningful feedback, exchanged and shared new ideas and constructed new understandings through discourse. Interaction and collaboration, Dykes suggests, were both social and cognitive (2001: 3), but they had to be planned, supported and encouraged. Collaboration, Dykes suggests (2001: 8), is particularly effective where learners have a clear goal and an identifiable outcome.

Tolmie and Boyle (2000) developed a list of seven critical factors which they considered necessary for successful use of computer-mediated communication (CMC) (cf. Cox 1997; Kowch and Schwier 1997; Cicco *et al.* 2000). They include:

1 Create small self-selected discussion groups, with a recommended size of around six.
2 Try to ensure that the members know each other and that a preliminary face-to-face session takes place.
3 Recognize that experienced users of CMC will interact more than non-experienced users or younger students.
4 Students must understand clearly, as a group, the task they are to accomplish.

5   Provide students with the opportunity to negotiate frameworks and understand their own and each others' roles within the group and the task.
6   Ensure that CMC is 'built in' to the work of the group – as a requirement rather than an optional extra.
7   Ensure that the technical aspects of ICT software and hardware present no obstacles to use.

Hattie (2009), using Cohen's d (a measure of effect size, often calculated as the difference in the means of the two groups, divided by the average of their standard deviations), notes the high effect sizes of factors influencing student learning and achievement:

- Formative evaluation ($d = 0.90$)
- Feedback ($d = 0.73$)
- Professional development ($d = 0.62$)
- Problem-solving teaching ($d = 0.61$)
- Help-seeking (from peers, from a teacher) ($d = 0.60$)
- Cooperative versus individualistic learning ($d = 0.59$)
- Peer tutoring ($d = 0.55$)
- Parental involvement ($d = 0.51$)
- Small-group learning ($d = 0.49$)
- Motivation ($d = 0.48$)
- Concentration/engagement ($d = 0.48$)
- Cooperative learning ($d = 0.41$)
- Reducing anxiety ($d = 0.41$)
- Inquiry-based teaching ($d = 0.31$).

In other words, the very elements of the innovation in the school in question here, many of which benefit from ICT, find support from Hattie's work (2009, 2012).

Claims made for ICT in learning and education

The Education, Audiovisual and Culture Executive Agency of the European Commission (2011) noted that ICT can exert a positive impact on learning (2011: 44) and that there are many benefits claimed for using ICT in classrooms. Principal amongst these are that it can:

- Raise student achievement in all subjects and for all students;
- Promote higher-order thinking in order to evaluate knowledge;
- Promote learning for capability and problem-solving;
- Foster collaborative learning;
- Raise students' motivation and engagement significantly.

Indeed, in an early document, the National Council for Educational Technology (1994) indicated many benefits from ICT in schools:

1. Children who use a computer at home are more enthusiastic and confident when using one at school.
2. Video games can be educational if they are well managed.
3. ICT can provide a safe and non-threatening environment for learning, and ICT gives students the power to try out different ideas and to take risks.
4. ICT has the flexibility to meet the individual needs and abilities of each student.
5. Students who have not enjoyed learning can be encouraged by the use of ICT, and interactive technology motivates and stimulates learning.
6. Computers give students the chance to achieve where they have previously failed and computers can reduce the risk of failure at school.
7. ICT allows students to reflect on what they have written and to change it easily, and using a computer to produce a successful piece of writing can motivate students to acquire basic literacy skills.
8. ICT gives students immediate access to richer source materials than a single textbook.
9. ICT can present information in new ways which help students to understand, assimilate and use it more readily.
10. ICT removes the chore of processing data manually and frees students to concentrate on its interpretation and use.
11. Difficult ideas are made more understandable when ICT makes them visible.
12. Computing programs which use digitized speech can help students to read and spell.
13. Computer simulations encourage analytical and divergent thinking.
14. ICT is particularly successful in holding the attention of pupils with emotional and behavioural difficulties.
15. ICT can often compensate for the communication and learning difficulties of students with physical and sensory impairments, and students with profound and multiple learning difficulties can be encouraged towards purposeful activity and self-awareness by ICT.
16. Using ICT makes teachers take a fresh look at how they teach and the ways in which students learn, and their students make more effective use of computers if teachers know how and when to intervene.
17. Computers help students to learn when used in well-designed, meaningful tasks and activities.
18. ICT offers potential for effective group working.
19. Giving teachers easy access to computers encourages and improves the use of ICT in the curriculum, and head teachers who use computers raise the profile of ICT in their schools.
20. Management information systems can help save money and time in schools.

LaJoie (1993) showed how ICT could support cognitive processes such as memory and sharing cognitive load. Hennessy (2006) shows clearly that this may only be possible if teachers have a clear grasp of how pedagogy and the use of ICT in classrooms are linked.

The Department for Education and Skills (2002: 3) notes that ICT can have a positive effect on students' academic attainment, and that within this, the teacher and pedagogy play a crucial role. ICT, it is claimed, enables students to take greater control of their learning and enhances learning on a variety of fronts (Higgins 2001). ICT can bring improvements on several fronts:

- Student outcomes
  o Performance increases, particularly when there is interactivity and multiple technologies (video, computer, telecommunications);
  o Attitudes improve and confidence increases, particularly in 'at risk' students;
  o Instructional opportunities are provided that otherwise might not have been possible.

- Educator outcomes
  o Moving from a traditional, directive approach to a student-centred approach;
  o Increased emphasis on individualized programmes of learning;
  o Greater revision of, and reflection on, curricula and instructional strategies.

Wegerif (2002) suggests that using ICT in classrooms, particularly in a constructivist approach, has great potential to develop students' higher-order cognitive skills, but that the relationship between ICT, thinking skills and pedagogy is complex. He notes that a review of the evidence suggests that using technology does not, by itself, lead to transferable thinking skills but that the success of ICT depends crucially on how the technology is used. Much depends on the role of the teacher.

The British Educational Communications and Technology Agency (BECTA) (2002) suggested that the effective use of ICT can lead to benefits in terms of greater student motivation, self-esteem and confidence, enhanced questioning skills and the promotion of initiative and independent learning, improving presentations, developing problem-solving capabilities, promoting better information handling skills, increasing 'time on-task', and improving social and communication skills.

Wagner (2012) indicates that innovative students using ICT develop and use their curiosity, enjoy collaboration and have heightened motivation, a view echoed by Fullan (2013: 24). Further, Prensky (2011) indicates that ICT can have an enormous impact on students' learning and on pedagogies, particularly in terms of student-centred, problem-based, enquiry-based and collaborative learning. In short, he indicates that these newer pedagogies constitute the end of teaching by telling and a fundamental change of roles for both teachers and students (2011: 6), with learning partnerships developing between teachers and students and between students and students. Teaching and learning using ICT (particularly video, cell phones and free visual communication media) become more closely connected to the 'real world' outside schools, and offer students far more choices rather than following a mandated single curriculum. Prensky (2012) further suggests that 'a new trio' of skills have heightened importance: working in virtual communities, making video and programming. Add to this Gee's comment (2005) that video games can be a powerful learning tool in themselves.

Moeller and Reitzes (2011) argue that ICT on its own will not bring reform, but that it has to be coupled with, and be part of, support mechanisms for ongoing comprehensive and systematic educational reform towards student-centred learning in which students can capitalize on their strengths, areas of interest and performance to date (2011: 7), and improve their performance (2011: 9) and motivation (2011: 12). Online learning, they report, is enhanced where learners have control over their interactions with the media in question and where they are prompted to reflect on their learning. The authors state that such reforms must ensure that learning is active rather than passive, with students taking responsibility for their own learning, all facilitated by ICT (2011: 6).

Bouffard (2008) reports a Harvard Family Research Project study which indicates that increased communication between home and school, facilitated by technology (2008: 27), thereby improves students' academic performance (though their report indicated that there was still a long way to go in this respect (2008: 4)). One of the purposes of the project in the school in question was to improve such communication.

Stoney and Oliver (1999) found that using an interactive microworld led to an enhancement of learners' cognitive engagement and autonomous, self-regulated learning and concentration, with greater emphasis being placed on the acquisition of higher-order thinking and problem-solving skills and less emphasis being placed on the assimilation of isolated facts and more facts. Further, they found that students' motivation, engagement and concentration improved when their higher-order skills were being exercised and developed (1999: 12–13). However, they offer a cautionary note. They report that interactive multimedia failed to deliver their potential where they were designed round the old (instructivist) paradigm (see also Fullan 2013: 61). Rather, they suggest that a well-constructed multimedia programme, with cooperative and situated learning, with an exploratory approach being adopted and with students working at their own pace and in their own sequences, can fulfil the potential of multimedia learning. Self-paced learning, they aver, can provide space for reflection and the integration of experience, understanding and conceptual development (Stoney and Oliver 1999: 8).

Deighton and Hocking (1999) found that, by introducing ICT into the learning environment, not only was interest in learning enhanced, but that this was as a consequence of making it more student-centred, collaborative and cooperative, with the involvement of creative problem-solving. Indeed, in such situations they found enhanced learner questioning they became more powerful thinkers.

Hattie (2009), from his review of meta-analyses, indicates several important average effect sizes of factors influencing student learning and achievement (introduced in Chapter 1: 0 to 0.20 = weak effect; 0.21 to 0.50 = modest effect; 0.51 to 1.00 = moderate effect; >1.00 = strong effect):

- Interactive video methods ($d = 0.52$);
- Computer-assisted instruction ($d = 0.37$);
- Simulations ($d = 0.33$);
- Visual/audiovisual methods ($d = 0.22$);
- Web-based learning ($d = 0.18$).

He notes that there is no *necessary* relation between computers and learning outcomes, but that computers 'can increase the probability of learning' and can be used to positive effect when diverse teaching strategies are present, all parties are given prior training in computer usage, plentiful learning opportunities are provided (with the student in control of his/own learning) and with optimum use of peer learning and feedback (2009: 221).

Similarly, Webb and Cox note that student-centredness does not follow automatically from the increased use of ICT (2004: 275). Rather, they argue for a more nuanced and complex approach to understanding the relationship, and that student-centredness is as much contingent on the teacher, the student and the subject matter as it is on ICT (2004: 276–7). The positive effects of ICT are not automatic, but conditional on a range of other factors. Fullan (2013: 43–54) notes some key findings from the research evidence of ICT and learning:

- Student-centred pedagogy, extending student learning beyond the classroom, were central factors;
- Innovative teaching was more likely to occur where teachers collaborated on instructional practices and were involved in engaging professional development;
- School leadership was a decisive factor in the success of ICT in schools, providing support for development;
- Rich, relevant tasks were essential, increasing student talk was significant, handing responsibility for learning to students was important and formative assessment was a key feature;
- Collaborative work between students was significant, with students controlling and taking responsibility for their own learning;
- Active learning and problem-solving were essential features.

A major claim for ICT in schools is its ability to foster social learning (see e.g. Crook 1994) which, as suggested earlier in the chapter, is a major factor in the development of higher-order cognition, and ICT can promote cooperative learning. Smeets and Mooij (2001) found that, in the majority of lessons they observed, some or all pupils were working in pairs at the computers and that in all the *innovative* learning environments that were referred to, cooperative learning was being stimulated.

Hawkins (2002) noted that ICT improved learners' abilities to work as team members and to share knowledge. Collaboration was not simply between students; rather, students felt comfortable in asking teachers questions and, conversely, teachers were less intimidated in seeking help from students. Teachers became more cooperative and convinced of the value of cooperative learning (Sandholtz *et al.* 1997; Sivin-Kachala 1998). Further, Deighton and Hocking (1999) found that ICT improved collaborative problem-solving, peer tutoring and collaboration, and technology-rich classrooms helped uncertain and reluctant teachers (Sandholtz *et al.* 1997).

Old and new pedagogies with ICT

The argument so far is suggesting that ICT has the potential to bring about significant improvements in collaborative teaching and learning, student performance, student motivation and attitude, and engaged, interactive, real-world, student-centred learning. However, it has also suggested that these require dramatic changes in pedagogy, from traditional didacticism to active and interactive teaching and learning strategies (see Table 2.3).

Within the new ICT-supported pedagogy it is possible to match key features of e-learning and collaborative learning (see Table 2.4)

Such changes in pedagogy bring about significant changes in how we view teaching and the teachers' roles (see Table 2.5).

Assessment and ICT

Much traditional assessment has taken the form of testing of recall, memorization and factual knowledge, leavened with some informed personal opinions. Students sometimes have to wait for several days or, in the case of public examinations, months for feedback in the form of a simple indication of the grade reached. ICT has the potential to develop and use alternative, and maybe more fruitful, assessment methods (see e.g. the ICT Cluster 2010: 30).

Assessment with ICT makes several positive claims (Jones *et al.* 1995; Pachler and Byrom 1999; Roschelle *et al.* 2000; Glazer 2000; Fetherston 2001; Liu *et al.* 2001; Department for Education and Skills 2002; Cohen *et al.* 2010; Moeller and Reitzes 2011):

- Feedback can be very rapid, even immediate;
- Feedback can be private, avoiding public humiliation;
- As students are working with ICT in groups, this frees time for the teacher to give feedback to individuals;

Table 2.3 Old and new pedagogies with ICT

Old pedagogy	New pedagogy
Know as much as there is in the book and as much as the teacher says	Use strategies to decide what is worth knowing in the head and what needs to be stored: not all information should be learned
Teachers uses lecture to pass on his or her knowledge to the students	Teacher helps students access, select, evaluate, organize, and store information coming from a wide range of sources
Students dump information or organize information by categories	Students organize by categories and according to a range of perspectives
Students put information on paper for the teacher to see or the paper is posted on the wall for the school to see	Students write to disks or publish on the web for parents, relatives and a wider audience to see
Paper journals and books as the source of knowledge	Online journals and books replacing established protocols for writing and publishing
Texts are set	Texts are editable
Students have limited choice of sources	Students' personal choices are expected
Goals using technology are not integrated or not present	Integrating classroom goals with the power of technology
Intellectual products such as reports are fixed on paper and finished	Intellectual products are revisable living documents subject to addition, subtraction and change
Report form tests with no connection to the persons producing them	A range of creative multi-sensory electronic forms, such as web pages, with movement, charts, and pictures with personal connections
Neat handwritten reports with every appearance of being produced by children	Intellectual product has a professional look printed with colour and attention to design
Students hide papers from each other, allowing only teachers to read the paper	Students exchange tips about editing and revising their products
Texts are brought home and shared with parents or others in person	Teacher asks students to share their products with friends and relatives in an attachment or on the web as a way to revise and publish for an audience
Knowledge is displayed in one form only	Knowledge is written in a range of forms such as web pages, paper reports, PowerPoint presentations, by cutting and pasting the information into different programmes
Knowledge is displayed only in a linear form	Knowledge is displayed in linear and hypertext formats. Class discusses advantages of each
Students who don't use technology at a young age don't have facility with electronic tools	Students use technology early and often, and discuss strategies for using tools

Table 2.4 Key features of e-learning and collaborative learning

Key features of e-learning support	Key features of collaborative learning
• Autonomy in student learning	• Learners have individual responsibility and accountability
• An environment which promotes collaborative learning	• Learning interaction takes place in small groups
• Moving beyond knowledge transmission to include communication as a real life skill	• Communication during learning is interactive and dynamic
• Promotion of personalisation and reduction of depersonalisation of learning	• Learners can identify their role in the learning task
• Support for learners in development of ICT and personal learning	• Participants have a shared understanding within the learning environment

Table 2.5 Traditional and newer teacher roles with ICT

Traditional roles	Newer roles with ICT
Teacher-transmission to passive learners who obey and receive	Process-based curricula with learners who question and analyze
Teacher-oriented	Learner-oriented
Teachers as task setters for individual learning	Teachers as managers of collaborative learning
An organizer of learning activities	An enabler of quality learning experiences
Dictating the learning	Creating enabling structures for learning
Technology as a tutor	Technology to promote interaction
Technology as a resource for enquiry	Technology to support creativity
Didactic teaching	Active learning
Low order retention and recall	Higher-order thinking
Teachers as providers of information and experts in all knowledge	Teachers as advisors, managers and facilitators of learning
Teachers as suppliers of knowledge	Teachers as developers of skills
Teacher as a distant authority	Developed student–teacher relationships
Teacher control of learning – its timing, pacing and contents	Teachers standing back to let learning happen and for children to solve problems
Prescriptions for what, when and how students will be taught	Responsiveness to students' cognitive needs and development
Teacher in narrow and unchanging range of roles	Teacher in many roles as required: designer, director-actor, facilitator, manager

- Feedback is richer because the computer can analyze the learner's performance in more detail and with more closely targeted feedback than the busy teacher;
- The computer can assess higher-order thinking and learning;

- Longitudinal assessment is possible through stored databases of each student, enabling progress to be tracked and presented easily;
- Authentic assessment is developed, and linked to real-world learning;
- Multidisciplinary tasks are able to be assessed;
- Assessment is based on performance of real tasks;
- Assessment can be more broadly based, including class participation;
- The links between learning, diagnosis and assessment are strengthened; assessment is linked to learning;
- Student self-assessment is facilitated;
- Examination anxiety is reduced, and less emphasis is placed on a single 'right' answer recalled at high speed;
- Non-academic achievement and skills can be accredited and recognized;
- The gap between learners and assessors is bridged; teachers, peers and individual students become both learners and assessors.

Rapid, rich and timely feedback improves learning and motivation (McClintock 1992; Roschelle *et al.* 2000), and in the school in question here, the teacher could gain immediate, electronic in-class feedback on who had or had not understood a matter in the class. Assessment and motivation are profoundly linked. ICT can indicate the number of attempts a student has made, the number of clues that needed to be supplied, the percentage of correct responses and the success of completion of the task (Pachler and Byrom 1999) (and, indeed, in the school in question the use of the computer by each student was automatically logged, so that teachers could see the kinds of uses made by the students, and when they were using them a lot – for example, in the run-up to examinations).

Moeller and Reitzes argue for ICT-supported, electronic assessment being regarded as a means to enable closer links between assessment and learning (2011: 6). Whereas traditional assessment frequently takes the form of summative, end-of-course testing, the provision of diagnostic assessments of strengths, weaknesses, difficulties, achievements and ways of learning and thinking is enriched and facilitated by ICT, in terms of speed and the quality of feedback. Assessment becomes the springboard into learning, having a strong formative potential. In short, assessment becomes assessment *for* learning and assessment *as* learning. These are familiar epithets of assessment, and ICT has considerable potential to provide timely (e.g. immediate) feedback to both teachers and learners to improve teaching and learning, respectively. This was a feature of the software used in the school in question here, wherein in-class polling, screen monitoring and feedback could provide the teacher with immediate feedback, so that, if necessary, further explanation and re-teaching could take place.

Authentic assessment embodies constructivist learning principles (Dykes 2001), for example through real-world simulations which enable students to demonstrate the extent to which they can transfer knowledge from classrooms to typical real-life situations (Simonson *et al.* 2000). Learning with

ICT is collaborative and requires multiple thinking strategies. To be able to reflect and embrace these forms of learning and to present evidence of learning, a suitable form of assessment is portfolio assessment, in which students compile their own portfolios of work, selecting what to include and how to present the material. Such portfolio assessment is motivating for learners (Liu *et al.* 2001), because it makes them agents of their own assessment, building in involvement and engagement. Portfolios require students to collect, select, present and reflect on their work and their learning (Grabe and Grabe 2001). Authentic assessment extends to in-class assessment (e.g. class participation).

Traditional assessment has usually been the task of teachers. Dykes (2001) suggests that this task will not be relinquished with the arrival of ICT. Rather, it will mutate, so that teachers set up learning activities and opportunities for rich assessment and so that students themselves become involved in assessment. This can take several forms. For example, Liu *et al.* (2001) suggest that a networked system enables peer-group assessment and self-assessment to be developed, through online submitted work, wikis, the opportunity for peers to comment on each others' work and for individual learners to learn from this, be it from comments or online grading to wikis and institutional platforms for sharing and contributing to comments (see also Collis *et al.* 2001).

On the other hand, Pachler and Byrom (1999) suggest that it becomes harder to find out whether the work is the student's own, whether students have been 'free riders' in group projects, and whether the student understands what she or he has written. Indeed, a surfeit of computer-assisted assessment might lead to student boredom, rote learning and cheating (Hartley *et al.* 1996; Sandholtz *et al.* 1997).

Leadership for promoting learning with ICT

Louis *et al.* (2010: 68) suggest that principals influence student achievement by:

- *Setting directions*: developing and sustaining a shared vision and consenting to group-developed goals, creating high expectations of performance and sharing the direction of developments;
- *Developing people*: supporting all participants as individuals, simulating intellectual development and being models of desired values, behaviours and practices;
- *Redesigning the organization*: developing cultures and infrastructures of collaboration, developing positive relationships between institutions, families and the community;
- *Managing the instructional programme*: developing and aligning human and instructional resources, instructional resources and support, monitoring procedures and protecting staff from unnecessary distractions.

In their study, teachers and principals identified effective instructional leadership practice in promoting student learning, comprising (2010: 71–2):

- Focusing the school on goals and expectations for student achievement;
- Keeping track of teachers' professional development needs;
- Creating structures and opportunities for teachers to collaborate;
- Monitoring teachers' work in the classroom;
- Providing mentoring opportunities for new teachers;
- Being easily accessible;
- Providing backup for teachers with student discipline and with parents;
- Staying current.

Leaders, avers Fullan (2013: 70), are both the drivers of innovation and the means for bringing about cohesion amongst the several dimensions of innovation, addressing eight major dimensions of innovation (2013: 66–71):

1. A clear focus (on, for example, content, process, roles);
2. Innovations that cannot be resisted;
3. Empathy with participants involved in the innovation;
4. Capacity building (knowledge, competencies, skills, attitudes and dispositions);
5. Contagion (through attention to innovating through groups and peers rather than individuals);
6. Transparency (e.g. in assessing the innovation and its implementation, and honesty in discussing how it is operating);
7. Elimination of non-essentials (e.g. removing elements which distract the innovation from its main purpose, drive and focus);
8. Leadership (which orchestrates the preceding seven dimensions into a harmonious whole).

Fullan (2013: 74), argues for the permeation of created coherence between the elements of the innovation (cf. Fullan 2001: 107), which involves identifying and focusing on priorities within the disturbance caused by the innovation.

Many of these eight dimensions are less about content and more about process, and, importantly, people and culture. As Fullan mentions (2005: 45), people are both the problem and the solution, and to effect change is to change their context, environment and conditions. As he notes (Fullan 2001: 79, 115), in a culture of change and innovation, leaders have to change the context and environment of participants to create those conditions in which innovation, change and learning can flourish. They set the conditions for change and guide participants through change in changed conditions and circumstances. In short, he remarks (2001: 43), the task is one of 'reculturing', and he argues that if leaders want to change participants' behaviour then they need to focus on changing their situation (Fullan 2011b: 45, 122–3). This happened in the school in question here.

With regard to leadership of change involving ICT, Tan (2010) notes that leaders in the school have a key role in providing the infrastructure which supports ICT usage, in actively promoting and supporting pedagogical change with ICT, and in developing a culture in the school that fosters extended ICT usage in the context of pedagogical change. Indeed, Tan notes that these could impact on the nature and level of computer use in classrooms (2010: 893). In introducing innovation in school with regard to ICT, leaders, then, have a key role in:

1 Infrastructural development;
2 Organizational and policy development;
3 Pedagogical innovation and change;
4 School cultural change (Tan 2010: 894).

Fullan (2011a: 35) notes that effective leaders of school development and reform focus on four areas:

1 Parents and community;
2 Development and sustenance of professional capacity;
3 Instructional matters (e.g. coherence and depth);
4 The safety of students (interpreted widely, to include intellectual and psychological safety).

These were main areas of focus in the innovation of the school in question. The combination of leadership and focus constituted a core dynamic in managing the multidimensional innovation in the school in question here.

Collaboration and respect combine with the leader's energy, optimism, enthusiasm, concern for people, persistence, resolve, resoluteness, confidence, purpose, trust, motivation of others and clear-headedness to effect the 'moral purpose' (Fullan 2011a) of increasing school, student and teacher improvement through collaboration, capacity building, sharing and the creation of professional learning communities. As will be seen in the later chapters of this book, persistence, determination and resolve became key features of the school principal's leadership strategy.

Conclusion

The chapter has argued that ICT has considerable potential to support a range of innovations, changes and developments in schools, teaching and learning. Whilst this is a commonplace truism, it has also suggested that there are no automatic guarantees of success here. Success is conditional on a range of deep-seated values, practices and changes being operational in schools, and behaviour may change before values, i.e. change affects and is affected by school culture, organizational health and climate (cf. Chapter 1). In turn, such changes require capacity building, support and development, and cultural changes; indeed, cultural change is the input, process and outcome of innovations in schools.

Further, the chapter has argued that the effective development of ICT in schools is premised on social constructivism, engaged learning, collaborative and interactive learning, active learning, student-centred learning, enhanced communication between parties and the harnessing of student motivation. Whilst there are many definitions of these terms, put briefly, these features themselves may constitute and require significant changes in pedagogy, classroom relationships, ways of working, ways of assessing students and providing feedback, and, importantly, organizational culture change.

The contents and processes of the many dimensions of innovation outlined in this chapter argue for the centrality of effective and sustained leadership of innovation, and the chapter closed with some indications of the tasks, qualities and roles of leaders in managing change and innovation here, not least in fostering the appropriate conditions and contexts of change. Indeed, leadership, as well as cultural change, is the input, process and outcome of the changes suggested, with shared leadership and the cultivation of the self-leadership of students being prominent.

The argument in this chapter has been couched in terms of possibility and prescription. Putting it into practice is neither as neat nor as comfortable as these prescriptions suggest, and the subsequent chapters of this book provide a case study of some of the challenges encountered and solutions adopted in one school.

3 The background to the case study

The school in question is in Macau, China. This chapter reports the background to schooling in Macau and to the school in question. It also describes the pilot project and its evaluation, which was part of its overall 'ESOS' project ('Empowering Students for an Open School'). The chapter sets the background for the particular school initiative within the context of schooling in Macau, in sufficient detail to indicate how the project in question constituted a major innovation in schooling in Macau. The chapter introduces schooling provision and the extensive decentralization of schooling in Macau, the majority role played by Catholic schools in Macau (of which the school was one), the nature of decision-making on curricula, pedagogy and assessment in Macau schools, and some current challenges facing Macau schools, including issues of student motivation and behaviour.

The school in question, Escola São Paulo (hereafter termed St Paul's school), commenced a project to address several challenges, both generally in schools in Macau, which obtained in the school in question, and specific to the school, and moves to an overview of the project designed to address them. This included the purposes, nature, contents and foci of the overall project, the methods and organization of the pilot project and the evaluation of the pilot project. This was an ambitious project that was designed to address very many challenges simultaneously. Hence it was, by its very nature, a multidimensional innovation which, where it worked effectively, integrated and synergized these different dimensions into a powerful movement for deep-seated change in the school. The pilot project was formally evaluated by a small team of university researchers from a local university, and the elements of the evaluation are set out in this chapter.

In short, this chapter sets the scene for the substance of the book: how to lead and manage multidimensional innovation in schools.

Schooling in Macau

Macau is a small territory which, although part of China, has its own jurisdiction. It is an unusual territory in that the government provides schooling for less than 7 per cent of the population, and the remainder is provided by other parties, particularly the Catholic Church.

Since the 1999 handover from Portugal to China, Macau has been a Special Administrative Region (SAR) of the People's Republic of China (PRC), operating the 'one country, two systems' principle, as in Hong Kong. Though Macau has a strong political affiliation to mainland China, it has very considerable autonomy, as does Hong Kong, and this extends to its schooling system. Macau's schooling is very distinct from that of mainland China, though, since the handover, principals and teachers have been taking part in many professional development activities in China.

Under the 450 years of Portuguese administration there was a tradition of extreme laissez-faire, non-interventionist practices with very few regulations and controls, and concern overwhelmingly for the schooling of the Portuguese, to the neglect of the resident Chinese (Tang and Morrison 1998). The positive legacy of the Portuguese is difficult to discern in Macau's schooling (Salcedo 2008: 539), with low standards in education, limited school development and large-scale private, and hence varied, provision of schooling, often by charitable, religious and political organizations (some of which latter have strong connections with the mainland political party) (Tang and Morrison 1998), 'no assistance from the government until 1987' (1998: 250), no public examinations, diverse curricula and very limited teacher training. Since the 1999 handover, the Macau government has taken immense strides to develop its schooling system, for example in school inspection, curriculum development and staff development, teachers' pay and conditions, workloads and school financing.

Despite many recent governmental reforms, Bray and Koo (2004), Tang and Morrison (1998) and Morrison and Tang (2002) characterize Macau's schooling as having: (a) an 'unstandardized', uncentralized (i.e. it has never been centralized) education system, adopting curricula from mainland China, Taiwan, Portugal and Hong Kong; (b) an inadequate data base and evidence base for monitoring education; (c) limited responsiveness to consumers and inadequate information to parents; (d) few quality assurance systems.

At the start of the project (towards the end of 2011) Macau's population was 557,400 (Direcção dos Serviços de Estatística e Census 2013), enormous in proportion to the land mass of Macau, which is 29.9 square kilometres, i.e. over 18,600 people per square kilometre. Macau is one of the world's smallest territories and its most densely populated place, a tiny territory with a proportionally enormous population. At over US$29 billion annual GDP in 2011, Macau's economy in absolute terms was comparatively small, but huge relative to its population. Its revenue derives mainly from tourism and the huge casino industry, with 28 million tourists in 2011 alone, and income from casinos amounting to over 270 billion patacas (local currency, some 33.8 billion US$ equivalent) (Direcção dos Serviços de Estatística e Census 2012).

Of Macau's population, an estimated 20,000 are Catholics, i.e. some 3.6 per cent of the population. By contrast, the Catholic schools in Macau provide education for some 40 per cent of the school population. A proportion of the Catholics are 'Macanese' (Parmenter *et al.* 2000), a term used to denote those who have both Chinese and Portuguese blood or ancestry. Parmenter *et al.* (2000) note that a strong distinguishing feature of this ethnic group is their self-chosen identification with the Catholic faith as well as their bilingualism (Cantonese and Portuguese). The number of Macanese is unclear. A review in 1999 gave a number of 10,000 (including the Macanese diaspora) (Chu 1999), and a review of 2009 (Wikipedia 2009) gave it as 8,000 (some 2 per cent of the Macau population) but with some 20,000 in the diaspora.

Most of Macau's school students are educated in private schools, the majority in Catholic schools, some in non-religious private schools, with government schools providing for some 4.5 per cent of the school population. Table 3.1 indicates the extent of the private and government sector provision of schooling in 2008 (latest data of this type available), whilst Table 3.2 indicates the overall number of students in private and government schools at the time of the project. Many schools have several thousand students each; such schools, by dint of their size, history of autonomy and private governance (the colonial legacy of Macau's schooling), exert considerable influence in Macau. Some of the largest private schools (over 6,000 students) are powerful, with close political affiliation to mainland China. There is a tradition of a 'hands off' approach to private education by the government (Bray and Koo 2004; Tang and Morrison 1998; Morrison 2006). Given the extent of the private provision of schooling indicated in Tables 3.1 and 3.2, having a government move into what are autonomous schools, and where the government schools are in a very small minority (both in number of schools and number of students) is a sensitive matter.

The extensive private schooling circumscribes the power of the Macau government to intervene directly in controlling education in Macau, and, indeed, it seeks harmonious relationships with schools. The private schools have freedom and autonomy to devise their own curricula and assessments,

Table 3.1 Students in schools in Macau, 2008

	Kindergarten	Primary	Junior secondary	Senior secondary	Special education	Total
All Schools	9,065	30,012	22,264	19,007	475	80,823
Government schools	316	959	996	851	262	3,384
Private schools providing free education	6,997	24,902	17,973	15,360	213	65,445
Private schools not providing free education	1,752	4,151	3,295	2,796	0	11,994
Catholic schools	3,892 (42.9%)	13,012 (43.4%)	8,720 (39.2%)	6,554 (34.5%)	0 (0.0%)	32,178 (39.8%)

Table 3.2 Schools and students in Macau, 2011–12

	Infant education		Primary education		Government schools Secondary education				Special education		Subtotal	
					General secondary education		Vocational-technical education		Total of secondary schools			
	No. of students		No. of students		No. of students		No. of students		No. of students		No. of students	
Subtotal:	317	2.69%	776	3.39%	1,333	3.59%	558	51.01%	1,891	4.95%	283	50.54%	3,267	4.45%

	Infant education		Primary education		Private schools Secondary education				Special education		Subtotal	
					General secondary education		Vocational-technical education		Total of secondary schools			
	No. of students		No. of students		No. of students		No. of students		No. of students		No. of students	
Subtotal:	11,470	97.31%	22,086	96.61%	35,789	96.41%	536	48.99%	36,325	95.05%	277	49.46%	70,158	95.55%
Total:	11,787		22,862		37,122		1,094		38,216		560		73,425	

Source: Direcção dos Serviços de Estatística e Juventude (DSEJ) (2012).

and to determine teacher recruitment and conditions of service (Tang and Morrison 1998; Morrison 2001, 2006; Morrison and Tang 2002). Principal power in Macau is immense, itself in part a legacy of the former Portuguese administration and the private schooling system (Morrison 2006).

In Macau's Chinese culture, personal connections are strong, together with face-giving and face-saving ('face' defined as 'the public self-image that every member of a society wants to claim for himself' (Faure and Ding 2003: 91)). This is particularly so in hierarchical, paternalistic leadership systems (Bond 1991: 78), and these exist widely in Macau's schools (Morrison 2001, 2002b, 2006; Morrison and Tang 2002).

Because Macau is a small, tightly networked society, and because secrets are hard to keep from the public about personal and professional matters, researching or releasing knowledge about schools becomes a high-stakes exercise. Much can hang on public opinion, knowledge or perception. Reputations and 'face' can be fragile (Faure and Ding 2003: 91). What, in other, larger societies, might go unheeded in connection with an individual's or school's actions (Puniani 2002: 27), is the subject of public scrutiny and knowledge in Macau. Hence, many Macau schools keep public information to a minimum; there is much 'producer capture' here – schools operating in their own interests rather than the interests of the students, and operating on a 'take it or leave it' mentality – if you do not like what your school offers then go somewhere else.

The Chinese features of saving, giving, sustaining and retaining face (Bond and Hwang 1986: 246; Bond 1991), widespread in Macau, contribute to self-protective and defensive behaviour, reinforced by bureaucratic and hierarchical structures in its schools and the 'hothouse effect' of small states and territories wherein small issues can be amplified and exert a disproportionate effect on public opinion and perception (Morrison 2001, 2002b, 2006; Parperis 2002: 271; Morrison and Tang 2002). Small wonder, then, that many of Macau's schools operate as relatively closed systems; they may have too much to lose if they 'open up' to the public. Levering open schools to public scrutiny is a significant issue in Macau – it is sensitive.

Features of Chinese culture (e.g. harmony, consensus, relationships, face-saving, avoidance of shame, the collective over the individual), all heightened in a small territory, render research and development of schools sensitive. In Macau, the collective identity is strengthened by close physical proximity: 577,000 people living in fewer than 30 square kilometres of land.

At the time of the start of the innovation (2011) there were 78 schools in Macau, of which 11 were provided by the government, educating 3,267 students (4.5 per cent of the school population) and 67 were private, educating 70,158 students (95.5 per cent of the school population) (Direcção dos Serviços de Estatística e Juventude (DSEJ) (2012)). De Robertis and Morrison (2009) noted that 39 were Catholic schools providing education for 32,178 students (39.8 per cent of students), and 15 private schools were providing education without receiving a government subsidy (14.8 per cent of the total). Other Christian groups run some of the private schools.

The Catholic Church in Macau is not a highly centralized religious institution in administrative matters. Thus, high levels of autonomy are given to each single school to organize, administer and run itself. The principle of 'subsidiarity' enshrined in Church law (Coriden *et al.* 1985: 450–2) is applied extensively. Most Catholic schools are the endeavour of international religious orders like the Dominicans, Jesuits, Salesians, Canossians, the Franciscans and others. These orders, following the principle of subsidiarity, are independent of the local Catholic diocese on administrative matters and form institutions apart in matters of governance and internal policies. The appointment of a principal in any of these schools comes from the major superior of each order that runs the school, and many of the Catholic schools in Macau have a priest or a nun as their principal. Table 3.3 indicates that, though the Catholic schools provide schooling for varying numbers of students, in fact most of these students and their teachers are not, themselves, Catholics. The situation has changed little since the 1999 date of Table 3.3.

The Catholic diocese of Macau also has its own schools; there are 10 of these, five of which are under one federation (Colégio Diocesano de São José: Diocesan College of Saint Joseph) which receive no subsidy from the government for providing schooling, i.e. they are run like fee-paying schools. This was done initially to ensure their complete independence from government and to have a clearly identified Catholic identity in Macau – a free voice.

School exclusion is a significant problem in Macau (Morrison and Ieong 2007): if students fail the end-of-year examinations they have to repeat the year; if they fail that repeat year then they are required to leave the school. In other words, marks play a significant role in Macau schooling culture.

The results of the Programme for International Student Assessment (PISA) for Macau

Dates from the PISA studies (Programme for International Student Assessment 2003, 2006, 2009), which include Macau, provide an insight into many features of schooling that obtained not only in the Macau school in question but more generally in the school system in Macau. In the case study school, the innovation project commenced with the subjects of mathematics and English, and these subjects have been addressed in the PISA

Table 3.3 Students and teachers in Macau Catholic schools in 1999 (latest data available)

	Baptized Catholics	Non-Catholics	Total	% of Catholics
Teachers	480	1,150	1,630	29.44
Students	1,798	41,483	43,281	4.15

Source: Macau Bishop's office.

studies over time. Further, the PISA studies provide data on key concerns in Macau's schooling, set out below.

The PISA 2003 data

The trend reported in mathematics education in Macau (a feature addressed in the innovation) is that it is traditional, marks-driven and emphasizes memorization. Only 29 per cent of Macau's students reported 'I get good marks' in mathematics (the lowest score but two of the 40 countries), despite Macau's high position in mathematics overall, and 63 per cent reported 'I worry that I will get poor marks in mathematics', with only 17 countries reporting a higher response here. Further, 39 per cent of Macau's students said that 'I feel helpless when doing a mathematics problem', with only 13 countries scoring more highly. Only 65 per cent reported that 'when I cannot understand something in mathematics, I always search for more information to clarify the problem', with 33 of the 40 countries scoring more highly on this item. Some 55 per cent of Macau's students reported that 'when I study mathematics I try to learn the answers to problems off by heart', with only 11 countries scoring more highly. To compound this situation, only 54 per cent of Macau's students reported 'I think how the mathematics I have learned can be used in everyday life', with 23 countries scoring more highly. Here is a mathematics curriculum largely disconnected from the real world, with students seeking to grasp marks for memorizing an irrelevant curriculum – getting the right results for the wrong matters.

Macau's students felt disconnected from their school (only three countries scored lower on the factor 'I feel I belong'). They keep silent rather than speak out, they are discouraged from having opinions, mathematics curricula are disconnected from the everyday world and the teaching of mathematics barely addresses individual students' needs. Only 57 per cent of Macau's students reported that 'the teacher gives students an opportunity to express opinions' in mathematics, with 28 countries scoring more highly on this issue. Macau's students were fourteenth highest out of the 40 countries in their response to the statement 'I feel helpless when doing a mathematics problem'.

The impact of school policies on performance in mathematics was the equal lowest of all 40 countries, and Macau was the third lowest country in having school resources make an impact on school performance in mathematics. This was an indictment of management practice in the schools: written mathematics policies simply did not exist in many Macau schools.

The PISA 2006 data

For mathematics, Macau's students scored higher than the OECD average in respect of level 3 upwards; for reading, Macau's students scored lower than the OECD average for the upper levels (4 and 5) and higher or much higher than the OECD average for the lower levels. For mathematical literacy, Macau ranked between seventh and eleventh, and for reading it ranked between eighteenth and twenty-second (varying according to which aspect of the PISA is being reported).

The PISA 2009 data

Macau's school students were average or above in mathematics, but their scores in English were poor or worse. Macau's students ranked between twenty-seventh and thirtieth amongst the 65 participating countries/economies on reading literacy. For mathematical literacy Macau's students ranked between tenth and twelfth (varying according to which aspect of the PISA tests are being reported).

Macau's school students and teachers live in a pressure-cooker system of constant assessment and examinations which they must pass or be forced to repeat a year, or, indeed, be kicked out of school. The use of student performance to judge teacher effectiveness in the OECD average was 46.9 per cent, whereas in Macau it was 73.6 per cent. Whereas the OECD average for using student performance to make decisions about student retention or promotion was 77.1 per cent, for Macau it was 93.7 per cent. In respect of using low academic achievement as a reason for students transferring to another school, whereas the OECD average for the response 'very likely' was 8.6 per cent, in Macau it was 31.7 per cent. In respect of using behavioural problems as a reason for such transfer, whereas the OECD average for the response 'very likely' was 8.5 per cent, in Macau it was 32.7 per cent. In considering a student's record of academic performance in admitting them to schools, whereas the OECD average for the response 'always' was 30.8 per cent, for Macau it was 64.9 per cent.

Repeating a year in Macau is a problem (see Morrison and Ieong 2007). To the question 'have you ever repeated a year', the PISA 2009 results showed that, for the OECD the numbers reporting 'once' or 'twice or more' was 7.8 per cent at the International Standard Classification of Education (ISCED) level 1 (i.e. primary), for Macau it was 20.6 per cent, at ISCED level 2 (i.e. lower secondary) for the OECD it was 5.4 per cent, for Macau it was 30.2 per cent.

In terms of standardized tests, Macau's students have more than twice the OECD average for 'monthly' tests and three times the OECD average for such tests 'more than once a month'. (Indeed, Tang and Morrison (2002) indicated that, on average, students encountered two tests per school day.) In regard to teacher-developed tests, they have nearly twice as many as the OECD average for 'more than once a month' whilst, for more authentic forms of assessment, such as portfolios, 46 per cent of the responses indicated 'never', nearly twice that of the OECD average. For assessment by use of homework, whilst the OECD average was 56.5 per cent, for Macau's students it was 97.1 per cent.

Whilst the OECD average for 'teachers not meeting individual students' needs' was 26 per cent for the response 'to some extent' and 2.7 per cent for the response 'a lot', for Macau the responses were 47.9 per cent and 8 per cent, respectively. Whilst the OECD average for the responses 'to some extent' and 'a lot' to the item 'students not being encouraged to achieve their full potential' was 23.5 per cent, for Macau's students it was 42.9 per cent. For the item 'the teacher encourages students to express their opinion about a text', for the response 'most lessons or all lessons', the OECD rating was: 54.3 per cent, whilst for Macau students it was 36.7 per cent. For the item 'the teacher discusses students' work, after they have finished the reading assignment', for the response 'most lessons or all lessons', the OECD rating was 55.4 per cent, whilst for Macau it was 32.5 per cent.

For the item 'the teacher poses questions that motivate students to participate actively' (and the innovation in question was designed to raise student motivation), for the response 'most lessons or all lessons', the OECD rating was 45 per cent whilst for Macau it was only 34.2 per cent. For the item 'school has done little to prepare me for adult life when I leave school', whilst the responses 'agree or strongly agree' were 23.8 per cent for OECD countries, for Macau they were 49.1 per cent.

In respect of using achievement data for publicly posted accountability procedures, whereas the OECD score for 'no' was 62.8 per cent, for Macau it was 86.1 per cent; Macau's schools do little to publicize their results. The use of student assessment to compare the school with other schools was only 23.3 per cent, compared to the average in the OECD of 45.5 per cent.

In terms of reading, for the item 'I read only if I have to' 40.1 per cent of OECD responses were 'agree or strongly agree', compared to 49.7 per cent of Macau responses, whilst 'agree or strongly agree' responses to the item 'I read only to get information that I need' were 45.3 per cent and 56.8 per cent for the OECD and Macau, respectively. Evidence of the recitation mode of learning was in the response to the item 'I read the text so many times that I can recite it': for the categories of 'often and almost always' the OECD response was 27.1 per cent, whilst for Macau it was 34.1 per cent. By contrast, for the item 'I make sure that I remember the most important points in the text' the response 'often' and 'almost always' was 74 per cent for the OECD and only 42.6 per cent for Macau; reading for many Macau students is seen as a chore to be put up with.

In terms of openness to change, for the item 'perceived hindrances to student learning: staff resisting change', for the responses 'to some extent' or 'a lot', the OECD countries rated 28.3 per cent, whilst for Macau the rating was 33.9 per cent.

Whilst criticisms may be levelled at the PISA methodologies and sampling, the picture from the data confirms other data on Macau's schooling, which is of students and teachers who are under immense pressure from marks and assessments, where marks and assessments play a critical role in students' school careers, where the pedagogy is traditional, where performance in some school subjects has a lot of room for improvement, where students' motivation is a serious problem, where the curriculum is regarded as often irrelevant to students and their future work and where there is little incentive to change.

ICT and the PISA 2009 data

The results of the 2009 PISA (OECD 2011) reported that, in Macau, most students have access to the Internet at home (97.1 per cent) and at school (96.7 per cent), and that 96.4 per cent of students used the Internet at home and 96.1 per cent reported using the Internet both at home and at school. Macau students playing computer games came to 47.1 per cent, 31.6 per cent reported using the computer for school work, 12.6 per cent reported using the computer for online chat at school, and 46.9 felt that they could use the computer 'very well' for multimedia presentations, 31.1 per cent for spreadsheets and graphs. Clearly, Macau students are familiar with many aspects of ICT.

By contrast, using the computer for more than 60 minutes per week in class, only 7.4 per cent of students in Macau reported this for language-of-instruction lessons, 2.3 per cent for mathematics, 6.8 per cent for foreign language instruction, 10.0 per cent for science, and only 2.8 per cent reported using laptops at school. These results obtained, even though 88.8 per cent of students reported that it was 'very important' for them to work with a computer.

The school and the inception of the project

In this context of Macau's schooling, one all-through (i.e. Kindergarten to Form 6) Catholic diocesan school in Macau in 2011 commenced a major innovation that was envisaged to take some five years.

St Paul's school is an all-through, private, government-subsidized Chinese medium school in Macau, with some 2,500 students, currently under the operation of the Dominican Order of Preachers, and it is one of the diocesan schools of Macau. It is a popular school, consistently over-subscribed and with waiting lists; and it has been involved in extensive new building and refurbishment operations, with new purpose-built suites, laboratories and teaching rooms. In 2012 it opened a vast purpose-built multi-storey block with solar electricity. The school has an open-door policy for parents, and they are free to sit in classrooms during lessons at will. The school is located in one of the poorer districts of Macau, and its students come largely from working-class and middle-class backgrounds.

The school enjoys a very high reputation in Macau, and it receives many visitors, from different parts of China and beyond, who come to understand the policies and practices of this enterprising establishment. It is widely regarded as giving a high-quality education in a caring and supportive environment for its students. Formal inspections and audits have shown outstanding leadership, a forward-looking management team, and 'continuous development' policy and practice. Its students take up university places in Macau and beyond; it has a stable staff, many of whom are long-serving. It aims to provide for the all-round development of its students, and it has an exceptionally wide range of out-of-school and extra-curricular activities across many domains, from sports to music, arts, culture, history, sciences and languages.

The school has developed its own all-through, 15-year curriculum, and it has copious resources to support this. Most students who start at K1 in the school follow their school careers through to the end of their schooling at Forms 4, 5 and 6 levels (the last three years of secondary schooling). In inspection and audit reports, the school has been praised for its curriculum, for its concern for the welfare and support of the students, for its attention to the all-round development of the students and for its initiatives in handing over responsibility for many of the school's functions to students as appropriate.

In contrast to many innovations in schools, and in the instance reported here, the school was under no external obligation to change, but its principal, with many years of leadership experience in schools, had decided to install a major, multidimensional innovation to change the pedagogy in the school from a traditional didactic approach to collaborative, interactive and student-centred learning, to improve the quality of teaching, learning, student achievement and motivation, parental participation, and to enrich the educational experiences of the students. A major lever of this change was the introduction of the extended use of ICT, coupled with – and intimately connected with – significant pedagogic change. In particular, the school focused on several key contents of innovation:

- A key role for advanced and extensive ICT;
- Radical changes in teaching and learning from didacticism and transmission teaching to collaborative, interactive and real-world learning;
- Raising student motivation, attitude and interest;
- Raising student achievement and performance;
- Promoting engaged, student-centred learning;
- Promoting higher-order thinking and problem-solving in students;
- Changing assessment strategies to provide formative feedback to students and teachers;
- Developing parental involvement and communication;
- Restructuring the curriculum and its development;
- Promoting staff development for sustainable change.

However, the starting points in the school were challenging, in that, like many schools in Macau, it experienced many problems:

- Motivating learners, particularly under-achievers and low-performing students, and particularly at secondary school level, was difficult, with under-achievers, poor attitudes to school, bored and disengaged students;
- The prevalence of exerting undue pressure on students in an assessment- and examination-heavy environment, reinforced by parental pressure for measured success in examinations;

- The existence of a pass-fail mentality which led to many students learning for the sake of gaining a minimum pass in examinations rather than learning for its own sake;
- The significant number of students repeating a year and failing in many subjects (in a subject-based curriculum);
- The ease with which students could gain post-school employment in Macau (as the economy recorded the second highest GDP in the world), rendering school knowledge and attendance as a 'rite of passage' rather than as a rich opportunity for learning;
- A perceived irrelevant curriculum in several areas;
- The prevalence of traditional, lecture-based, mechanistic, didactic, rote-and-repetition based teaching and learning, with little student involvement or active, engaged learning; the observable presence of passive students with negative/uncaring attitudes; a facts-driven rather than skills-driven curriculum, with skills that had only selective relevance to the real world; limited higher-order thinking or problem-solving pedagogies; inauthentic learning;
- Students having little or no control over their learning;
- Students' interest in books was limited;
- Many students were 'switched off' from learning, and this increased as they progressed through the school;
- Large class sizes presented a challenge for teachers to break out of a lecture-based style, and imposed considerable demands in terms of everyday marking and assessment;
- Limited, if any, differentiation of teaching and curricula for different abilities within a class, i.e. whole-class teaching with limited interactivity;
- Over-emphasis on low- and middle-order thinking to the neglect of higher-order thinking, problem-solving and practical application of learning;
- A long tail-down of under-achieving students;
- Though the amounts of homework that the school set were very reasonable, parents sent their children for private lessons and tutorials, some for many hours each week, in evenings and at weekends;
- A concentration on academic performance to the neglect of other aspects of all-round learning and student development;
- Though there was staff willingness to change, most staff had limited or no experience of alternative, collaborative and more interactive pedagogies;
- Many of the innovations to date had been led by the principal (rather than other members of the school);
- Limited use of ICT other than to buttress up delivery and transmission models of teaching and learning;
- Some staff were resistant to change.

The task that the school faced was to identify a lever of change, an intervention, which could address these several features simultaneously. It did this through the extended use of ICT in the school and the accompanying changes in pedagogy (from didacticism, rote memorization and recall to collaborative, interactive, engaged learning and problem-solving approaches to learning), assessment (away from marks-driven learning and assessment of learning towards assessment *for* and *as* learning), curriculum, communication and student-centredness that it brought. Further, it was anticipated that the huge increase in the use of ICT would act as a motivator of students, particularly the lower performing students, and that the move from teacher-domination of teaching and learning would give way to student empowerment and autonomy in learning, and engaged learning along with the higher-order thinking that would accompany this. The advent of ICT in the school was not unheralded; rather, the school had been preparing for it over the preceding months and years. Further, the project built on ongoing curriculum and pedagogic development that had commenced in the school prior to the project:

- Developing an all-through curriculum for the school (such that, for example, the lock-step curriculum – which is a familiar practice in Macau schools, with all the students in a particular class going through the same material at the same rate and time – is replaced by teachers and students having greater flexibility and differentiation in deciding the content, rate, progression, differentiation, matching and timing of the curriculum;
- Nurturing positive and open relations between the school/teachers and parents;
- Encouraging greater student empowerment (e.g. in handling several school-related matters);
- Promoting group work and encouraging collaborative learning (the school had instituted a requirement for group work in many lessons each week).

However, these were in the early stages of development, and, in some cases, were embryonic and under-developed. The school found in ICT and its associated pedagogies an instrument that, it hoped, could address simultaneously and in a multidimensional approach, several of the challenges that it faced. In other words, a lever of change – ICT and its related pedagogies – was used to open up and address wider areas of concern facing the school, including, for example:

- Improving student motivation, attitude and behaviour;
- Enhancing student achievement and performance;
- Significantly more interactive and non-didactic teaching and learning, with the reduction in emphasis on rote and memorization;
- Increasing staff development for active and interactive learning;
- Promoting distributed leadership and management in the school;
- Enhancing parental participation in the education of their child(ren).

In many ways, as indicated later in the book, this high-profile project was successful and effective. For example:

- It attracted international attention and worked with leading international ICT companies and agencies;
- It greatly enhanced students' ICT skills and competencies from an early age;
- It improved the motivation, attitudes and confidence of many students;
- It promoted collaborative and interactive learning and group work;
- It promoted engaged learning;
- It promoted student-centred learning and higher-order thinking;
- It drove in new pedagogies;
- It enhanced staff pedagogical expertise;
- It promoted e-learning and blended learning;
- It brought in online submission of assessments and online marking;
- It enabled students to review classroom lessons;
- It improved student behaviour;
- It brought in more adventurous homework;
- It exceeded the leaders' expectations in bringing in quite rapid change.

On the other hand, the project faced many unexpected challenges (reported later), including:

- Practical matters (e.g. equipment not arriving on time, Internet instability and lack of connectivity out of school, short e-tablet battery life and recharging needs, students encountering problems in using the e-tablet out of school, clearing copyright problems);
- Human and managerial matters (e.g. staff resigning and leaving the school, late commitment from funders, very significant work overload on teachers, limited understanding and communication of the project);
- Leadership matters (e.g. over-expectations for the benefits of the project, determination to continue when several negative aspects of the project arose, limited communication with parents, a culture of obedience (under the sobriquet of 'respect') to the senior officers of the school);
- Pedagogical matters (e.g. limited staff expertise (and horizons) in the new pedagogies and ICT, fewer than anticipated opportunities for staff development, lack of e-resources at the start of the project);
- Student performance matters (e.g. fewer gains than anticipated in measured performance were found; some hoped-for improvement to students' attitudes and motivation did not occur, or did not occur as much as hoped; students (and their parents) were still concerned with marks in assessment; online assessment proved difficult for all parties);
- Improvements were not uniform or even across and within classes, i.e. there were some gross differences in effects;
- Parental matters (e.g. some open hostility from parents who felt 'left out'; limited parental involvement);
- ICT matters (e.g. using ICT to reinforce traditional teaching rather than to bring in new pedagogy).

This was a very wide range of challenges, with deep-seated obstacles to change, both within the school culture and the wider external culture. The question which the later part of this book addresses is how the school addressed these challenges through a multidimensional innovation project. More broadly, the book addresses the question, 'How can schools manage multidimensional, multiple innovations to address deep-seated obstacles to change?' The later chapters of this book report the school's success in addressing this, and draw out from the case study several key implications for leading and managing change.

The purposes behind the overall school innovation project

In 2011 the school initiated a large-scale project, described below, which was to roll out over some four years. Given the size, depth and number of dimensions to the innovation, the school decided that its first year should act as a pilot, working with only three classes (Primary 4, Secondary Forms 1 and 4) and on two subjects only: English and mathematics. It was recognized that some of the features of this comparatively small-scale start would not be scalable to the larger scale project as it unfolded over the years, for example in terms of: the ICT technology, equipment and support, and the financial issues involved; the number of subjects addressed; the number of students, classes, teachers and parents involved; the teaching and learning resources required; the different degrees of expertise of the teachers.

Nevertheless, the early stage of the project was designed to identify, in a safe environment (i.e. where challenges and problems could be contained), the key benefits, difficulties and issues to be addressed in rolling out the project in full over the years. This conforms to the important benefits of 'trialability' and 'divisibility' of an innovation (Morrison 1998: 17), i.e. conducting the change on a partial and limited 'basis' so that lessons can be learned without too many adverse affects.

To enable the school to learn from the first year of the project, the school commissioned an in-depth formative and summative evaluation by a small team of evaluators from a local university. The evaluation data were used to present one full initial oral report and two large written reports to the school, and the evaluators also made presentations to parents and local government education officers. This book reports on the pilot.

The evaluation project was multi-method, in order to catch the complexity of the innovation, and the later chapters of this book provide an extensive worked example of mixed methods research.

In relation to ICT, the school wished: (a) to keep abreast of developments in ICT; (b) to enable its staff and students to become increasingly proficient in their use of ICT *per se*; and (c) to reduce reliance on paper-based operations. The school saw ICT as having a major potential to address key features of the school's mission and operations in many fields:

- To break with over-reliance on traditional didactic teaching and learning strategies;
- To further the school's mission of providing equality of opportunity, access, resources, uptake, outcome and impact of the curricular and learning opportunities for all students in the school, rather than providing an educational experience in which a minority achieve highly and excel but in which the majority do not;
- To raise and work with, and on, the motivational levels of students for learning, involvement, feedback and communication;
- To enhance communication, collaboration and cooperation between teachers, students and between other parties inside and external to the school;
- To increase collaborative planning, sharing and operations amongst groups of staff, i.e. to increase the collegial work and ethos of staff and students;
- To increase active and interactive learning by staff and students;
- To enable formative assessment to lead into curricular and pedagogic development;
- To empower students to take control of their own learning, supported by extensive resources from the school;
- To provide parents with accurate, ongoing and up-to-date information about the operations of the school, the class and their child;
- To reduce the emphasis on marks and a pass-fail mentality;
- To increase higher-order thinking in students so that they could become critical thinkers, problem-posers and problem-solvers, collaborative learners, and technologically literate;
- To differentiate teaching and support for students with different needs.

However, ICT alone would not, either deliberately or automatically, bring about these changes. Rather, the ICT was embedded within other innovations intended in the school, for example in pedagogy, collaborative planning, assessment and curriculum structure and organization.

The contents of the pilot intervention

The innovation was multidimensional. For example, one part of the innovation was the introduction of extensive interactive and collaborative pedagogies. Whilst this might be commonplace in some parts of the world, in this school it was not and, indeed, this could be argued to be a powerful cultural phenomenon in this part of the world (Morrison 2002b, 2004; Tang and Morrison 2002). However, to bring about a change in pedagogy alone required, for example, significant staff development in these pedagogies to develop understanding, expertise, willingness and confidence to put them into practice. Further, sufficient material resources were needed to enable the new pedagogy to work (as pedagogy on its own cannot work in a vacuum, it requires appropriate resources – the resources required for a lecture are very different from those required for collaborative, interactive and project-based learning); reliable equipment and immediate in-class support were needed in case of failure of equipment; appropriate and timely leadership and management were required to facilitate and support the changes; changes were required in students', teachers' and parents' expectations of each other, teachers, teaching, learning and assessment; changes were needed in assessment and its consequences; changes were needed in the organizational culture of the school (from teachers working in isolation to teachers working collaboratively and collegially) and, indeed, in the wider cultural expectations for how teachers and students work.

In this one sphere alone one can see that a single innovation entails many deep-seated features. A single source of innovation opens many concerns, and once the genie is out of the bottle, it cannot be put back easily if things go wrong.

The intervention in the school was designed to work on many fronts, all facilitated through the use of an e-tablet for every student and appropriate software for class-based interactive and collaborative work in classrooms. However, it went further than this, as the ICT aspect of the project was designed to bring about a range of new inputs, processes and outcomes for the school:

- For curriculum:
  - Greater attention to differentiation and matching, away from a lock-step curriculum in which all students learned the same given material in the same way at the same time;
- For resources:
  - The provision of materials to support real and virtual classrooms;
  - The provision and use of revised instructional materials to broaden the range of reference materials beyond paper-based resources;
  - The provision of a virtual classroom bookshelf on which would be stored multimedia resources to support the subjects and session taught, suitably differentiated by skill levels, subjects, etc.;
  - The provision of a content management system to enable effective organization and storage of, and access to, thousands of pages of resources;
  - The provision and use of instructional materials and resources for every session taught, available to teachers, students, parents and other permitted parties;
  - Online access to resources and web sites;
  - The provision of interactive activities, such as quizzes and problems;
  - Differential levels of access to different parts of the system by different parties: teachers, parents, students, administrators;
- For pedagogy:
  - The move towards much more interactive and collaborative learning inside and outside the classroom;
  - The move towards greater student-centred learning and classrooms;

- Enhanced student-driven learning, engaged learning and student autonomy;
  - The increase in higher-order thinking;
  - The facility for students to annotate materials in class and outside class, for personal use;
  - The facility for students to compile their own notes in class and outside class, for personal use;
  - 'Lesson capture' through in-class video recording and playback, to enable permitted parties to review every class session on demand and as appropriate;
  - The elimination of electronic distractions in class sessions, through screen capture, blocking and blanking, under the control of the teacher who has access to these in class;
  - The facility to conduct in-class and outside-class activities such as quick surveys, collaborative work, projects and group-based learning;
  - Discussion boards for staff and students, to encourage participation;
  - The ability to post/upload materials by teachers and students, to submit homework and assignments and to enable feedback to be given and received;
- For assessment:
  - The revision of assessment, not only towards online assessment, but towards formative assessment and away from an emphasis on marks and a pass/fail mentality;
  - The enabling of teachers to conduct formative, in-class assessments to check students' understanding and to modify their teaching as appropriate;
  - The implementation of online assessment and feedback;
- For teachers:
  - Greater collaboration between teachers;
- For parents:
  - Greater communication with parents and involvement of parents in their child's education;
  - Access by parents to their own child's materials and information;
- For students:
  - Enhanced motivation of all students, particularly the low-performing students;
  - Improved attitudes towards, and interest in, schooling by all students, particularly the low-performing students;
  - Student guidance system;
- For communication:
  - The provision of a platform for teacher, student and parent collaboration and communication on curriculum development and sharing;
  - The provision of weekly and daily planners/journals/summaries, for teachers and students, of activities, assignments and homework, made available to relevant parties;

- Management of document/message flow/posting/reviewing/organizing/managing by administrators and staff;
    - Access to announcements and newsletters, policy documents, curricular websites and resources, and discussion boards;
    - Access to administrative networks (e.g. finance, facilities, meetings);
    - Remote access for relevant/permitted parties;
    - Email access for notifications and messaging;
- For records:
    - Records of student attendance and conduct.

Here was a project that was designed to operate on very many areas of school practice, with the lever of change being the use of ICT, together with ongoing changes in pedagogy and assessment.

The ICT content of the school project

In 2009 the school had commenced a major new, multi-million pataca (1 pataca = 0.125 US$) project to move the school from a conventional paper-based environment for students, staff, parents and stakeholders, to an electronic/ICT-rich environment for all aspects of its work, including teaching, learning, assessment, internal and external communication, administration, management and collaboration (e.g. between staff, staff and students, students and students, all parties with parents). The school, partly sponsored by the government's Department of Education and Youth Affairs (DSEJ), had devised a thoroughly worked-out plan to convert the premises to an all electronic environment with wi fi, and it provided every student and member of staff with his/her own e-tablet.

On the e-tablet were stored all the curriculum and supporting resources for the students and staff. It had Internet access for searching, reviewing, uploading and downloading materials, submitting and receiving feedback on homework, together with a virtual classroom, on-screen note-taking and annotating facilities, screen capture and blanking facilities for everyday classroom use, communication channels with several parties, a classroom lesson playback facility from the school's lesson-capture system, sharing facilities for collaborative work between different parties, and materials for parents to have a transparent understanding of the activities in the school by curriculum, resources, subject, teacher, class, their own child, etc. The e-tablet was highly flexible and adaptable for all parties, including, but not limited to, each class, subject, teacher, student, form and working group. There were several levels of password-protected security and access together with suitably installed firewalls. In other words, the system was highly professionally designed, had enormous capacity (and not only for existing functions, but to be able to add functions over time), capability, flexibility, security and access. The school had set up a management team to work on this project, comprising technical, curricular, pedagogic and assessment expertise.

Each classroom had video-recording facilities, to catch every classroom session, with a default setting of focus on the teacher, and each classroom session that the teacher agreed to have recorded was stored, protected access to which was available through the e-tablet. This enabled students and their parents to review the sessions for revision and understanding purposes (as will be reported later, this required a courageous stance from teachers).

The e-tablet also enabled teachers to check students' understanding of key points as the lesson proceeded, through quick polls and surveys, immediate questions and quizzes, application tasks, etc. The teacher could see what each student had on screen, could capture each student's screen and post material on their screen where necessary or important, thus enabling the teacher to monitor progress, understanding and student activity.

At its inception, the project was believed to be the first of its kind in South East Asia, and was supported by, and received technical advice and instructional technologies and software from, Automated, DyKnow, H3C, HP, Lenovo, Mediasite and Microsoft. The hardware architecture and platforms for the project were developed and implemented in the school in cooperation with these international organizations and with the specific requirements of the school as central. All the ICT facilities could accommodate ongoing developments in hardware and software.

The purposes of the evaluation of the pilot

The purposes of the evaluation of the pilot were managerial in three senses:

1 To provide data on how, where and how well the project was, and was not, operating in maximizing teachers' roles as facilitators of learning;
2 To provide the leaders and managers in the school with formative and summative data on the successes, key issues, challenges and problems which emerged in the pilot in respect of the planning, implementation, curricula, pedagogy, resourcing, programme evaluation, student assessment, leadership and management of the intervention in the school, which would inform and enable the development of, and training/preparation of, teachers and other parties for the project as it unfolded inside and outside the school;
3 To make recommendations to the leaders and managers of the project for managerial, curricular and developmental issues to be addressed for the full project, within and outside the school.

This evaluation of the pilot project served formative and summative functions. *Formatively*, it provided the school with ongoing feedback on the operations of the intervention, so that the development and further implementation of the project could be improved. It identified where the intervention was and was not proceeding well and meeting the problems/needs/challenges that it was designed to address. As mentioned earlier, this was undertaken *before* the whole project went on stream over time in the school (i.e. incrementally, adding subjects, classes/forms, teachers and resources each year). The evaluation included recommendations for adjustments to be made to the hardware, software, usage, pedagogy, staff development, etc., as appropriate, for issues to be addressed and development activities to be installed. It identified problems to be addressed in the fields of curricula, pedagogy, resources, assessment, management (of the project), staff development, communication and collaboration and matters concerning students, parents and teachers.

Summatively, it provided the school with a summative evaluation of the extent to which the objectives of the pilot had been met, where, and with what degrees of success (judged against the success criteria), for the relative improvements to students' performance and achievements in the areas of focus.

The foci of the evaluation

The evaluation addressed such questions as:

- In light of the pilot, what needs to be done to ensure that the main programme is sufficiently and effectively prepared for, operates to maximum efficiency and effectiveness and avoids problems encountered in the pilot?
- What are the main difficulties in the programme, as found in the pilot, and how can they be addressed?
- What staff preparation and training needs to be provided in order for the programme to operate to maximum efficiency and effectiveness?
- In what areas, and to what extent, has the programme in the pilot:
    o Reduced traditional didactic, rote-and-repetition teaching and learning strategies?
    o Increased student involvement in their own learning and active learning?
    o Reduced the curriculum from a facts-driven to a skills-driven curriculum?
    o Enabled the teachers and students to increase equality of opportunity, access, resources, uptake, outcome and impact of the curricular and learning opportunities for the students?
    o Raised the motivational levels of students for learning, involvement, feedback and communication, particularly for low-performing students and students with uncaring/negative attitudes?
    o Reduced the tail-down of under-achieving students?
    o Enhanced communication, collaboration and cooperation between teachers, students and between other parties inside and external to the school?
    o Increased collaborative planning, sharing and operations amongst groups of staff?

- o Increased active, interactive and engaged learning by staff and students?
- o Increased formative assessment, leading to curricular and pedagogic development?
- o Empowered students to take greater control of their own learning?
- o Provided parents with accurate, ongoing and up-to-date information about the operations of the school, the class and their child?
- o Increased higher-order thinking in students?
- o Reduced assessment pressure in the pilot classes?
- o Increased the differentiation of teaching and learning to students' different needs?
- o Enhanced the perceived relevance of the curriculum in students' eyes?
- o Reduced the demand on teachers in respect of marking and assessment?
- What are the major and minor strengths, weaknesses, areas for improvement and development, problematic areas/areas of concern and matters of perceived importance to be addressed in the running of the full project?
- How, where and how well is, and is not, the project operating in maximizing teachers' roles as facilitators of learning, and what needs to be done to address development and improvement needs?
- What are the successes, key issues, challenges and problems which have emerged in the pilot in respect of the planning, implementation, curricula, pedagogy, resourcing, programme evaluation, student assessment, leadership and management of the intervention in the school, such that it informs and enables the development of, and training/preparation of, teachers and other parties, within and outside the school, for the full project to be conducted more effectively?
- What recommendations come from the pilot for the leaders and managers of the school and the project in respect of the further development of the full project in the school, in developmental, curricular, managerial, preparatory and implementation aspects?

The evaluation focused on three main areas: programme operations; teaching, learning and the curriculum; and productivity.

i   *Programme operations*

To what extent, and in what areas, did the programme in the pilot:
- Provide a positive experience for students, parents and teachers? Did it promote learning motivation and student learning?
- Provide an engaging, creative and interactive learning environment that matched and complemented the students' learning styles?
- Expand material availability and timetabling flexibility (i.e. providing access to information that otherwise might be unavailable)?

- Use electronic equipment, e-tablets and networks for accessing information to enhance communication (teacher–students, students–parents, teacher–parents)?
- Enhance parental involvement in the education of their children?
- Enable teachers, students and parents to have sufficient knowledge, skills and appropriate methods to use the resources in the pilot? What additional professional development is required?
- Enable students, teachers and parents to find the programme useful?
- Provide adequate support for the teachers and students by the school?
- Encounter problems? How can they be solved and addressed, and how and where can the programme be improved?

Added to these were two further questions:
- What variations were there the way the pilot affected different students?
- What proportion of parents benefited from the pilot?

ii *Teaching, learning and the curriculum*

To what extent, and in what areas, did the programme in the pilot:
- Provide opportunities to enrich the curriculum that would be possible outside the programme?
- Enhance and meet the curriculum goals?
- Improve the curriculum, instruction and teacher effectiveness?
- Assist in planning the curriculum and meeting individual needs effectively?
- Impact positively and negatively to influence student learning?
- Help teachers to understand the progress being made by students, their difficulties and problems, the standards they achieved and what they needed to do to improve further?
- Develop closer links between teaching and learning in ways that will help the progress of each individual learner?
- Challenge and engage all students?

Added to these were two further questions:
- What were the problems and challenges in relation to the pilot – learning, teaching, curriculum, etc.?
- How can they be addressed and solved?

iii *Productivity*

To what extent, and in what areas, did the programme in the pilot:
- Cater for differences in students' needs, interests, concerns, capabilities and learning styles?
- Enhance student achievement and attainment?
- Help high-performing students to increase their achievement and attainment?

- Help low-performing students to increase their achievement and attainment?
- Help students to demonstrate their understanding by thoughtfully applying their knowledge and constructive cognitive processes?
- Help unmotivated students to have a better disposition/attitude to learning?
- Address and develop higher-order thinking skills?
- Improve student behaviour?

To answer these questions not only required a lot of data, but these data could not be confined to either numerical or qualitative data; both types of data had to be integrated, i.e. a mixed methods approach in which the methods, whilst running in parallel, were also combined. This conforms to the 'fully integrated mixed design' of Teddlie and Tashakkori (2009: 151) in which mixed methods are used at each and all stages and are integrated at each stage.

The methodologies of the evaluation of the pilot

A mixed methodology for the pilot was adopted, as follows:

1. A 'true experiment': this was undertaken in the school, with three classes comprising the experimental groups and three other classes comprising the control groups (see Figure 3.1). Students were assigned randomly to either the control or *experimental* groups (the experimental groups were termed the 'pilot' groups in the school: three experimental classes (Primary 4, Form 1 and Form 4) and three control groups (Primary 4, Form 1 and Form 4), see Sampling section below. These groups were all involved in pre-testing and post-testing of their performance in mathematics and English. The performance data collected here were examination and assessment data together with data addressing changes over time (e.g. in students' attitudes and motivations to learning, their ability to engage in higher-order thinking, etc.).
2. A survey methodology, using *interviews* and *questionnaires*. An experiment operates on an input-output model, measuring starting points and end points. As the pilot had a formative intent, it was important to catch *process* variables that were impacting on the operation of the pilot, and so qualitative data were collected through interviews and questionnaires, together with staged quantitative surveys administered to staff and students at the start of, during and at the end of the pilot; the data from which were processed with the Statistical Package for the Social Sciences (SPSS) and which were analyzed by the evaluation project team.
3. Ongoing *journals*. Since the data collection took place at fixed points during the pilot project, there was a risk of memory loss of key events/issues/ matters arising. Teachers in the pilot were asked to keep an ongoing record

88 *The background to the case study*

of such key events/issues/matters arising during the interim periods, and these were discussed with the evaluators at the interviews. This enabled not only such key factors to be identified but emergent issues to be identified and placed into a time frame.

4 *Logged data*: These comprised data that were automatically logged by the computer system in the school, e.g. how many times the student had used the e-tablet, and for how long; how many times the student had used online links, for what and for how long; what the student had uploaded and downloaded; how many times the teacher captured screens and for whom; how many times quick surveys were conducted in class, the incidence of collaborative work and sharing; the usage of online chat and discussion; how many times the daily/weekly assignment journals and plans/week-at-a-glance were accessed, and by whom; attendance records.

The *interviews* were designed: (a) to identify the parties' key purposes of, perceptions of, aspirations for, concerns in, agendas in, priorities for, responses to, anxieties in, challenges in, problems with, difficulties in, (dis)satisfaction with, worries about, perceived areas of effectiveness and ineffectiveness in, benefits of, disappointments in, advantages from, anticipated and unanticipated outcomes of and processes in, practices in, recommendations for, implications of and needs within and from the pilot before, during and close

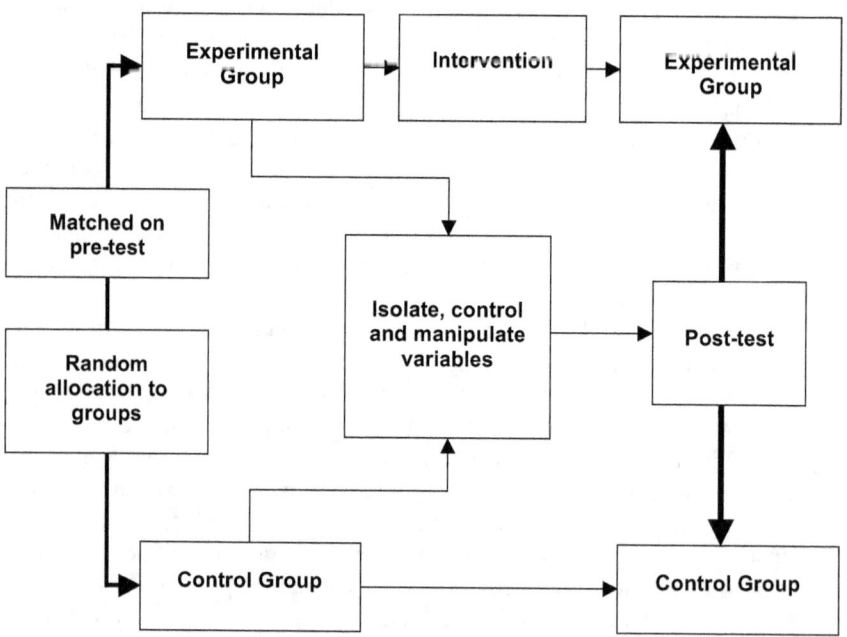

Figure 3.1 The 'true' experiment

to the end of the pilot; and (b) to identify emerging key issues of concern and focus over the duration of the pilot.

In order to enable different perceptions on the same topics to be gathered, wherever possible there was a deliberate match between the topics addressed, and the questions put to: the principal and senior officers of the school and the project, the teachers involved in the pilot, the students involved in the pilot (control and experimental groups) and the parents of the experimental group of students involved in the pilot. These interviews took place at three points in time (beginning, middle and end of the pilot), to catch the evolution of and emergent issues in the pilot and its implications for the preparations for and operations of the full project (which expanded incrementally over time by subject and the number of classes). The interviews were intended to gather qualitative data.

The *questionnaires* were designed largely to gather numerical data, which were analyzed to yield comparisons between the parties involved on key issues and topics of focus in the evaluation. As with the interviews, the questionnaires were designed to enable different perceptions of the same topics to be gathered. Hence, wherever possible, there was a deliberate match between the topics addressed and the questions put to the same participants as for the interviews, with the exception of parents (who did not receive the questionnaires). Additional to the common questions across the parties, the questionnaires to each of the parties included qualitative questions together with questions specific to the party in question. The questionnaires enabled pre- and post-pilot data on perceptions, concerns, issues and so on to be gathered.

The *experimental* data were derived from two main sources: (a) pre-test and post-tests of students' attainment data, using the school's standard examinations; and (b) additional questionnaire items (included in the questionnaire survey) to gather numerical data on pre-test and post-test perceptions of the pilot and its effects on aspects of concern as set out in the purposes and success criteria for the pilot.

The *journal* data were kept by the teachers involved in the pilot. They were not intended to be over-detailed or exhaustive, as this would over-burden the teachers. Rather, they were designed to enable teachers to record key/significant/unanticipated/notable/interesting/important issues, concerns, practices, etc., as they emerged and in order to record these rather than risk losing them to busy teachers' memories. Teachers kept these on an ongoing basis, although they only reviewed them with the evaluators twice during the pilot project.

The *logged data* comprised data that were automatically logged by the computer system in the school. These yielded numerical data on frequencies and duration of different kinds of usage of the e-tablet, and by whom.

The data collection instruments were:

1   *Individual interviews* with the principal and senior officers of the school and the project. These comprised the same people each time.

2   *Individual interviews* with each of the teachers involved in the teaching of the pilot. These comprised the same people each time.
3   *Group interviews* with students in each of the pilot classes involved. For each class at each round of interview, there were three groups of no more than eight students in each group. It was important, where possible, for the same students to be grouped and interviewed at each round of the interviews. Selection of the students was under the guidance of the school with informed consent from the relevant parties.
4   *Group interviews* with parents of students. For each round of interviews, there was one group per class of the pilot classes, of no more than eight parents in each group. It was important, where possible, for the same parents to be grouped and interviewed at each round of the interviews. Selection of the parents was under the guidance of the school with informed consent from the relevant parties.
5   *Survey questionnaires* to (a) the principal and senior officers of the school and the project, (b) all the teachers involved in the pilot, and (c) all the students involved in the pilot, both as experimental and control groups (but for students in the control group, questions relating to the operation of the intervention were excluded, whilst questions on items relevant to both control and experimental groups (e.g. attitudes, motivations, teaching and learning strategies etc.) were included, so that comparisons could be made between the control and experimental groups).
6   *Pre-test* and *post-test examination scores* on all the students in the pilot, in both experimental and control groups.
7   *Journals* kept by each teacher involved in the pilot.
8   *Logged data* automatically generated by the computer system.

The database comprised numerical and qualitative data, gathered over time and from the various parties. The data from these multiple methods form the basis of the empirical part of this book. Data for the project were collected at three time points, and were reported in three rounds, as indicated in Table 3.4.

The success criteria of the project

The success criteria lay in two domains, both in respect of the pilot project itself and the evaluation of the project:

1   Measured improvements in many areas of staff and student performance, behaviour as set out in the experimental methodology below;
2   The provision of comprehensive, detailed and useful formative and summative data to enable the parties in the school to prepare for, develop, implement, improve and evaluate the operations of the full project.

Table 3.4 Data collection, instrumentation and reporting

Time point Sample	Beginning of September 2011	September 2011 to January 2012	January and February 2012	End of February 2012	31 March 2012	Final week of May 2012	May and June 2012	February 2012 to May	Last week of June 2012	31 July 2012
Principal and senior Officers	Interviews and survey 1		Interviews and survey 2				Interviews and survey 3			
Teachers: English: P4	Interviews and survey 1	Journals	Interviews and survey 2				Interviews and survey 3	Journals		
Teachers: English: F1	Interviews and survey 1	Journals	Interviews and survey 2				Interviews and survey 3	Journals		
Teachers: English: F4	Interviews and survey 1	Journals	Interviews and survey 2				Interviews and survey 3	Journals		
Teachers: maths: P4	Interviews and survey 1	Journals	Interviews and survey 2				Interviews and survey 3	Journals		
Teachers: maths: F1	Interviews and survey 1	Journals	Interviews and survey 2				Interviews and survey 3	Journals		
Teachers: maths: F4	Interviews and survey 1	Journals	Interviews and survey 2				Interviews and survey 2	Journals		
Students: P4 (English and maths)	Pre-test attainment data Interviews and survey 1		Interviews and survey 2			Post-test attainment data	Interviews and survey 3			
Students: F1 (English and maths)	Pre-test attainment data Interviews and survey 1		Interviews and survey 2			Post-test attainment data	Interviews and survey 3			

(Continued)

Table 3.4 (Continued)

Time point Sample	Beginning of September 2011	September 2011 to January 2012	January and February 2012	End of February 2012	31 March 2012	Final week of May 2012	May and June 2012	February 2012 to May	Last week of June 2012	31 July 2012
Students: F4 (English and maths)	Pre-test attainment data Interviews and survey 1		Interviews and survey 2			Post-test attainment data	Interviews and survey 3			
Logged data		Data summaries						Data summaries		
Parents	Interviews 1		Interviews 2				Interviews 3			
Reporting				Interim oral report to principal	Interim written report to principal				Oral report to principal	Final written report to principal

The background to the case study

In terms of measured improvements, given that the pilot lasted for one year – i.e. sufficiently long for the Hawthorne Effect to have reduced – the experimental methodology within the evaluation had several success criteria.

For teachers and students, the evaluators investigated: (a) whether the pilot scheme reduced traditional didactic, rote-and-repetition teaching and learning strategies statistically significantly more than in the control classes; (b) whether the ICT modalities and affordances increased equality of opportunity, access, resources, uptake, outcome and impact of the curricular and learning opportunities for the students, as measured on given instruments, and more than in the control classes. For parents, the evaluators also investigated whether the pilot provided parents with accurate, ongoing and up-to-date information about the operations of the school, the class and their child.

The evaluators investigated whether the pilot scheme *increased* the following:

a   Student involvement and engagement in their own learning and active learning statistically significantly more than in the control classes;
b   The motivational levels of students for learning, involvement, feedback and communication, particularly for low-performing students and students with uncaring/negative attitudes, statistically significantly more than in the control classes;
c   Communication, collaboration and cooperation between teachers, students and other parties inside and external to the school statistically significantly more than in the control classes;
d   Collaborative planning, sharing and operations amongst groups of staff statistically significantly more than in the control classes;
e   Active and interactive learning by staff and students statistically significantly more than in the control classes;
f   Formative assessment, leading to curricular and pedagogic development;
g   Empowering students to take greater control of their own learning, more than in the control classes;
h   Higher-order thinking in students;
i   The differentiation of teaching and learning to students' different needs;
j   The perceived relevance of the curriculum in students' eyes.

The evaluators investigated whether the pilot scheme *reduced* the following:

a   The curriculum from a facts-driven to a skills-driven curriculum statistically significantly more than in the control classes;
b   The tail-down of under-achieving students statistically significantly more than in the control classes, in terms of measured performance;
c   The demand on teachers in respect of marking and assessment statistically significantly more than in the control classes;

d   Reduced assessment pressure in the pilot classes statistically significantly more than in the control classes.

For the surveys and interviews, the evaluation of the pilot worked with teachers, students, parents and other relevant parties (as appropriate) inside and outside the school. The success criteria for the evaluation of this aspect of the pilot were:

- The evaluation identified major and minor strengths, weaknesses, areas for improvement and development, problematic areas/areas of concern and matters of perceived importance to be addressed in the running of the full project;
- The evaluation provided data on how, where and how well the project was and was not operating in maximizing teachers' roles as facilitators of learning, and what needed to be done to address development and improvement needs;
- The evaluation provided the leaders and managers in the school with formative and summative data on the successes, key issues, challenges and problems which had emerged in the pilot in respect of the planning, implementation, curricula, pedagogy, resourcing, programme evaluation, student assessment, leadership and management of the intervention in the school, such that it informed and enabled the development of, and training/preparation of, teachers and other parties for the full project, within and outside the school, to be conducted more effectively;
- The evaluation provided data and recommendations for the leaders and managers of the school and the project in respect of the further development of the full project in the school, in developmental, curricular, managerial, preparatory and implementation aspects.

Sampling

All the students in three classes in the school were involved in the pilot intervention. They were in one class in each of Primary 4, Secondary Form 1 and Secondary Form 4. Each class in the experimental groups comprised around 40 students, i.e. a total of 120 students.

A parallel class in each of Primary 4, Form 1 and Form 4 formed the control groups. Each class in the control groups comprised around 40 students, i.e. a total of 120 students. Students were randomly assigned to either the control or experimental classes, and pre-tests indicated a very high level of congruence between each pair of control and experimental groups in terms of measured attainment.

A volunteer sample of parents of students in each of the experimental groups (one group of around eight parents for each class: Primary 4, Form 1 and Form 4) participated in group interviews, and all the parents of the students in the experimental groups were circulated with survey questionnaires for completion and return to school.

All the teachers involved in teaching mathematics and English with the three experimental groups participated in the interviews and survey questionnaires.

The principal and senior officers in charge of the school and of the overall ICT project participated in the interviews and survey questionnaire.

Reliability and validity

Content validity of the evaluation was addressed through the in-depth and in-breadth contents of the instrumentation and their comprehensive coverage of the key issues and areas of focus in the evaluation of the pilot.

Concurrent validity was addressed through triangulation of:

- *Perspectives*: as the instruments and issues were used with, and addressed by, different sub-samples, respectively;
- *Instruments*: there were several instruments which focused on identical and similar contents;
- *Timing*: the data collection period was long, spread out, multiple and ongoing;
- *Investigators*: the evaluation was conducted by a team, not an individual;
- *Theory*: different theoretical premises of the evaluation were employed, including: Norman's theory of complex learning; Fullan's, Hall's and Hord's theories of change and its management; social and cognitive constructivist theories of learning (Vygotsky and Piaget, respectively);
- *Methodologies*: a 'fully integrated mixed design' methodology (Teddlie and Tashakkori 2009) was employed;
- *Data types*: qualitative and quantitative data were gathered;
- *Models of evaluation*: the evaluation included several models: an objectives-driven model, an experimental model, Stake's (1967) countenance model, Stufflebeam's (1971) CIPP model, Brinkerhoff's *et al.*'s (1983) comprehensive model.

Construct validity was addressed by rooting the foci of the evaluation, methodologies and instrumentation in appropriate theoretical foundations and research literature (see also above: theory triangulation).

Reliability was addressed through statistical means where they applied (Cronbach's alpha), through multi-instrument approaches with the same sub-samples, through mixed methodologies and through involving several different sub-samples.

Interviews were conducted in the language medium of the participants' choice (Cantonese or English). Translation and blind back-translation of data collection instruments were undertaken to ensure reliability. With the exception of the survey questionnaires to parents (which parents were asked to complete at home and return to the school), all the data collection was undertaken in the school (cf. Morrison 2013). Respondent validation of data interpretation was not used, as the responsibility for the data analysis and reporting lay with the evaluators.

As the experiment was undertaken in the same school, it was recognized that contamination effects may have arisen in that teachers and students in both control and experimental groups may have communicated with each other and the same or different teachers may have taught both the experimental and control groups, and their behaviour may not have been consistent. Some controls were possible in the experiment, for example:

- The same textbooks were used with both the control and experimental classes, the only difference being the medium through which they were accessed (hard copy/e-tablet electronic copy);
- The classes in the control and experimental groups were matched in terms of age and range of abilities;
- The curricula were the same for classes in the control and experimental groups;
- The teaching periods, session duration and timing, and the amount of time spent in class were the same for the control and experimental classes.

Though it was not possible to isolate and control the variables in this natural (rather than laboratory) experiment (e.g. the same teachers teaching the control and experimental groups), nevertheless the size of the classes (40 in each), the number of classes (6 classes: two each from P4, F1 and F4) and the randomization and random allocation of students to the pilot and control groups all strove to address some degree of randomization in the distribution of personally related variables that were involved in this experiment, and this was designed to partially overcome some of the problems of isolation and control of variables.

The pilot intervention ran for one school year, during which time reporting to the school, the parents and the local government education officers took place.

As can be seen, the intervention was ambitious in its scope, in terms of both breadth and depth. How far this was realized in practice, and what challenges were occasioned, is addressed in the subsequent chapters, and it is to these that the book turns.

Having set the scene here, the narrative now moves towards reporting what actually happened and what can be learned from this for the leadership and management of multidimensional innovations.

4 Starting points and rules of engagement

Introduction

This chapter reports, analyzes and draws implications from the early stages of the school's project for the leadership and management of multidimensional innovations in schools. The chapter provides a narrative which is derived from many data sources in the school project: questionnaires, interviews and documentation. Though many of these data sources were numerical, the chapter studiously avoids reporting the detailed tables of data that were used in the evaluation of the innovation, as these present unnecessarily local, parochial close-grained data. Rather, the chapter reports the key findings in textual form, combining numerical and qualitative data.

The chapter indicates how participants were engaged in the process and contents of the innovation, what their concerns were and how the parties and the leader developed and promoted commitment to the project as it began to unfold. Indeed, the term 'engaged' is used in several senses in this chapter:

- What leaders and managers of complex change must be and do;
- Involvement and intrinsic, committed motivation of learners, teachers, leaders, parents and planners;
- Putting together, connecting, attaching and interlocking the elements of the innovation: contents, people, processes and resources;
- On-task activity;
- Commencement of a new commitment;
- Busyness and business.

Coupled with this is the reach of engagement: engaged learners, engaged teachers, engaged parents and engaged leaders. Their views are presented separately in the chapter and then lessons learned for managing complex change are drawn together at the end of the chapter.

The innovation project, part of the school's ongoing ESOS project (Empowering Students for an Open School) was to use extensive ICT and blended learning in parallel with significant changes in pedagogy – from teacher-centred didactic teaching to student-centred collaborative and active, engaged, interactive learning – in order to raise students' performance, motivation and interest, particularly for the low achievers in the school, one hoped-for outcome of which would be improvement to their behaviour in school. This was coupled with planning for, and implementation of, increased parental involvement and communication, changes in curriculum and assessment, increased staff collegiality, distributed leadership, higher-order thinking in students, student autonomy and decision making. The two significant drivers of these changes were:

1   The ICT, with each student having his/her own e-tablet (hereafter termed the 'tablet') coupled with:
    a   highly interactive, tailor-made software from the DyKnow instructional technology organization;
    b   extensive resources loaded onto each tablet;
    c   online access in class and at home;
    d   video recording and playback of classroom sessions;
    e   a sophisticated electronic environment for students, with online submission of homework and classroom work-share.
2   A push towards collaborative, active, engaged and interactive student-centred learning, inside and outside class, building on existing moves that the school had already started to introduce in group work.

These twin main concerns echo the comments in earlier chapters of the need for simplicity in managing change (Kluger 2007) – keeping to a small number of core, visible priorities, purposes and strategies – and combining these with the complex task of managing the contents, people, capacity building, collaboration, processes, resources and dimensions of change contained within these simple purposes.

There were three rounds of data collection: at the beginning, middle and end of the pilot intervention. This chapter focuses on the first round of data collection, and uses quantitative and qualitative data to present a picture of the situation at the start of the project. Data were collected from initial assessments of students, interviews and questionnaires, as set out below.

Numerical data were gathered from the pilot group teachers (N = 6), the students of the control groups (N = 117) and the students of pilot groups (N = 116). For questionnaire data there were 75 numerical questions for students of the control group, 91 questions for students in the pilot groups and 142 questions for teachers. Many questions asked respondents to award a mark out of 10 (with a zero) for the item in question. Wherever possible, the questions asked of the three groups (pilot group students, control group students, teachers) were matched so that comparisons could be drawn between the perceptions of the three parties on the same issue. These data were perception-based, operating on Thomas's (1928) principle that 'if men [sic] define their situations as real, they are real in their consequences'. Numerical data were processed with SPSS.

Qualitative data were gathered from semi-structured interviews with a range of parties and semi-structured, open questions in the questionnaires for students and teachers. Some 60 hours of interviews were conducted with different parties, thus:

- Twenty-four of the pilot group students from each of the three classes were interviewed in three groups of 8, i.e. 72 pilot group students in total;
- All six teachers involved in the pilot were interviewed individually;
- Fifteen individual interviews were conducted with a range of senior and middle managers in the school (principal and deputy principals, heads of sections, treasurer, head of IT, head of curriculum, subjects heads of mathematics and English, counselling and student management staff);
- Three groups of parents were interviewed, one from each of the pilot classes.

These data set a baseline, an early context, for the innovation project and constituted in part a situational analysis and a needs analysis, charting the situation from different perspectives at the start of the project (teachers, senior staff of the school, students in both the pilot and control groups and parents). The data addressed a range of early issues, for example:

- What happened in the run-up to the pilot and the very early stages of the pilot;
- Strengths and weaknesses of the pilot for students, leaders, managers, teachers, support staff and parents;
- Successes and problems in the early stages of the pilot;
- Handling challenges and problems – anticipated and unanticipated – in the early stages of the pilot;
- Leading and managing the project in its early stages;
- Meeting multiple and conflicting demands in the early stages;
- Implications for different parties in the planning, leadership and management of multidimensional changes and innovations in schools.

The project targeted four main parties: the students, the teachers, the senior and middle managers and the parents. There were similarities and dissimilarities of view and strength of feeling within and between each of these parties, and part of the early management of the innovation was the need to manage these adroitly and fairly. This presented a significant leadership challenge and called for strong and decisive leadership in the face of different views and degrees of support for the project, as indicated later in this chapter. Effective management of innovation calls for the management of perception, and the early round of data collection, reported to the school, indicated the different perceptions of the project that had to be handled.

As the four parties had different views, this chapter reports the results from each of the four parties and then draws common threads from them and implications for the leadership and management of multidimensional innovations, the dimensions of which were laid out in the previous chapters.

Beginnings

Launching a multidimensional project is hazardous. It is like stepping off a cliff, a leap of faith. There is no perfect time to commence; one has to take the plunge and the leader has to take the risk. The analogy is potent, not only as innovation may lead to ruin but, when one reviews the literature on educational innovations, after the initial trumpeting of the innovation it is likely to bring setbacks and an initial downturn in performance: Fullan's (2013) 'implementation dip' (discussed in Chapter 2). The curve of innovation often starts at an initial high, followed by a plunge, followed by a more sustained rise – the U-curve of innovation (discussed in Chapter 5). Living through the downturn is challenging. Keeping with the analogy of the cliff, one can support the stepping-out by belaying, fixing some matters securely and keeping some control over what happens. The familiar mountaineers' saying of 'don't look down' can apply here – the leaders must keep a firm eye on possibilities rather than be fixated on obstacles. This chapter charts the opening stage of the innovation, and teases out leadership and management implications.

At the start of the project, students in Primary 4 (P4), Form 1 (F1) and Form 4 (F4) were randomly assigned to either the experimental (hereafter termed 'pilot') or control groups and these groups were very closely matched in terms of their scores on mathematics and English from the school's end-of-semester scores from their most recent assessments. Each class had approximately 40 students: two classes for P4 (pilot and control classes); two for F1 (pilot and control classes) and two classes for F4 (pilot and control classes). The syllabus was the same for each pair of experimental and control groups, and so was the subject teacher.

Before the semester commenced, the teachers and students had been given their own tablets and some preparatory training on them. Parents had given their permission for their child to be involved in the innovation, and where they had not given their permission, that student was not involved in any way. Meetings with parents had been held in advance of the start, and other communications about the innovation had been given to parents.

Six teachers were involved in teaching in the innovation:

1 One teacher of mathematics to the two P4 groups (pilot and control);
2 One teacher of English to the two P4 groups (pilot and control);
3 One teacher of mathematics to the two F1 groups (pilot and control);
4 One teacher of English to the two F1 groups (pilot and control);
5 One teacher of mathematics to the two F4 groups (pilot and control);
6 One teacher of English to the two F4 groups (pilot and control).

Additionally, key persons involved in the project from the school were the school principal, the head of ICT and the head of curriculum. Several other parties were involved to lesser extents, e.g. heads of primary mathematics and English, heads of secondary mathematics and English, deputy principals, counselling and school discipline staff, heads of sections (primary and secondary), and the school treasurer.

Each teacher taught the pilot and control group for each parallel class (P4, F1, F4). The same syllabus was covered by the pilot and control groups in each parallel class, the only major difference being that the pilot class was taught using the ICT equipment and software to support, even to drive, the collaborative, active, engaged and interactive learning. The textbook materials that each class had were the same for each parallel class, though soft copy only was available to the pilot groups whereas hard copy only was available to the control groups.

Each student had his/her own tablet, with individual password-protected security access, onto which was loaded all the software used in the innovation (including software for sharing and online, real-time communication and sharing), and all the multimedia resources prepared by the school, including lesson materials, extension materials, quizzes, a range of subject-related resources, information for parents and students about weekly planning, facilities for online submission and marking of homework, software for in-class surveys, online assessment provision, video playback of classroom sessions, Internet access and communication facilities for students and parents to contact and discuss matters with the teachers.

Many students, particularly the younger students (P4), were very enthusiastic about the innovation at its inception. They were proud to have their own tablet, they liked ICT and they felt that their ICT skills would improve. They liked access to the Internet, to the much wider range of online resources made available to them and to the opportunity to take their tablet home each evening, where it could be used not only for school-related matters. Some of the older students were a little more cautious of or, indeed, indifferent to the tablets; others were suspending their judgment. Older students (and their parents) were concerned about whether students would slow down in their learning and whether their performance/marks would suffer; parents of younger children were concerned about possible damage to students' eyesight and to the lowering of their child's marks.

There was generally a positive sense amongst all the pilot groups of being chosen to be in an innovation which gave them a 'free' tablet. However, many students encountered difficulty in using the tablets at first, particularly the young children, and time was taken in solving problems rather than in moving on with curriculum content. The school intervened rapidly to address this, providing extra tuition classes for any students in the pilot groups who wished to attend, on using the tablet and on curriculum content. This ran for several months.

It had been intended that each teacher and each student would be provided with his/her own tablet, and that these would arrive in good time for teachers and students to have the necessary training in their use. In the event, the suppliers delivered them late, only very shortly before the start of the semester. This put immense pressure on staff in respect of learning how to use the tablet and its software, and, at the start of the project, they felt under-equipped to handle these. Training was thus telescoped into a very short window of time towards the end of the school vacation, and was intense. Students were brought into school for several days before the start of the term, to be taught how to use their tablet, but time was short.

Though the other ICT equipment was installed, there were many teething difficulties with the equipment and the software. The school was in constant touch with hardware and software providers and all parties were able to respond very rapidly and helpfully so that the system could stabilize and avoid crashing, hanging or freezing. In classrooms, if the teacher, system or software encountered any problems, the school took immediate action, placing ICT staff on stand-by call to be able to go into classrooms at a moment's notice to rectify any problems with the equipment, the software and its use, both for teachers and students.

From the very beginning, the teachers involved came under intense stress in preparing their sessions, culling materials from the Internet and preparing classroom resources, spending a huge number of hours of their private time on this in the evenings and weekends. They spent hour after hour in planning lessons for the increased student interactive and collaborative learning in tandem with the tablets and their software. Indeed, they spent more time on resource preparation than on preparing pedagogy. Teachers felt that they did not have sufficient curricular resources to support their collaborative, interactive, engaged and active teaching and learning, both with and without the tablets, so much of their time was spent in finding and preparing resources from the Internet.

Though the school had been introducing collaborative learning since before the commencement of the project (as part of its overall ESOS project), in fact it was partial and inconsistent, and teachers, on their own admission, did not have much expertise in this. They did not know well how to 'do' collaborative, interactive and engaged teaching in their classes. When new ICT equipment and software for collaborative, interactive, engaged and active learning were introduced on top of this, it meant that teachers felt doubly disadvantaged and under pressure, and so they, perhaps understandably, retreated somewhat to their comfort zones – or survival mode – in spending hours preparing PowerPoint slides and other materials to reinforce a 'delivery' mode of teaching, uploading many materials onto the tablet. Despite this, most of them remained in favour of the innovation and its hoped-for benefits to students.

Teachers and students had to digest a vast amount of information about the functioning of the DyKnow interactive software in a very short time, and had to overcome teething problems with the ICT equipment, e.g. battery life and recharging of students' tablets, variable online connectivity and access, screens freezing, the tablets 'hanging', students' and teachers' errors in using the new software and the new tablet, teachers and students not knowing what to do if an unfamiliar command came on screen or the tablet did not do what was intended, losing information/screen/files, not knowing how to navigate between screens and functions and so on.

Young children (P4) were nervous of using the software, even though they were proud to be included in the innovation. Not only did they make many mistakes with the software but, if they were using it at home, they could not rely on their parents to help them.

The early stages of the project got off to a somewhat shaky start, with considerable staff and student goodwill, enthusiasm, optimism and momentum being tempered by the reality of limited preparation, overload of novelty, increased stress, increased workload, lack of knowledge of how to make the innovation work effectively and a multitude of early practical problems encountered.

Teachers worked on different dimensions of the multidimensional innovation, but in a piecemeal fashion, focusing on immediate priorities and preoccupying elements rather than necessarily synergistically. For example, though clear links could be drawn between changes in pedagogy and all of the ICT elements of the innovation, such that they would be mutually potentiating, in practice the greater part of the early stage was fragmented: how to ensure that the tablet would work, how to gather and prepare resources, how to solve technical and practical software usage problems. Whilst links could be drawn between ICT usage and parental involvement, in practice these were divorced from each other, and the attention given to parents was slight. Whilst links could be drawn between assessment and pedagogy, in practice, with the exception of teachers trying to be fair and consistent in awarding marks for class participation, what actually happened was that teachers were attempting to retain and put the old wine of traditional forms of assessment into the new bottle of the tablet. Whilst links could be drawn between curriculum and the new pedagogy, in practice the new pedagogy was reframed as using the tablet, particularly as a means of easy storage and retrieval of 'transmission' types of resources, i.e. the tablet buttressed up existing traditional views of teaching and learning (this is, perhaps, an over-statement of all the practices reported, as some collaborative and interactive learning did take place, but it was limited).

The lesson here is that, for multidimensional change to be effective, it is advisable to see how the different dimensions can be used *together*, to reinforce and strengthen each other rather than being used in relative isolation. Whilst the exigencies of the moment often require attention to priorities, this does not preclude the advantages of planning for how the several dimensions of a multidimensional innovation might be usefully linked and run simultaneously.

One corollary of this is the need not only for careful, holistic planning, but also for adequate preparation of participants and the ensuring of expertise in all the key elements before an intervention commences, such that they can maximize the benefits of such synergies. Clearly, this is an innovation in itself, but it sends a clear signal that an innovation is not only what is transacted in situ but what is prepared in advance: the innovation begins before the intervention is rolled out to all those affected and involved. This, in turn, can establish a stronger fortress to withstand emergent challenges and unanticipated events.

The rest of this chapter reports data from the first formal round of data collection by the external evaluators. It deliberately reports these from several perspectives, as they press home the point that different parties have different views and concerns, and the management of multidimensional innovation has to take account of this phenomenon. At the end of each subsection which reports each main party's summary data, some key lessons for management of multidimensional innovation are listed. The end of the chapter draws these together in making key recommendations for the leadership and management of multidimensional innovations.

The student data

The numerical data indicated that students generally felt positive towards the school, and liked it; they generally felt that the standard of teaching was good, that many students tried to work hard, not least because of pressure of examinations and family, and that there was a considerable amount of traditional, didactic teaching in the school with very considerable teacher talk and concomitant student silence in the classrooms. These data suggested that, in terms of the school's intention of the ICT project to change pedagogy, there would be a considerable amount to do here, though there appeared to be a willingness and positive attitude towards ICT on the part of students for the project to be successful. The data indicated low or very low use of ICT in teaching, with the exception of using ICT as a presentational device, typically using PowerPoint.

The students' numerical data suggested several important features in the school:

- There was a lack of challenge in tasks set by teachers, but with students not speaking out about this;
- Students found it quite easy to understand their teachers;
- There was limited group activity and inter-student discussion in class;
- There was a limited variety of teaching strategies used;
- There was domination of the class by teacher talk and student silence;
- There was limited student autonomy, choice and opinion in class;
- There was limited student motivation for follow-up on learning;

- There was limited out-of-class support for learning (by both teachers and parents);
- There was very limited coverage of the range of ICT possibilities for use in class;
- There was limited use of ICT in the classroom apart from PowerPoint;
- The underuse of a range of ICT in the classroom, together with an overemphasis on PowerPoint as the main use of ICT, were detrimental to effective teaching and learning;
- There was a very considerable amount of traditional, didactic teaching;
- Students reported feeling unmotivated to follow up their studies outside school, and they reported little direct support from parents in their learning.

It appeared, then, that the aspirations of the project – to enhance student motivation, use of ICT, communication with, and involvement of, parents and promotion of more adventurous, less traditional, didactic teaching, collaborative, engaged and interactive learning, and problem-solving activities – were well founded; the school had identified a real need and had taken action to focus on this.

The pilot group of students overwhelmingly felt positive about this innovation and were looking forward to it, and this augured very well for the project. Indeed, at this early stage, the students felt that the school had prepared them adequately, though not outstandingly, for the project to date, and had prepared the parents less well. Regression analysis of data indicated that, for the dependent variable 'generally, how good is the teaching in the school?' the message was very clear: students noted that relevance to everyday life, arousing student interest, and using a variety of teaching strategies were important for effective teaching. Students noted that having challenging tasks and active learning were important contributors to effective learning.

Part of the project was designed to address student motivation in the school. For the dependent variable 'generally, how motivated are you to learn at school?' the message from the students was clear: student interest, ease of understanding the teacher, and student voice were important for student motivation.

For the dependent variable 'how much do you like school?' the message, too, was very clear:

- Student interest and the perceived relevance of curricula to students' everyday lives were important to how much they liked school, with teachers charged to make the learning interesting;
- Student voice was important to how much they liked school;
- Too much pressure from parents and family was counter-productive for how much they liked school, and pressure generally was related to how much they liked school (in a culture of significant parental and family pressure to achieve high marks).

For the pilot group of students, with regard to the dependent variable 'generally, how good is the teaching in the school?', the data suggested that the use of ICT was related to effective teaching, but that teachers should reduce reliance on PowerPoint alone and that they should consider carefully the negative aspects of discussion boards and forums before embarking on them to any great extent.

Some of the purposes of the project were to make school more relevant to students' lives, to raise their motivation and interest, to enhance and extend the pedagogy and teaching strategies, to make learning active and interactive and to increase student engagement and voice. The student data indicated that this project would address significant challenges in the school, in that there was much traditional, didactic teaching.

Difference tests (t-test, ANOVA and the Tukey test) were conducted to investigate differences between the pilot and control groups in respect of their questionnaire data at this early stage of the project and between the three pilot groups (P4, F1 and F4). Understandably perhaps, given that one feature of the project was extended use of ICT, differences were found between the pilot and control groups in respect of ICT. It was also found that the youngest group (P4) was generally more positive in its responses to the questionnaire items than the older children, and there was also considerable homogeneity of responses. The questionnaires addressed issues of teaching and learning, student motivation, homework, assessment, levels of intellectual challenges in lessons, classroom processes, talk in classrooms, teaching strategies, collaborative, interactive, active and individual work, learning through memorization, pressure on students, parental involvement, views on the innovation and ICT inside and outside the school,

Key factors repeatedly reported by students to make for effective learning, and motivation for learning, were:

- Relevance to outside life and the 'real world';
- Deliberate attention given by teachers to engage student interest;
- Reducing concern for behaviour in favour of interesting, active, interactive and ICT-rich learning;
- Having teachers set realistic challenges for student learning;
- Increasing student voice, autonomy, opinions and choice;
- Increasing attention given by teachers to student understanding of what is being taught;
- Reducing reliance on delivery models of teaching and learning, together with a reduction in reliance on PowerPoint.

These very items were reported to be under-represented in pedagogical practices in the school; they consistently received low scores from students.

The declared purposes of the project were several, including:

- To make school more relevant to students' lives;
- To raise students' motivation and interest;

- To make learning more meaningful, relevant, active, interactive and engaging for students;
- To give students greater control over, and autonomy in, their learning;
- To replace traditional, didactic teaching with student-centred, interactive learning;
- To enhance and extend the pedagogy and teaching strategies;
- To increase students' higher-order thinking;
- To increase communication with parents;
- To facilitate students' out-of-hours learning;
- To replace over-emphasis on summative assessment with greater emphasis on formative assessment;
- To make learning active and interactive;
- To increase student engagement and voice.

Students were adept at identifying these issues for attention in the school. The student data indicated that these features were under-represented in the school at the start of the project. The data indicated that the intentions of the project were well placed, and that it was urgent that the school addressed these issues. The data also indicated that addressing these challenges would be an immense task, and that the school's intentions in the project, including to change pedagogy, student motivation and relevance, and to increase parental involvement, were going to require a considerable amount of innovation, at many levels and in many spheres of operation in the school. In short, to address the problems identified would require multidimensional innovation.

Semi-structured group interviews were conducted with 24 pilot group students from each of the three classes, interviewed in three groups of eight, on the strict understanding that none of the comments reported would be attributed to, or traceable to, any individual student. These results are grouped under key emergent headings below.

Motivation and performance

There was interest and excitement in the project amongst nearly all pilot group students, particularly the younger students, and many felt positive towards the project and the tablet (but this excluded a significant number of older students who felt less enthusiastic). Many, but not all, were looking forward to trying the tablet, and they hoped that the project would improve their learning. Many students felt positive about being chosen to be in the pilot, but a significant number did not care, particularly the older students.

Students were excited by the ability to submit homework electronically. Some older students indicated that they did not feel as though the tablet would improve their performance or motivation, and that the teacher was more important than the tablet in these respects. There was a split here: many students felt that their performance might improve, many felt that it would not and, in some cases, whole groups of interviewees felt that it would not improve their performance or motivation.

Use of the tablet

Students used the tablet overwhelmingly for doing homework, playing games and sending emails, less for searching for information, and even less for reviewing homework with their parents. The older the student, the more they reported using the tablet for online browsing and reviewing PowerPoint and courses at home, and checking and reviewing points that they had not understood clearly in class. Many students indicated that they would use a cell phone to communicate with their peers (e.g. for help with work) rather than email.

Preparation

Their teachers had shown them how to use the tablet, and a large number felt sufficiently prepared by the school in how to use it, though the older the students, the more of them wished that they had received more preparation. Indeed, the majority of the older students felt insufficiently prepared by the school to use the tablet or for the project generally. Many students felt that they needed more preparation, over a longer period of time, and in shorter sessions. Many students indicated that they would like to have more, and shorter, preparation sessions for using the tablet.

Almost all of the students indicated that, even though they had received a briefing session, they were not clear on the purposes of the innovation, and all felt that they had not been told about it and were ignorant or confused about it, and that they needed much more briefing on it. A direct consequence of this was that the school ran more ongoing training sessions for the students on the tablet and its functions, spread over many weeks.

Over-reliance on the computer

Very many students were worried in case they could not use the tablet and what would happen if the system broke down (e.g. connectivity and stability) or if the upload and download speed was slow (slow enough for the computer to time out); indeed, some of them indicated that they had already had problems with connectivity. Some students indicated that they felt that too much might depend on the tablet, and if it broke down in the class then the class would come to a standstill (as had happened in the classes in the early stages of the innovation). Some students were worried about losing material on the tablet (e.g. their homework).

Parents

Almost all the students indicated that their parents did not use the tablet, did not know how to use it, or could not – or did not – help them with the homework, and only checked that they had done the homework. Very few students indicated that their parents had discussed the project with them. Many students indicated that their parents did not have time to help them with homework and, anyway, students would seek help from their peers rather than their parents. Some students indicated that their parents used the tablet to watch the video of the class session. Some students indicated that their parents were worried about a decline in their child's performance.

Surveillance

The school had installed video cameras to record the classroom sessions so that students and their parents (who had security-protected access to their child's tablet) could watch the lesson again in order to review points that they had not understood or only partially understood. The video camera was a fixed installation, with a fixed focus on the front of the classroom, i.e. focused on the teacher. The older the student, typically, the less they liked being videoed in the classroom, particularly as their parents would be able to watch the video and also because the teachers could re-watch the video, i.e. many students felt under heavy surveillance; and the older the student, the stronger and more widespread was the negative feeling about being videoed, mounting to outrage in some of the older students. Such students wanted the tablet to be used for study, and nothing else. In this early stage of the innovation, videoing the class appeared to be highly unpopular, though the school principal was determined that this would continue as it was designed to be in the students' interests and for their benefit rather than to be used against either them or the teachers.

Lessons from the students' data for the leadership and management of multidimensional innovations

There are many direct lessons to be learned from the student data for leading and managing multidimensional innovations. These are set out below. The later part of the chapter draws these together with those from other parties in making recommendations for the effective leadership and management of multidimensional innovations.

- Identify and focus on real needs and the underlying causes of problems;
- Identify a project that can address the underlying causes in a single, multidimensional project;
- Identify a lever of change that can focus on many dimensions simultaneously;
- Recognize that an innovation begins before an intervention, through initial-needs analysis and situational analysis;
- Effective innovation addresses big challenges;
- Listen to, and act on, students' views for informing innovations;

- Focus on important, central and deep-seated areas of school work in an innovation;
- Identify whether a problem is singular and confined, or whether it is multi-dimensional, and, if it has many dimensions, identify what these are;
- Ensure that multidimensional innovations are fit for purpose, rather than, for example, singular and single-dimensional innovation;
- Identify initial perceptions of different dimensions of an innovation, and look for commonalities and differences between participant groups, in order to give a differentiated response to the challenges faced;
- Be realistic in the expectation of where the innovation might have impact;
- Communicate, communicate, communicate the purposes and contents of the project to those immediately affected by it, and provide training and preparation, suitably timed, targeted to content and the reduction of negativity, and organized in time periods and durations that are suitable for the participants;
- Provide ongoing, timely and sustained training for students in the early stages of an innovation;
- Identify students' concerns early in an innovation and take action to allay these concerns;
- Persuade with evidence;
- Be realistic about what can be expected from different parties in a complex innovation;
- Provide plentiful ongoing multimedia, multi-channelled briefing to parents involved in a school-based innovation;
- Be prepared for resistance from some parties, some of it strong. Anticipate where resistances might be, and from whom, and how to address these resistances and participants;
- Act quickly to address immediate problems.

The teachers' data

At this early stage of the innovation, though the teachers were generally optimistic about the ability of the project to handle key challenges in the school, in respect of both teaching and learning, and of teachers and students using ICT, their optimism was guarded rather than high.

Teachers reported effective teaching of high-performing students, with the level of challenge for these students being moderate but no more. Teachers felt that they were working moderately well with medium-performing students but that they were experiencing problems with low-performing students. As the performance level of the students decreased (from high-performing to low-performing), so the teachers indicated that challenges increased.

In respect of pedagogy, teachers reported a low incidence of active learning, group work, whole-class activities, individual activities and of how much their teaching was responsive to student-driven initiatives. In many ways, the teacher data reinforced the numerical data derived from the students, indicating the high incidence of the lecture method, with much teacher talk, much teacher direction and limited student autonomy and activity, an emphasis on assessment and its communication, and on the use of examinations to motivate students.

The teachers were often more positive than the students. For example:

- Teachers indicated that they used a range of teaching strategies, whereas students did not feel so strongly that this was the case;
- Teachers indicated that they emphasized students' higher-order thinking more than the students acknowledged;
- Teachers acknowledged that they took students' abilities into account, whereas the students saw many of the lessons as undifferentiated;
- Teachers saw that the knowledge students learned was applicable to the real world, whereas students saw this as a problem;
- Though teachers indicated that they did not use whole-class activity a lot, the students' views contradicted this.

It became clear very early in the project that the management of different perceptions would present challenges, not least as too threatening a set of feedback to teachers at this point could demotivate them and could influence their initial willingness to be involved in the project. A key leadership matter, then, became how to keep teacher motivation in the face of some negative feedback and difference of views.

Generally, the teachers reported a positive level of communication between parents and teachers, and between parents and their children, though they recognized that the levels of parental involvement in the school with respect to matters of curricula, teaching, learning and student achievement and progress were not strong, and parents were currently not able to help their children much in their learning. These data suggested that, potentially, the level of actual involvement of parents in the school could be expected to be quite low in respect of important features of the project (curricula, help for children, supporting their learning), and this, in turn, suggested that the school might need to provide considerable support for parents on these areas. Teachers also reported that students were under pressure from examinations.

Teachers were generally positive towards the project and hoped that it would benefit the school, even though they were anxious about it. However, they reported having received only small amounts of training for the project and its associated ICT and they felt that this was inadequate to the point that they felt under-prepared for the project in terms of knowledge of its aims, goals and contents and of their own ICT knowledge and abilities; in short, they felt that they had received inadequate preparation for the project. They recorded low scores for questionnaire items asking them about how comfortable they felt in understanding and using the tablet and how well equipped they felt to handle the project.

The teachers reported that the intended outcomes of the project were only moderately clear, and its organization and management were even less clear to them. The teachers felt that, because of limited training, communication and clarity, they were insufficiently prepared for the project, even though they were positive about wanting it to bring benefit. Indeed, they reported being more worried about the project than they were positive about it in respect of their own and their students' abilities to undertake the project.

On the other hand, teachers were strong in their positive feelings on the parents' views of, and participation in, the project, in how it would be led and managed, about working with other teachers in the project and on the project's consequences for improving student performance and parental involvement. These are significant points, as it shows trust in the leadership of the school and an indication that the expressed benefits of the project would impact on the students. There was faith in the leadership and management of the school to handle the innovation.

In terms of the ICT aspect of the innovation, the teachers' data supported the earlier comments that they largely operated in the lecture mode of transmission teaching and that, overall, their current use of ICT was limited, or very limited, in respect of using ICT for audio, video and DVD materials, discussion boards and forums, emails and online communication with parents and students. Clearly, the purposes of the project, to increase and enhance the use of these and other forms of ICT, was both timely and promised much to address these current shortcomings in the school.

Overall, at this early stage of the innovation, whilst the teachers were generally positive and optimistic that it would bring benefit and that the managers of the school would be able to lead and handle the project, they were also apprehensive or very apprehensive about it and, indeed, several scores on indicators of anxiety were higher than for positive feelings. This apprehension derived in part from lack of clarity and communication about the innovation, in part from the lack of preparation for the project, and in part from their long-standing practice of traditional teaching and their current use of ICT. There was a significant problem in that teachers reported themselves to be under-prepared and under-trained for the ICT project; they felt anxious, ill-equipped and uncomfortable about this matter.

The teachers' data indicated that they felt better equipped to handle high-performing students than low-performing students, indeed that the lower the performance level of the students, the greater the challenge for teachers, and that large class sizes were a significant problem. Low-performing students – a particular target for the ICT intervention – posed many challenges for teachers, in terms of their motivation, interest, involvement, homework, engagement, application and attitude to learning. In this respect, the expressed intentions of the project, to lift the attitudes, motivation and performance of the low-performing students, were well placed.

Though the teachers reported that they used a range of teaching strategies, other responses to questionnaire items did not support this, and a 'delivery', didactic model of teaching, largely undifferentiated to individual students' needs, was found in very many responses, with much teacher talk, limited student involvement and emphasis on assessment and examinations, and this was compounded by parental pressure on students. Though teachers reported that they encouraged higher-order thinking in students, this was not confirmed by their responses to other questions. Teachers' responses indicated limited active learning, group work and individual work in class. The teachers' responses also indicated limited student choice and autonomy, and, indeed, one of the purposes of the project was to address this challenge. In these respects, the teachers' data were similar in views to those received from the students, though, generally, the teachers had a more optimistic view of what was happening than did their students.

Teacher pressure

The teachers were committed to working hard to make the project succeed, very aware that they were 'under the spotlight' and that many people were watching them and the project, and that they were in the front line of developments here (Macau is a small city, and reputations can be fragile). They felt under very considerable pressure.

Many teachers commented on the very heavy, unsustainable workload pressure that they were under to prepare materials for the tablets and classes. They were spending very large amounts of time (many hours a day, and at weekends) in searching for materials and information, and their health and family/outside life were suffering. Despite being given some remission of teaching loads, they felt that this was negligible in the face of the hours they were taking to prepare materials and utilize the tablet.

Innovations almost inevitably increase workload. Many teachers might be persuaded to increase their workload in the short term, but, as the teachers here expressed, it may be unsustainable beyond this (indeed one of the six teachers left during the course of the innovation, as discussed in a later chapter).

Benefits of the project

Teachers indicated that student commitment to the project was critical to its success. Many teachers were curious to know whether the project would actually achieve its aims. Some comments indicated that the use of the tablets might benefit most of those students who enjoyed ICT, but that it might have less effect on other students who enjoyed ICT less, i.e. the success of the project might hinge on student-related factors rather than on teaching methods. Indeed, the use of the tablet might disadvantage those students with poorer reading abilities.

Surveillance

Many teachers did not like the idea of being videoed in class, though some were less opposed than others. Some teachers were considering leaving the school if this happened as it brought 'suffering' (their word) and stress. The teachers felt that the surveillance issue as felt by students was a lesser problem, as the intention was pedagogical rather than acting as a 'spy' in the classroom. There appeared to be a hiatus here: videoing was acceptable for some parties but not for others. Teachers were concerned that video material might be re-recorded and posted on YouTube, and that students had not been briefed sufficiently.

Teacher preparation

Preparation for using the tablets had been provided by the school, but many teachers felt that it was too little, too short, and in too telescoped a time frame, such that there was considerable overload and teachers could not remember everything. Teachers were worried about using the tablet, its functions and the ICT approach generally. Many comments were received about this, including the need to spread training over a month or even a year. Though the innovation focused on a wide range of areas, the ICT area was the one that preoccupied the teachers, and, to a lesser extent, having pedagogical expertise to promote collaborative and interactive learning.

Pedagogical issues

Though teachers were aware of the need to employ interactive teaching strategies, many teachers were using the tablet to reinforce a delivery mode, i.e. to prepare PowerPoint slides from a wider range of sources than previously. Teachers were aware that the project was intended to bring about more interactive and collaborative learning, and that this was not contingent on the ICT but on teaching strategies in themselves. Some teachers felt that the ICT usage in the class could facilitate much greater interactivity between students and with the teacher. Teachers commented that issues of teaching methodology were serious problems for inexperienced staff and that it was taking a lot of private time to prepare for this or to keep up with lesson preparation.

Teachers working on the project needed greater preparation on pedagogy; it was the pedagogy rather than exclusively the tablet that required greater attention, focusing on interactive and collaborative teaching strategies *and then* with the tablet to reinforce and serve that pedagogical practice. Some teachers were planning for interactive work whilst others were not. Comments indicated that the teaching methods and students' learning methods needed more preparation, with concrete examples, followed by how ICT worked within these teaching strategies, i.e. so that the teaching strategies were not exclusively ICT-driven but ICT-facilitated and so that it could be seen how ICT integrated with these teaching strategies.

These comments indicated that a main parallel dimension to the ICT aspect of the innovation – the pedagogical area – was itself a serious cause for concern. Though the school had been taking deliberate steps to promote collaborative, interactive and active learning prior to the inception of the project, striving to lay the ground for the ICT dimension of the innovation, nevertheless clearly this was still relatively embryonic. Then to lay the ICT on top of this was to risk building a larger edifice on a weak foundation. Adequate staff development in the key dimensions of the innovation became a key concern here.

Initial reactions

Teachers raised a paradox: in a situation in which they felt that they were required to increase the amount of collaborative and interactive teaching and to cover certain materials on given sessions (incorrectly for this latter point, it turned out) they increased the amount of transmission teaching using PowerPoint to present material rather than using the ICT to promote collaborative and interactive teaching and learning, and they increased the amount of testing that took place as they feared that their classes were falling behind in their coverage of the syllabus, that teaching time was being lost to technical matters with the tablet and that teaching generally had slowed down.

Parents

Teachers felt that parents, who were concerned about their child's performance and marks, had been given considerably insufficient preparation for the project, even though there had been information material in print form and a face-to-face session. The school principal had made it clear that the innovation would bring in newer forms of assessment, whereby there would be the inclusion of class participation in assessing a student's performance (and marks played a very significant role in determining whether a student would be promoted to the next class or would have to repeat the year) and that this would benefit all students, particularly the poorer-performing students. Nevertheless, the parents continued to voice their anxiety about this.

Teachers indicated that parents had told them that they (the parents) felt that insufficient preparation and information had been given to them, and their views had been inadequately solicited on the innovation. Some teachers reported that they had received comments from students to say that the students would not tell their parents how to use the tablet, as this would lead to increased surveillance and, thereby, reduce student freedom.

Lessons from the teachers' data for the leadership and management of multidimensional innovations

As with the student data, there are many direct lessons to be learned from the teachers' data for leading and managing multidimensional innovations. These are listed below. The later part of the chapter draws these together with those from other parties in making recommendations for the effective leadership and management of multidimensional innovations.

- Identify how to handle different perceptions of a situation from different participants, and how to present potentially demotivating feedback;
- Be realistic in identifying problems and the limits of support in introducing an innovation;
- Communicate, communicate, communicate, from the very earliest part of an innovation, even before any classroom intervention commences;
- Do not lose staff motivation early on through inadequate preparation and training for an innovation and its contents;
- Ensure that staff are able to experience success right from the beginning of an innovation, particularly in the key dimensions of the innovation;
- Identify and address participants' worries and anxieties at the start of an innovation;
- Ensure that the benefits of the innovation are made clear to all participants, and that participants are resolute in their trust in the leadership of the innovation;
- Ensure that the innovation is timely;
- Ensure that the innovation brings tangible benefits in terms of knowledge and skills to participants;
- Focus on chalk-face problems, as they can signal anticipated problems and inject realism into a proposed innovation and this can enhance teachers' motivation for involvement in an innovation, even in the face of apprehension;
- Identify common areas of agreement on perceptions of situations, as this enables an innovation to be recognized as having an agreed potential for impact;
- Identify and work on areas where differences of perception and of positive and negative feelings are found to exist between participants;
- Utilize positive feelings and work on removing the negative feelings for an innovation;
- Consider the increased workload that innovations bring, and how to address these immediately and beyond. Increasing workload to an

unacceptable level, regardless of reward, is a significant demotivator for participants;
- It is essential to take participants' views seriously and act on them in a way that makes a difference;
- Provide ample training in areas not only identified by the innovation leaders but also in response to participants' foremost concerns;
- Identify the uppermost concerns in the participants' minds, and act on them;
- Make training and development realistic in terms of contents, timing, duration and the avoidance of overload;
- Provide ongoing support and development;
- Ensure that each dimension of the innovation receives adequate initial preparation before being joined with another dimension;
- As dimensions of innovation become integrated, so greater preparation and staff development have to be provided in how to integrate these, with concrete examples and support;
- Anticipate what might backfire in the early stages of an innovation and how regression to more intensified forms of earlier practice might occur, and intervene to prevent this;
- Ensure that key players who have key concerns have those concerns addressed;
- Reinforce the messages of the innovation repeatedly to key participants and relevant parties;
- Provide plentiful information, repeatedly, multi-channelled to key parties involved in, or affected by, the innovation;
- Work with, and work on, parents' real-life concerns.

The parents' data

Three groups of parents, one from each of the pilot classes, were interviewed in groups, on the strict understanding that none of their comments would be attributable or traceable to any individual.

Before the project commenced, the school had provided parents with a comprehensive introduction to the project through written and face-to-face channels, and the school had made it clear that participation in the project was entirely voluntary – i.e. the parents had the entirely free and open option not to have their son or daughter involved in the project – and the school had secured in writing permission from the parents for their child to be involved. In other words, fully informed consent had been obtained.

Generally, the parents reported feeling positive about the project and were happy to give their approval for their child's participation, though they felt they knew only a little about it. They felt that the parents should have been given a much bigger role and voice in the project. They accepted the case for increasing ICT and for the tablet, feeling the development to be positive. They indicated that the project had the potential for them to gain more information about their children and the teaching and learning, but they commented volubly on the need for more support and training on a wide range of aspects of the project and the uses and functionality of the tablets. It became clear that some parents thought that the innovation comprised only the tablet, and they were unaware of the full project. They were worried whether the teachers had been sufficiently trained to handle the project.

Most of the parents commented that they had been given very little information or preparation by the school. There had been some briefing, but they needed considerably more on how to use the tablet, the overall project, how to help their children, how to use the tablet for communication and on the performance of their children. They felt that the briefing was too little, too short, too rushed and did not indicate any potential difficulties with the project, how to address them and where to get help. They reported not knowing where and how to look for help with the project and in using the tablet. They reported limited understanding of the tablet or the whole project. They were critical of the school for this, feeling that the school should have prepared them more. Some parents were fearful that they would not be able to help their child as they did not understand how to use the tablet or how to use the different functions on it. They needed examples and simulations, perhaps with a manual or CD to help them for their review and subsequent learning and follow-up. They reported needing hands-on training. Some comments suggested that the communication with the school was currently too one-way.

Parents said that their own time was limited for such consultation (as they were at work). Some comments indicated that, with the project, the communication between parents and school might actually reduce rather than increase, as parents did not know how to use the tablet for communication. Several parents said that they would continue to use the channels of communication that had existed prior to the project, and which they had found to work effectively, e.g. visits to the school, telephone conversations to the school, comments in their child's logbook.

Parents reported being worried about the performance of the children, particularly if they were at risk of failing or if the project turned out not to be working, as the parents would be unable to help them (many parents had few, if any, ICT skills). They were worried about their children being expelled from the school or repeating a year because of poor performance in the project (Chapter 3 indicated that these two problems are widespread in Macau). Parents reported different degrees of currently helping their children: as their children grew older they helped them less.

Parents thought that the video capture and replay were useful. They did not regard the communication function as a major feature, as they had other ways with which to communicate with the school. They indicated that their children had not told them very much about the project, and they were worried that their children would be wasting time on the tablet, e.g. playing games or downloading undesirable materials. They were worried, too, that, in an examination-oriented environment such as Macau, with university entrance dependent on examination performance, their children would be disadvantaged.

Lessons from the parents' data for the leadership and management of multidimensional innovations

As with the teachers' and students' data, there are many direct lessons to be learned from the parents' data for leading and managing multidimensional innovations. These are listed below. The later part of the chapter draws these together with those from other parties in making recommendations for the effective leadership and management of multidimensional innovations.

- Provide copious information, repeatedly, multi-channelled to parents involved in, or affected by, the innovation;
- Arrange frequent opportunities for face-to-face meetings with parents;
- Work with, and work on, parents' real-life concerns;
- Make clear, repeatedly, the potential benefits of the project, and cite evidence from outside the school which indicates how different aspects of the innovation bring benefits, and what these benefits are;
- Allay concerns about measurable changes in key areas of concern, e.g. students' performance, the consequences of the innovation on students' futures;
- Indicate what steps have been taken to prevent failure or negative aspects of key parts of the innovation and its consequences.

The senior staff

A multidimensional innovation stands or falls on the leadership and management of the institution and the innovation itself. In this instance, the innovation was led by the school principal, and the main part of it was undertaken by the head of ICT and the head of curriculum. Fifteen initial interviews were conducted with senior and middle managers of the school, including the principal and deputy principals, treasurer, head of ICT, head of curriculum, the subject heads (primary and secondary) of mathematics and English, and counselling and student management/discipline staff. Each interview lasted around one hour, and some lasted considerably longer. The intention of these was to understand their views and gather information on the early stages of the innovation. In most cases the remarks below are deliberately unattributable and non-traceable to individuals, even though different levels of senior managers were involved in the data collection (e.g. principal to heads of departments). Where remarks are attributable, permission was gained to include them in this book.

The comments from the senior and middle managers of the school are arranged in terms of key issues from their interviews and presented in terms of key areas of focus that emerged.

Vision, mission, leadership and commitment

Key criteria for the success of the innovation project were whether, and how much, it raised the performance, motivation and attitudes of students, particularly the poorly performing students, how it increased communication with parents and how it increased interactive, engaged and collaborative learning and extended ICT use. These were felt to be realistic criteria. Indeed, it was reported that benefits could come to all students, not only the poorly motivated and low performers.

It was very clear that the principal, the treasurer and the head of ICT were very clear, very positive and in agreement about the purposes, nature, scope and development of the project, with a clear vision and strategy for its leadership, management and unfolding. This clarity was not always shared by other members of the staff and, indeed, some of the latter's comments about the purposes of the project did not accord with the 'official' version as set out in the introductory materials on the project.

Some comments noted that there was a risk that some teachers would be 'left behind' if the pace of changes and innovations was too quick. Many comments indicated that all the senior staff were positive about, supportive of and positively concerned for this project to succeed, to bring benefit to students and increase communication with parents, and they supported the principal in his efforts at reform and development in the school. They were aware that the project really had to succeed. Some were more optimistic and committed than others here, but the senior managers of the school were united and clear.

Some comments about the innovation were more guarded than others, and it was clear that the project had less support from some senior staff; there were some indications of staff suspending judgment or not being in full support of the project (not all of these comments were negative, they were more in the nature of suspending judgment.) At the early stages of this project it was unclear as to the impact of these views on the actual operation of the project.

The school principal was aware of these views, differences of opinion and commitment, and the stance taken by some staff to suspend judgment. Nevertheless, he stood firm and unwavering in his insistence that the project would happen.

Management practices

With regard to the strategy for implementing the project, there was widespread consensus that the policy of 'drip-feed' developments – i.e. avoiding overloading participants with too many requirements and information all at once – and introducing more and more over time, was suitable. Several comments were received to indicate that the 'drip-feed' model of development was, in reality, the only one possible, that alternatives were unworkable, and that not giving participants the full picture of the project was not necessarily a negative feature. The deliberate strategy of 'seepage' and networking, wherein the informal diffusion of the project to other staff, parents and teachers, was seen to be operating to advantage as it helped to set the ground for the fuller unrolling of the innovation in subsequent years.

It was widely acknowledged that, even with incremental increase (e.g. starting with allowing time for teachers to become familiar with the tablet and then moving on to issues of pedagogy), there was an ongoing and serious problem of overload on teachers who were already very exposed and visible and, in retrospect, the sequence of planned rolling out of the project could have been different and, thereby, more targeted to necessary pedagogical change.

Comments indicated that more should have been done in the preparatory stages for teachers, students and parents (even though teachers knew that the project was coming), and that not all of this was contingent on the presence of the ICT equipment.

Quite a lot of communication between the senior officers was reported, both formally and informally, though communication between different levels of the senior officers was reported to be more mixed. It was reported that the use of informal communication was deliberate and, indeed, this was an intentional strategy to ensure not only collegiality but dissemination of the pros and cons of the innovation.

Several comments were received about the need for the school to ensure that all staff, students and parents were 'on board' with the project, understood it and agreed with it. This required effective and full communication, clarity, involvement and full information to all relevant parties, and full preparation of all parties. This was seen as a major challenge for the school, with mixed views on how well these had been addressed, with particular concerns registered in terms of how well the needs of the parents had been addressed and how familiar the teachers were with the functions and operations of the tablet. Many comments noted how the project had been rushed and hasty (a view which the senior officers recognized but which they over-rode, given the factors operating on the situation – such as the late delivery of the tablets and the need to make a start somewhere). Though the organization of the project had been planned well, gaps were exposed in how it was running and being managed, with increased communication between all parties, together with more ongoing, planned development activities in pedagogy and assessment, being seen as important to rectify this.

Preparation of all parties

All the staff commented that they were aware that the initiation of the ICT element of the project was rushed and delayed, for reasons outside the control of the school. It was very widely reported that the lack of time at the start had had serious knock-on effects on the project. That said, some features of the project could have been started much sooner without the tablets being present or the ICT system being ready, e.g. much more work could have been done on collaborative, active and interactive teaching and learning. Even though many comments indicated that the school had been introducing this for some years, in fact, from comments received, the extent of it was questionable. The innovation was predicated on this style of teaching and learning, together with alternatives to examinations for assessment purposes, and the extent of these prior to the ICT project was very mixed, and, in some cases, under-developed. This was a problem which undermined the ICT-nature of the innovation. There was talk of interactive teaching, group work and less conventional teaching in the school, but its actual practice was reported to be much less than mentioned or hoped for at the commencement of the project.

Many senior staff were very aware of the very high strain and massively increased workload that this project was placing on the teachers involved, and they hoped that the outcome would justify this. Similarly, many were taking care to keep themselves and each other fully briefed about the project. Several comments, however, indicated that more needed to be done here so that all parties understood what was happening.

Benefits to students

Some managers doubted the extent to which the ICT project would really benefit students, reduce homework and reduce testing. Whilst consequences were unknown at this early stage, nevertheless some doubts were being harboured. Several managers indicated that the hope of the potential benefits of the project to poorly motivated and poorly performing students was widely shared and that it was a realistic hope. Others were more guarded, indicating that the project might be more beneficial to those students who already had a good commitment and attitude to the school and to learning. It was suggested that maybe only the already-motivated students would review lessons through the video function and that it was unrealistic to expect a tablet alone, or in large part, to improve the motivation of poorly motivated students. Yet, other comments indicated that student motivation might be less important than student understanding, and that the system enabled students to review and understand more, and teachers to be able to ascertain quickly those parts which the students had not understood well.

Some comments indicated some positive benefits that had already been noticed with some poorly motivated students, in terms of raising their motivation, and that some students in the pilot groups were already improving in their attitude to school and taking a pride in their membership of the pilot group.

Parents

Many comments reported that insufficient action had been done to prepare parents, and this increased the risk of losing their commitment. Several comments indicated the need for more to be done to brief, train and develop the parents in and for this innovation and for the parents to be made aware that this was a longer-term rather than a shorter-term project, i.e. that results may take more than one year to show their benefits (and it was recognized that this was a potential problem, as many parents wanted short-term benefits as well). Most of the comments received here were critical, some heavily critical, and some comments indicated that some parents were considering withdrawing their children from a pilot class. It was reported that parents were concerned with outcome and performance, and that they had not been informed of the problems with the project to date. Several comments reported the need to educate parents about alternative views of effective teaching, learning and assessment, not only in connection with the innovation, but more widely, and to break the marks-orientation of teaching, learning and assessment. Further, many parents had insufficient expertise to be able to judge if their children were telling the truth about their use of the tablets, and were less able to supervise their homework.

In response to these quite strong comments, the school took immediate action to communicate with parents and involve and inform them more about the project. However, it was recognized that some parents (and the school's catchment drew from many less-educated parents) would have difficulty in understanding some aspects of the innovation, and anyway, as many incomes were low, both parents would be working and so would be unavailable to come to the school for training and meetings.

Pedagogy

Some senior staff indicated that the tablet was being regarded as a substitute for the whiteboard, i.e. still reinforcing a transmission model of teaching, and that it was going to be very difficult to break the culture of the teacher being the centre of the lesson and doing all the talking. Assessment was going to include class participation, and this was seen as being difficult to arrange, given the class sizes. Much teacher development work still needed to be done to change mentalities and practices of assessment.

Some comments indicated that it was perhaps unrealistic to expect the project alone to change teaching and learning strategies and that the changes needed to be deeper than at the project level. Many comments expressed hope that the project would change teaching and learning strategies; how realistic this was as a lever of change was questioned by others, as the changes to teaching and learning required deeper-seated changes than the introduction of a particular project. Several comments suggested that the tablet alone would probably not motivate the low-motivation students, as, for many of them, what happened at school was already boring regardless of the equipment and that, if there were fewer tests, students would study less (in a marks-oriented culture). The lack of motivation was a critical issue that required attention to pedagogy, levels of understanding and individual attention to students, i.e. motivation was not just about the blanket introduction of a tablet but about how to handle mixed abilities within a single class.

The need was stated for many parties to regard the tablet as a *tool* for learning, rather than as an end in itself; this point was made several times, with indications that some parties had misperceived the nature of, and priorities in, the whole project.

Comments were made that some parties were relatively blind to the need to change pedagogy or how to do this. Teachers did not know enough about non-transmission teaching, student-centred teaching and learning or collaborative and interactive pedagogies and they needed much more support and development on this, regardless of the project. Comments were received that, at that moment, the teachers were somewhat blind – they did not know where and how to go in student-centred teaching. It was widely suggested that the challenges were pedagogical and concerned class management rather than being ICT-based. They indicated that there was an urgent need for *pedagogical* leadership, and this required attention to the cultures of teaching in the school. Key senior and middle manager figures needed to spend more effort on developing pedagogy and on bringing into classrooms new pedagogies, developing pedagogical expertise in teachers.

Several comments suggested that the key figures in the project, the teachers, had not been sufficiently prepared for the project, and that this could threaten its overall success if pedagogical changes were not sufficiently supported and developed. A cultural change was required in teachers, and this was a long-term development which could have been started sooner; even though classes were supposed to have interactive teaching already, this was not happening sufficiently to be the bedrock of the project.

Several comments were received to suggest that a cultural change was required in teachers, and this was a long-term development which could have been started sooner.

Lessons from the senior officers' data for the leadership and management of multidimensional innovations

As with the preceding parties, there are many direct lessons to be learned from the senior officers' data for leading and managing multidimensional innovations. These are listed below. The later part of the chapter draws these together with those from other parties in making recommendations for the effective leadership and management of multidimensional innovations.

Vision, mission, leadership and commitment

- It is critical for the leaders of the institution and of the innovation to be clear and united in their views of and intentions for the innovation, and not to be easily swayed or put off by others. This is decisive:

- Leaders of the innovation need to be aware that not everyone shares their views, and they need to decide how to handle this;
- Leaders of the institution and of the innovation must be positive about it and convey this to relevant parties;
- The management of innovation is often largely about the management of perception and opinion. The leaders of an innovation need to understand and handle opinions and perceptions;
- Leaders' absolute and unwavering commitment is essential, backed up by taking a stand when challenges raised by the innovation and participants occur.

Management practices

- Plan how to prepare the ground for those coming into the project later;
- Identify where overload might occur and plan how to avoid or reduce it;
- Plan the strategy for introducing the different dimensions of the innovation over time;
- Consider the wisdom of not disclosing the full picture of the innovation at the start of the innovation in order to avoid overload and anxiety of participants;
- Provide essential, staged training and development before and during the intervention;
- Communication is key. Aligned communication of senior officers is vital;
- Recognize that informal communications are often more powerful than formal communications, so plan for how informal communications might be used to support and develop the innovation and to spread the messages of the innovation to those who will be involved later in the innovation;
- There is no perfect time to start an innovation, only a 'good enough' time: 'satisficing' rather than perfect conditions;
- Encourage concerns, anxieties and dissent to be aired and promote openness and voice;
- Identify what preparation can take place without certain resources being in place;
- Identify what is the minimum level of expertise, training, development and preparation required for each dimension of the innovation to commence, and ensure that it is present.

Preparation of all parties

- Whilst some aspects of innovation only emerge as it unfolds, others can be anticipated, so anticipate and handle them;
- Ensure that the foundational conditions for each dimension of the innovation are well established before the intervention commences;

- Plan for what to do if essential resources, experience and expertise for some aspects of the innovation are not ready;
- It is not enough to recognize a problem, action has to be taken to address it;
- Leadership and management of an innovation benefits from informed understanding and sharing of what is happening in each dimension of an innovation, and by different parties.

Benefits to students

- For leaders of innovations, identify where doubts and different expectations exist, and decide how to respond to these. Do not be swayed by opinion alone, be informed by evidence and data;
- Celebrate and disseminate early success to all parties;
- For leaders, decide whether to have ambitious, 'stretch' goals and expectations (maybe with a 'fall-back position'), or to be more modest in expectations;
- Take ongoing soundings from staff as to where the innovation is working effectively, and less effectively, and the reasons for these.

Parents

- Do not lose the support of powerful stakeholders. Take active steps to keep them not only on board, but supportive and positive;
- Consider making the innovation part of an ongoing parent development strategy;
- Be prepared for resistance and criticism from parents (and other stakeholders), and plan how to address these;
- Provide sufficient initial training and preparation for parents to be able to take part in the innovation as planned.

Pedagogy

- Consider how one dimension of the innovation relates to other dimensions of the innovation, and how the combined strength of resistances in several dimensions might impede the overall progress of the innovation;
- Be realistic about what might or might not be achieved (though clearly, in some cases, it may be a genuine unknown);
- Gather different participants' views on the purposes and roles of different parts of the project;
- Convince participants of the need for change, what needs to change and why, and make it clear what support and development will be assured for the innovation;

- Consider the management of the project with a view to appointing named persons responsible for different dimensions of the project, particularly in key areas of the project and in areas where there are current weaknesses.

Key lessons for leading and managing multidimensional innovations

In drawing together the lessons for effective leadership and management of multidimensional innovations from different parties, summarized in previous pages, some common themes emerge. These do not replace the detailed lessons learned, as set out in the preceding subsections; rather, they highlight some features of leading and managing effective multidimensional change.

The chapter focused on the perceptions of four main parties (students, teachers, parents and leaders and managers of the school). What became clear was that there was no single, unified view of what the innovation was, what it was for, how it was operating and how well it was operating. Though this existed in the minds of the leaders, it became much more blurred in the minds of different participants.

One of the opening messages of this book is the need to address 'simplexity' (Kluger 2007; Fullan 2013): keeping a fixed eye on a few core purposes and priorities in the project, not being swayed from them by circumstances and coupling these with the complex task of working with people and connecting people and content in the innovation. What, then, were the core key lessons as the innovation commenced?

- Identify and stick to the core purposes and priorities of the innovation.

What was happening in the innovation, and what people's reactions were to it, were not only a matter of perception but a matter of practice: the teachers were doing things differently from that which the project leaders had in mind, and the best of intentions were not always realized in practice. Managing innovation is not only about managing content, or people, but also about perceptions and processes. In the case here, some of the key initial conditions for the innovation to take place were not in good shape, e.g. resources (human, material, technological, temporal); expertise; experience; shared understandings of the innovation; anticipation of problems; appropriate middle management of all the main dimensions of the innovation; effective communication; awareness of people's concerns, anxieties, needs, stresses, pressures and workload; and links between the different dimensions of the innovation.

- Engage, align and connect people, groups, processes, contents and dimensions of the innovation.

If the task of leadership is to provide the conditions for an innovation – the soil into which the innovation is planted – then some of these were in embryonic form only here. This resonates with Hoyle's (1975) analogy of 'tissue rejection': if a new heart is to be transplanted into a patient then not only does that heart need to be compatible with the patient but the patient's body has to be prepared to accept it, otherwise rejection will occur.

- Set the conditions for the start of the innovation.

The innovation commenced even before intervention (practice) was started. There is an essential planning and preparation stage before anything happens in practice, so that necessary training, development and resources are in place.

- Ensure that capacity building is built in from the beginning.

This aligns itself with the research, development, preparation and trialling model of innovation where, well before the innovation is put into practice, the initial preparations and trialling are completed.

- Have adequate start-up development and resources.

At the start of the innovation there were repeated references to the need to ensure that not only were needs identified (a situational analysis), but that they were real needs, going to the heart of the problem for which the innovation was designed to be a remedy, and that the different dimensions of the problem were matched by different dimensions of the innovation, but preferably in combination. This suggests that the innovation needs to establish what the links are between its different dimensions, how they are understood and addressed in the minds and practices of the participants and how they will be developed and addressed in practice. In short, there needs to be 'joined-up thinking'; problems need to be linked and different dimensions of an innovation need to be linked not only to address the problem but also so that the benefits of synergy can be obtained. A tug of war is won by people pulling at the same time and in the same direction. Alignment of understanding and effort is essential.

- Establish and make clear, visible and practical the connections between the different dimensions of the innovation – contents, people, processes, resources – and work with their synergistic power.

There is not only a need for alignment but also for commitment from all parties. Whilst the staff participants in the school here had deep commitment to the innovation, some students and some parents were more hesitant. There is a need to persuade people by evidence, rational argument, educational expertise and celebration of successes, that the project is on track and working, that it is bringing benefit and that it is worth the considerable expenditure of effort put into it.

- Communicate and collaborate.

A recurrent theme from all parties was the need to communicate, or, rather, communicate, communicate, communicate. Whilst the defining features of the leaders was their clarity and unity of vision for the innovation, and their commitment to it in the face of serious setbacks that were out of their control, that clarity and unity was not shared by all participants. Many participants had no or little understanding of the innovation, or differing, selective, incorrect, incomplete and unbalanced (in terms of priorities) understanding of the innovation. This is something that can be handled both formally and informally, but the message from the start of the innovation is that it has to happen.

- Make the commitment worthwhile.

The work of Hall *et al.* (1986) and Hall and Hord (1987, 2011) (see Chapter 1) indicates that participants have different concerns at different stages of an innovation, and that, in the early stages of an innovation, they are typically concerned with 'awareness', 'information' and how the innovation will affect them personally (the 'personal' stage in their Stages of Concern model). It is for the leaders to ensure that correct, clear and full understanding of the innovation exists in the minds and practices of the participants. That this seems simplistic and platitudinous is contradicted by the practice found in the early stage of the innovation in the school reported here.

- Start where the participants are but move them quickly.

Effective leadership of an innovation is not only a matter of communication but also of careful planning and practice of the content, media and directions of communication. In the case reported here, many were the calls for greater openness and expression of concerns from and to all parties. Whilst the leaders of the innovation were persuaded of the value of a 'drip-feed' leadership and management strategy in the interests of overload avoidance for staff, nevertheless many staff felt under-informed and unable to detect whether their voices were heard and/or were making a difference save for immediate priorities (e.g. equipment failure).

- Balance necessary information and information overload.

The leader of the innovation – the school principal – was decisive, unwavering and strong in his leadership style, deciding that, even though there were serious setbacks at the start of the project, nevertheless it would start at the time already decided. That requires courage. He recognized, as the comment earlier in the chapter has indicated, that there is no perfect time to start an innovation, only one that is 'good enough'. Indeed, the knock-on effect of delay to the start of the innovation would have been enormous in terms of when the full project would roll out in the school, and over what period-of time. The principal had an overview of the whole scenario of his school's development and where this innovation fitted into it, and initial setbacks were not strong enough to sway him from this. These suggest several key features of leading and managing multidimensional innovation at the start of the project, organized into three main areas: personal robustness of the leader, working with others, and leading.

1. Personal robustness
   - Maintain tenacity, resolve, resoluteness and persistence;
   - Tolerate setbacks;
   - Be deliberate and deliberative;
   - Maintain optimism, confidence and determination;
   - Identify what will and will not be conceded as the change unfolds;
   - Refuse to admit or tolerate failure;
   - Balance patience and impatience;
   - Be assertive in different ways and at different levels;
   - Balance empathy and distance.
2. Working with others
   - Promote engagement and commitment;
   - Harness the power of connected people with the connected elements of a complex change (integrating different people and different parts of the change);
   - Promote ownership and commitment, starting with the leader's visible and practical commitment;
   - Keep up forward momentum and pressure;
   - Work on and with the intrinsic motivation of participants;
   - Energize participants by example and practice;
   - Develop passion and commitment through success and personal example;
   - Work collaboratively with groups: practice what is being preached.
3. Leading
   - Learn by, and from, doing;
   - Think big and small;
   - Identify the connections between interlocking parts of the innovation and make these visible;
   - Identify a few key related elements (the core purpose and core priorities) of the innovation, making them very clear and keeping to them through thick and thin;
   - Practice simplexity;
   - Build in recognizable success;
   - Set the context and conditions for change to occur;
   - Enhance and use communication and multidirectional feedback;
   - Support risk taking and experimentation and learn from these;
   - Build capacity for sustainability;
   - Create safe conditions for creativity and change;
   - Distribute leadership;
   - Balance hands-on and hands-off leadership;
   - Combine authority and democracy in innovations.

These points are formidable in their challenge.

The innovation was complex in two key ways. First, it was complicated, with several different elements combining in different ways. Second, it accorded with key elements of complexity theory: it was self-organized rather than externally imposed; order and practice emerged through the interaction of the different dimensions of the innovation (contents, people, processes, resources); it developed and required the creativity of the participants; it progressed through feedback, communication, collaboration and cooperation; it addressed emergent, unanticipated matters; it recognized the multiple and multidimensional connections of all parts of the innovation; order emerged through feedback and development; and qualitatively new situations emerged. In short, though the principles of complexity theory were not germane or deliberate in the planning and implementation of the innovation, nevertheless, faithful to the inexorable, behind-the-back-of-agents nature of complexity theory, they were at work. Whether we like it or not, complexity theory is present. If leaders can work with its key tenets then it can promote powerful complex, multidimensional change; the 'is' of what actually happens can become transformed into the 'ought' of planning and implementing complex change in schools.

Conclusion

At this early stage of the innovation many of the key areas for improvement in the school had been effectively diagnosed by many of the key parties, and it was clear that the innovation was designed to address these, including:

- Raising student motivation, attitude and interest, particularly with low achievers and those with a negative attitude to school;
- Teaching and learning (from traditional to collaborative, engaged, interactive and active);
- Student achievement and performance (raising both);
- Assessment strategies (from examination and a marks-orientated/marks-driven curriculum to formative and more comprehensive assessment to incorporate class participation and more authentic assessments);
- Parental involvement (greater involvement and communication, facilitated by online communication on the tablet);
- Curriculum development (to move towards greater differentiation);
- Extended use of ICT (both *per se* and as a tool for promoting collaborative, engaged, interactive and active learning);
- Staff development (to bring changes in pedagogy, assessment, collegiality and curriculum).

The declared purposes of the innovation were several, including:

- To make school more relevant to students' lives;
- To raise students' motivation and interest;

- To make learning more meaningful, relevant, active, interactive and engaging for students;
- To give students greater control over, and autonomy in, their learning;
- To replace traditional, didactic teaching with student-centred, interactive learning;
- To enhance and extend the pedagogy and teaching strategies;
- To increase students' higher-order thinking;
- To increase communication with parents;
- To facilitate students' out-of-hours learning;
- To replace over-emphasis on summative assessment with greater emphasis on formative assessment;
- To make learning active and interactive;
- To increase student engagement and voice.

In these areas the initial data indicated that there were significant challenges in the school, and, in turn, the project and its ICT elements faced considerable challenges in overcoming them.

There was a widespread agreement on the importance of these, and optimism that the different dimensions of the innovation could address these. Further, there was strong, committed and well aligned leadership of the school and of the overall innovation, though this was not always translated into the daily workings of some parts of the innovation. Many were the hopes and much was the optimism for the project. The leaders of the school had a very clear and very clearly expressed strategy for the implementation of the early stages of the innovation and kept steadfast to the purposes, contents and benefits of the innovation even in the face of challenges, setbacks and criticisms.

However, there were some key setbacks and challenges as identified by the evaluators. The delivery of the tablets was delayed (out of the control of the school) and they arrived only in time for limited preparation of teachers and students. Staff preparation, experience and expertise in key aspects of different areas of the innovation (e.g. pedagogy and alternative forms of assessment) were insufficient. Workload and overload were immense. Staff and students encountered problems in using the tablets in class (technical, software and functional problems). The power of transmission teaching was so deep-seated that the interactive and collaborative purposes of the tablets were hijacked into serving didactic teaching. Parents, though supportive, felt under-prepared and somewhat excluded; they did not know what was happening and did not understand the tablets. Despite communication to the parents, parents felt that this had been insufficient. Many parents were concerned about their children's performance and how it might suffer, and many felt that the hopes and expectations for the power of the innovation to really solve the deep-seated problems in the school were unrealistic. There were varying degrees of enthusiasm and support for the innovation from the students and the teachers. Much of the intervention took place with avoidable, insufficient preparation: the start of the innovation was before the intervention commenced in practice, yet the lead into this was insufficient. Links between different dimensions of the innovation were not made sufficiently strongly, particularly between ICT and pedagogy and between pedagogy and assessment. The leaders of the school and the innovation were quite some distance in front of the followers and implementers. Not all concerns were voiced out in public in the school, and not all staff participants understood the project sufficiently clearly. The organizational culture and climate of the school were not propitious for the innovation, there being limited openness to people and change in some quarters, and informal cultures of hesitancy to be committed entirely to the innovation – a wait-and-see attitude from some participants. Teachers felt exposed and vulnerable, and there were no innovation managers in some key dimensions of the project (e.g. pedagogy, assessment, parental participation). The conditions and foundations for the innovation to commence and run were insufficiently met in some key areas (e.g. pedagogy, assessment, ICT abilities, teacher preparation).

The school had prepared for several key aspects and, when problems arose, it intervened very promptly to address them, for example:

- It set up and ran more training sessions, on an ongoing basis, for students and staff;
- It brought parents together in face-to-face meetings, to ask questions and to give them information on the implementation of the project and its early findings;
- It took active steps to ensure that all aspects of the ICT equipment stabilized and operated smoothly to the immediate benefit of the students and the staff;
- It provided immediate in-class ICT support for teachers, so that such problems were solved instantly;
- School leaders and innovation leaders took a very strong and visible position on supporting the innovation;
- It took more steps to ensure that online work was facilitated for staff and students (including in respect of homework);
- It provided time for teachers to be released from some of their teaching in order to prepare materials;
- It clarified to all parties the use and control over what would be videoed and uploaded;
- It reinforced the key messages, purposes and contents of the innovation, to promote clarity;
- It provided feedback to staff on how the innovation was proceeding, what challenges were being faced and how;
- Senior managers took steps to ensure that staff were really able to keep up with the speed of the innovation, e.g. by slowing down or speeding up as necessary;

- It ensured that concerns were raised by all staff in means other than face-to-face meetings, so that staff would speak out without fear of recrimination;
- It took steps to communicate to all parties, so that all staff were 'on message' about what was to be achieved in the project and what it was doing;
- Senior managers reviewed their expectations of the project and what it might achieve, whilst holding fast to their intention that the project would lead to improvements in all the areas initially intended and planned;
- It communicated clearly to dispel concerns about health and safety;
- It took further steps to ensure that all the functions of the tablet were used fully;
- It built tablet use into homework.

In many of the key dimensions of the project, the commencement of the intervention was not as intended and not as sufficient as intended in several areas:

a   Pedagogical expertise and experience of teachers for collaborative, interactive and active teaching and learning;
b   Alternative assessments and how to assess class participation;
c   Electronic resources: their purchase, usage, preparation and the use of the e-tablet: how to use it, how to maximize its functionality, and how to use it as a tool to support new pedagogical developments and practices;
d   ICT abilities and experience of staff and students;
e   Parental support, involvement and communication, how to bring parents more into their roles, aspects of the innovation and how to link these to pedagogy, assessment and ICT usage;
f   Student motivation, attitude and interest, and how to link these to pedagogy, assessment, ICT and tablet usage, and changes to curricula and resource usage;
g   Management positions, operations, implementation, clarity and dissemination for all the different dimensions of the innovation;
h   Collegial working by teachers;
i   Staff development and training foundations and preparations;
j   Organizational culture: of openness to people, to change and to sharing and dialogue;
k   Preparing and implementing the links between the dimensions.

What has become clear in this chapter is that leading and managing multidimensional innovations concerns setting the conditions for the innovation to work, to identify tangible and intangible factors, and it hinges in large part on the ability of leaders and managers to understand and work with multiple perspectives, opinions, views, agendas, interests, constraints, parties and emergent issues. Whilst this is not necessarily confined to multidimensional innovations, nevertheless they are felt very sharply in multidimensional innovations. Further, it has become clear that key factors in effective leadership and management of innovations is to establish, develop and work with the linkages between different dimensions, e.g. contents, processes, people and resources. When these are bound together, they can withstand challenges and setbacks, but they require immense resolution from the leaders to ensure that these linkages occur.

The early stages of the innovation rode in on the back of some quite serious setbacks and disadvantages. Yet, it is testimony to the commitment and strong leadership of key players – the school principal, the leaders of the ICT and curriculum aspects, the teachers themselves – and to the optimism borne out of vicarious hopes for benefits to students that the project not only commenced, but that many positive outcomes manifested themselves quite soon, and it is to this mid-term stage of the innovation that the next chapter turns.

5 The project in mid-stream
The U-curve of innovation

It is to be expected that innovations will not proceed smoothly or exactly as planned. That is the norm and the project reported in this book is no exception. However, the project moved on in the face of this, and how this happened is testimony not only to the leaders of, and participants in, the innovation but also to the will for the project to succeed. Fullan (2013) refers to the 'implementation dip', in which, after the start of the innovation, it initially encounters setbacks and poorer than-hoped-for results. It can be represented as a U-curve, as in Figure 5.1. Indeed, he argues (2011b: 71) that it could not be otherwise, as 'new skills and understandings' are being learned. Here the immediate upturn in outcomes (results) or gains at the start of the innovation is followed by a dip in outcomes and the experience of negative gains, e.g. student performance, implementation success (i.e. whatever measures are used), and then the performance of the innovation climbs again. The innovation reported here follows a similar trajectory wherein the initial upturn in performance (e.g. student motivation and attitude, collaborative group work) entered a dip in results (e.g. students' assessment results, teachers' extended use of collaborative learning).

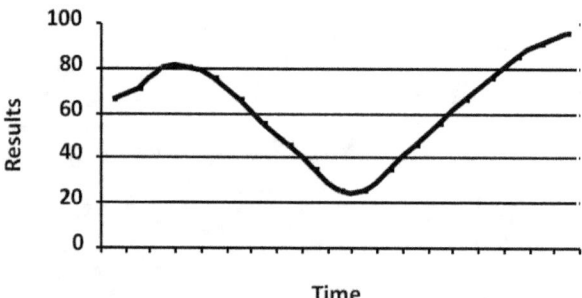

Figure 5.1 The U-curve of innovation

This chapter reports the second phase of the evaluation of the project, wherein the dip in outcomes was experienced. Indeed, there was a double-dip or, rather, a doubly reinforced dip, in that the innovation commenced at the start of the school year, and it is common for student performance in a school year to have an initial increase when students start the new class in the new year, followed by a dip towards the end of the first semester, followed by a rise towards the end of the second semester. Certainly, the results from both the control and pilot groups showed this to be the case, and this was explained to parents who were concerned about their children's marks, though the fall in marks for the three pilot groups was, on average, higher than for those in the three control groups. For one group of students (Form 1), not only was it the start of the new year, but the start of a new phase of schooling (from primary to secondary), and they encountered very different ways of organizing their classroom sessions, subjects, learning and homework; for this group one could suggest that there was a triply reinforced dip in performance: new innovation, new school year and new phase of schooling.

This chapter reports the results of the second round of data collection in the innovation, from multiple perspectives (as in the previous chapter), and draws lessons for the leadership and management of a complex innovation in its post-initial phase. It shows how, six months into the innovation, the project encountered several challenges, some of which could have been anticipated but others which could not. The initial phase of the innovation had seen it commence with limited preparation, for reasons out of the control of the school, and now, in this middle stage of the innovation, some of these initial difficulties were coming home to roost. Coupled with these were: downturns in student performance; some, although limited, effects on important spheres of the innovation such as improved student attitude and motivation; continuing staff reservations about the project; unclear and mixed effects on students; continuing lack of expertise in newer forms of teaching, learning and software use; and the rise of negative parental reactions to the innovation.

The chapter shows, however, that the innovation continued apace, and demonstrates that, in the face of setbacks and unfulfilled aspirations, the carry-through of determined leadership, staff commitment and their learning-by-doing enabled the best intentions of the innovation to prevail. Such effectiveness contains important messages that committed leadership and followership, a belief in the value of the innovation and resoluteness are essential ingredients of innovation, and that, together, they are powerful antidotes to negativity. In short, it is the human side of an innovation that enables it to succeed, not simply the contents of the innovation itself. People are both the problem and the solution to effective innovation.

The project had many dimensions and purposes:

- To have ICT play a key role in the teaching and learning of the pilot groups;

- To effect radical changes in teaching and learning from didacticism and transmission teaching to collaborative, active, interactive and real-world learning;
- To raise student motivation, attitude and interest, achievement and performance;
- To promote engaged, student-centred learning;
- To promote higher-order thinking and problem-solving in students;
- To change assessment strategies and contents;
- To further parental involvement and communication;
- To support the restructuring of the curriculum and its development;
- To promote staff development for sustainable change.

Central to these several dimensions were the twin – core – features of (a) collaborative, active, interactive, student-centred and real-world learning, and (b) ICT usage, both *per se* and to support collaborative, active and interactive pedagogies, the consequences of which would be improved student motivation, attitude and achievement which, in turn, would feed back into enhancing student-centred learning and achievement. Figure 5.2 maps the web of dimensions here (the thick lines indicate strong connection). Whilst engaged learning is at the core of the innovation, the connectors in Figure 5.2 deliberately have no directions of causality, as each area feeds into, and feeds from, all the others. It is a genuine web of learning rather than a simple input-output model of learning.

At the time of the second round of the evaluation of the project, many of the initial teething troubles with ICT hardware and software had been solved, though, as reported below, problems still arose. Six months into the innovation the students and teachers were using the tablet and the DyKnow software extensively, both in class and out of class. Students were using the tablet for doing homework and for submitting homework, and teachers were marking homework online. Interactive and collaborate teaching were progressing, though teachers admitted that they felt less than fully equipped to handle this, as they had little experience in planning and implementing extended collaborative learning, let alone with ICT. Though the school had run a training session for parents, it had been poorly attended. If parents had any questions or concerns about the innovation, they typically used the methods of communication that they had used heretofore, e.g. telephoning the school or coming in person. More training in the use of the software had been provided for both students and teachers.

Figure 5.2 can be used to indicate where the project was and was not working effectively. For example, those parts which were closely linked – (a) collaborative, active, interactive, student-centred, real-world learning; (b) ICT competencies, skills and usage and (c) raised student motivation, attitude, behaviour and interest, the parts which are connected with the thick lines in Figure 5.2 – were working more effectively than those parts which were less strongly linked. 'Parental involvement and communication' were

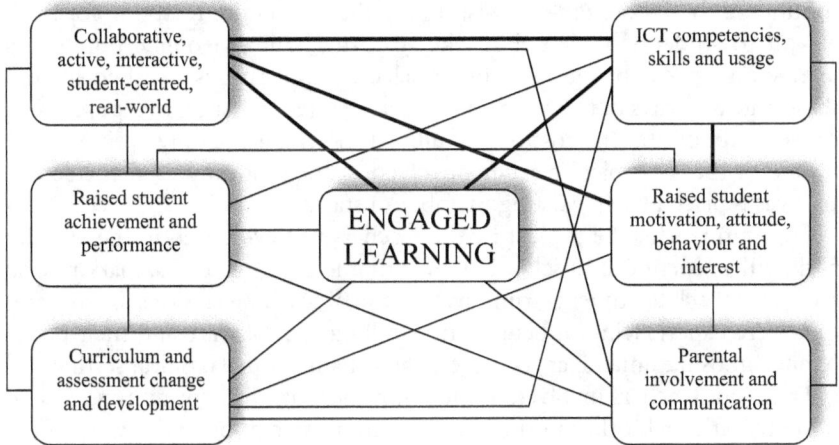

Figure 5.2 The web of engaged learning

less coherent with (a), (b) and (c), and were more marginal and less logically linked to (a), (b) and (c); the school did not concentrate heavily on parents at this stage and it did not develop as much as the other areas. Fullan (2001: 64) argues that effective innovations demonstrate 'program coherence', i.e. elements are coordinated, focused on explicit goals for learning and sustained over time; those parts which are not central to the 'coherence' may become marginalized, and this was the case here.

The innovation had started to attract the attention of local schools and, more widely, schools from the Greater China region and from other countries beyond. The number of visits from other school staff, government officers and other parties increased, and they were welcomed at the school and were able to see demonstrations of the innovation in practice in classrooms. The school was in touch almost daily with the software designers of instructional technology in the United States, and, indeed, the designers from Automated, DyKnow, H3C, HP, Lenovo, Mediasite and Microsoft flew in for the formal opening of the innovation. The heavy workload on teachers continued, with teachers spending hours searching for useful Internet resources, typically preparing PowerPoint slides to upload onto students' tablets, along with other electronic and online resources.

Access to, and control of, the video option for students to re-watch classroom lessons at home had been adjusted to give greater control to teachers over what could and could not be videoed. Early problems of e-assessment and e-submission of homework were being addressed, as were very practical matters such as charging up the tablets, how to handle the tablets 'hanging', unstable connectivity outside school and suchlike.

An ongoing debate between textbook copyright holders and the school continued: the school did not wish to purchase an entire textbook for loading on to students' tablets, but, akin to other kinds of online purchasing (e.g. sound tracks of music or other selected applications), wished to purchase selected parts of texts. The publishers resisted, insisting that purchasing entire textbooks (at the cost of the full textbook) was the only option.

One of the six subject teachers involved in the innovation left the school and was replaced by an existing member of staff.

Commitment to the project by the teachers was evidenced in the amount of time they spent out of school in preparing lessons, materials, marking and giving feedback to students, running additional teaching sessions for students who were experiencing difficulties in handling the software and their perseverance in using unfamiliar software in an unfamiliar pedagogical setting.

That said, teachers involved in the innovation had little or no time to collaborate with each other in the planning, implementation and review of the innovation and their work in it; parents were only very scantily involved in the project, and, indeed, to a large extent, had not been included in that part of the innovation which was designed to increase parental involvement and communication.

Much was riding on the innovation. It was hoped that it would raise student motivation and improve attitudes to learning, integrate ICT with collaborative, active and interactive pedagogies, break the culture of didactic teaching, promote collegiality and cooperation between staff, enhance parental involvement in, and communication with, the school, lift student performance, promote engaged student-centred learning, stimulate higher-order thinking and problem-based learning, prompt curriculum and assessment change, increase real-world, authentic learning and provide significant staff development. A key aspiration for the project was that it would particularly help the lower-performing, disaffected students in the school, those with a negative attitude to school.

In many ways the multiple aspirations of the projects demonstrated the optimism of enthusiasm; how realistic it was for a single, if multidimensional, change to deliver on all of these expectations turned out to be somewhat attenuated over time. However, the light of commitment, singularity of purpose and determination to proceed in the face of setbacks was not extinguished when early results showed some difficulties in the innovation. What happened at this stage echoes Fullan's remark that a school and its leaders must focus on the smallest number of key matters which have to be done effectively (2011a: 41), identifying a limited numbers of key priorities and following them without letting up, keeping the goals clear in mind and not being distracted from achieving them (2011a: 69). He adds to this (2011b: 18) the need for leaders to pursue these 'core priorities' by capacity development in the participants in a climate of openness and without blame or recrimination.

This chapter reports, analyzes and draws implications from the evaluation of the middle stage of the project (six months into the innovation). The data collected at this stage came from test data (from pilot and control groups from Primary 4 and secondary Form 1 and Form 4 students), survey questionnaires (staff and students), interviews (students, teachers, parents, middle and senior managers of the school), automatically logged data on computer usage by students and teachers, and teachers' own diaries/logs. The chapter summarizes key findings from the data from the second round of evaluation of the pilot, indicating the 'implementation dip' (Fullan 2013) in the innovation and the performance dip for some students, and how the school responded to these, and the successes, challenges, strengths and weaknesses of the pilot in terms of: students, leaders, managers, teachers, support staff and parents. A key issue at this stage was the apprehension, indeed hostility, of some parents towards the innovation, or, more precisely, their role in it, and the ways in which the school reacted to this. Throughout, and summarized at the end of the chapter, will be 'lessons learned' for the leadership and management of multidimensional change in school.

A key finding at this stage of the innovation was that the innovation was beginning to become differentiated in terms of participants' views and what was unfolding within and between the parties involved. There were some, but few, consistent findings across the participant groups, by the age of the students, and within some of the groups. Differences were emerging within and between groups – of parents, teachers, students and senior staff – in terms of pedagogical practices, enthusiasm and support for the innovation, student performance and effects of the innovation on different parties. The evaluators noted the following:

> Overall, at this stage the project is perceived to be having mixed results, with both improvements and decrements. In many cases, with some exceptions (e.g. ICT-related matters), at this stage it is difficult to state unequivocally that the pilot is bringing widespread improvements to students, though the signs are positive and, in some cases, very positive. ... There is a very mixed and wide-ranging response to whether and where the project is operating well. Many comments indicated that the project was working more successfully in English than in Maths, and with older rather than younger students; several concerns were raised about the suitability of the project for primary students. Many respondents indicate that the project is on track and going according to plan, though there was some significant dissent to this view from several parties, or only partial consent from several parties (i.e. the project is working well in some parts rather than others). ... From perception-based data from students, the pilot groups' results on the questionnaire items are generally and specifically higher than those for the control groups. The older the students, the more frequent and greater were the differences found between their pilot and control groups, and there is a clear trend, whereby the older the students, the greater the benefits appeared to be. ... Teachers are mainly positive about the project though they

> have reservations about the project's positive effects on students. ... Whilst very many students are positive about the project, many are either negative or indifferent. Given that the project is intended to be the same in all three pilot classes, the considerable differences found between the three classes suggest that the intervention itself is making only a limited (if significant) impact in comparison to other factors. ... The senior staff were generally more 'on board' with the project at round two (in comparison to round one) and felt that it was on track. Many senior staff still had a lot of reservations about the project even though they supported it.

This part of the evaluators' report contains many important features for managers of multidimensional change:

- Judging the success or failure of an innovation is time-sensitive: too soon and one is caught up in short-term gains or losses, overlooking the longer-term outcomes; too late and one misses important emergent issues that need to be faced immediately;
- It is to be expected that there will be a U-curve in innovations. After the sparkle of the introduction of an innovation many eagerly expected positives may encounter drops, less-than-hoped-for gains, or no change: decrements and flat-lining;
- It is unrealistic to expect the outcomes of a multidimensional project to be unequivocal and uniform. Rather, perceptions, outcomes and practices may differ on several factors. Participants – teachers, students – 'do something' with an innovation, rendering it less antiseptic and teacher-proof in practice than the written plan might suggest;
- Different parties have different views, some of them differing widely;
- The commitment and alignment of commitment from the senior staff and leaders of the innovation is essential;
- Some reservations may stem from experienced practice in the innovation;
- There is a difference between alignment and support.

The students' views

The evaluators reported a mixed picture from the students' perceptions (from questionnaire survey data and interviews with groups of students from each of the three pilot classes). The evaluators reported that there were:

> a few clear positive gains from the project, whilst in many other areas there are either no perceptible gains or even losses from the project, and there was evidence of the continuing prevalence of 'traditional teaching: pressure of tests and examinations and much teacher talk from the front of the class' ... However, there is considerable use of ICT in the

> pilot classes, and generally the students like the school and feel that the teaching is good. There is evidence, though comparatively slender, that the intervention is related to increased means for the pilot groups in relation to the control groups, and that the differences between the means of these two groups become stronger as the students become older. ... The pilot groups deem themselves to have improved over time since round one on the areas of: motivation; liking for school; positive attitudes; teaching and learning; communication with parents; interest; engagement and involvement in lessons; active, interactive and collaborative pedagogies; encouragement and support for learning; teacher explanation; and realistic challenge.

The pilot groups reported that there had been improvements over time, since round one, in the areas of: motivation; liking for school; positive attitudes; teaching and learning; communication with parents; interest; engagement and involvement in lessons; active, interactive and collaborative pedagogies; encouragement and support for learning; teacher explanation; realistic challenge. Effect sizes (using Cohen's d) calculated for questionnaire items indicated that, even at this early stage, the students in the pilot groups had a slightly more positive view of the school than those in the control groups. The older the students, the more frequent and greater were the differences found between the pilot and control groups.

Several comments across all student pilot groups indicated that they liked school a little more with the innovation. On the other hand, a significant body of pilot group students across the board indicated that there had been no real change in their attitude to school or their motivation to learn. However, no comments were received to indicate that attitudes and motivation had worsened as a result of the project.

Though the pilot groups overall felt positive about the innovation, the data indicated that they did not fully understand its purposes and what they had to do in it. Further, the student data indicated that there were several enduring features in the school:

- A lack of challenge in tasks set by teachers;
- Limited group activity;
- Students tending not to speak out if they did not understand, or if the work was too easy or too difficult;
- Limited student talk and discussion in lessons;
- Student opinion was generally not much solicited or encouraged;
- There was still a moderate amount of learning by repetition and limited real-life application of knowledge;
- There was little student choice of materials, and students continued to have difficulty in finding materials to help them to learn;
- Communication with, and involvement of, parents continued to be low.

Many students commented that the pilot had brought no changes to their performance, as their performance was contingent on how difficult the course was and how hard they worked, rather than on the tablet and/or the pedagogy. Many comments indicated that students felt that their performance was dropping. Some comments indicated that students felt the new assessment (including marks for class participation) was better because it made their performance look better.

Several students' comments indicated both attractions and teething problems with the use of the tablets. They felt that the tablet looked 'cool' (their word) and was usually easy to use, though Internet connection at home and stability and speed of connection were problems, and the signal was often weak. Several students commented that the tablet screen 'froze' and 'hung', particularly at home. Some students were worried about breaking the tablet, and other comments reflected their concern that they might accidentally delete their own work (and that they may not know how to fix a problem). Many comments indicated that students felt that using the tablet was useful in keeping them up to date on ICT, and that they felt that they had more time for homework with the tablet. Most students, across all the pilot classes, commented that the tablet had made few, little or no difference or change to the teaching or learning, had not done much for them in this respect and had not improved teaching and learning.

The evaluators reported that 'given that the project is intended to be the same in all three pilot classes, the considerable differences found between the three classes suggest that the intervention itself is making only a limited (if significant) impact in comparison to other factors'. On the other hand, the evaluators, by calculating effect sizes using Cohen's d, found large effect sizes between the pilot and control groups of students for two questionnaire items: 'generally, how much do your teachers use many different ways to teach you?' and 'generally, how much group-based work takes place in class?' Moderate effect sizes were found for the following differences between the pilot and control groups of students, indicating that the innovation was producing some positive results:

- How much do you like school?
- Generally, how interested are you in reading for your school subjects?
- Generally, how interesting do you find the lessons?
- Generally, how much do your teachers encourage you to be active in the lessons?
- Normally, do you tell the teacher if the work is too easy?
- Normally, do you tell the teacher if you have already learned the work before the lesson?
- Generally, how much do your teachers encourage you to discuss the contents of the lesson with your classmates during lessons?
- How much do your teachers really encourage you to think hard in your lessons?

The project in mid-stream 145

- How much do your teachers let you learn in the way that you want to learn?
- How much do your teachers really encourage you to think of problems and how to solve them in your lessons?
- How much do your teachers make you interested to know more about the subject?
- How much do your teachers really encourage you to have your own opinions about the contents of the lessons?
- How much do your teachers find out during a lesson if you have understood the lesson?
- How much do your teachers explain again if a lot of students have made the same mistake in homework or in a test?
- How much do your teachers explain a point again if a lot of students have not understood a point during in the lesson?
- How much do your teachers give you the chance to apply your learning in real-life situations?
- How easily can you find materials to help you to learn as soon as you need them in the school?
- How much support do you feel that you get from the school, outside lesson time, to help you to learn well?

These were important findings, as they suggested that, at round two of the evaluation, six months into the innovation, pilot group teachers were using more active, interactive, collaborative and varied pedagogies in the classroom, students in the pilot groups were becoming more engaged and involved in their learning, the learning in the pilot groups was becoming more 'real-life', students in the pilot groups were becoming more motivated and had a more positive attitude to the lessons, classrooms were becoming more learner-centred and learning was becoming more interesting, with greater student follow-up outside lessons.

Lessons from the students' data for the leadership and management of multidimensional innovations

The comments from the students touch a range of topics (often as a consequence of the questions asked by the evaluators) and indicate a range of reactions to the innovation, not only by group (there were three age groups of students) but also by dimension of the innovation. For leaders of complex innovations, the lessons from these end users are salutary:

- Expect a differentiated rather than a uniform or singular result by areas of the innovation and parties involved;
- Explain and repeat the purposes of the innovation;
- Expect a range of levels of change, from a lot to nothing, from superficial to deep;

	Apathy	Resistance	Acceptance	Enthusiasm
Deep/ extensive				
Moderate				
Superficial/ limited				

LEVEL OF USE OF THE INNOVATION

DEGREE OF COMMITMENT TO THE INNOVATION

Figure 5.3 Levels of use and degrees of commitment to an area of an innovation

- Expect a mixed response to the innovation from its target groups, from apathy, indifference and resistance to enthusiasm and commitment;
- Be sure to know whether it is the innovation that is making a difference or other factors;
- Expect changes to be both tangible and intangible;
- Expect an innovation dip – the U-curve of innovation – after its initial launch;
- Communicate, communicate, communicate.

Indeed, for each dimension of the innovation one can plot different degrees of use and reactions (Figure 5.3) for each group in question. Though the chart is perhaps simplistic, nevertheless it enables innovation leaders to chart changes over time. Into each cell of the matrix can be entered the members of a particular group, or, indeed, the entire group, depending on the level of generality required.

The teachers' views

Data gathered from the teachers at round two were unsettling. Teachers reported that they continued to spend huge amounts of their private time in preparation. Even though there had been some slight easing in terms of time spent outside school in preparation, it was still immense.

The comments received from the teachers were very mixed, from very positive to much more cautious and reserved, and indeed negative, though nearly all of the teachers indicated that the project generally was going according to plan. Whilst many of the teachers supported the purpose and spirit of the project, they felt that there were many shortcomings, worries, problems and challenges to be met, and, indeed, some comments were significantly negative about the project and its effects. Several comments indicated that there was a huge gap between the wished-for and the actual benefits, and significant room for improvement.

Many comments from teachers indicated that student motivation and attitude towards learning had increased and improved respectively and visibly over the time of the project to date, in some cases considerably. For some students this was because of the new assessment system, in which, because of assessment of class participation, they could earn marks towards their final results and this encouraged low-performing students to try hard and work hard as this could enable them to avoid obtaining a failing mark. In other words, students were still very marks-oriented. For other students the increase and improvement were on account of the active and interactive classroom processes in themselves.

Many comments indicated an increase in active, interactive and collaborative work in classrooms, with greater levels of student participation and involvement in class, and that the tablet had helped to promote this both for teachers and for students. Indeed students liked this style of teaching and learning, enjoyed it and were pleased with it. Other comments indicated that students, aware that class participation attracted marks, were motivated by marks to become involved and more active; group work was reported to have improved, with far fewer 'free riders' in groups, because of the new marking system.

The teachers' data did not support the hypothesis that the intervention had made significant changes to the attitudes, motivation and interest of the students, as measured by the proxy indicators, be they low-performing students or high-performing students. This suggested that there was a deep-seated trait emerging: students still clung to the traditional ways of teaching and learning, reporting textbook-driven teaching, limited student choice, repeating knowledge, reduced active learning and a preference for learning on their own. In turn, these findings suggested that addressing these challenges was going to be an immense task, and that it was perhaps unrealistic to expect all the wished-for changes stated by the school to be realized by the project alone. The school's intention in the innovation, including to increase ICT, change pedagogy, student motivation and relevance, and to increase parental involvement, was going to need a considerable amount of innovation and working on deep-seated preferences and mentalities of students.

In terms of overall teaching and learning, the teachers' data indicated a reduction in traditional teaching methods, problems created by having large classes, passive learning, teacher direction and pressure of tests and examinations, together with an increase in student talk and teaching that was responsive to students' needs. The data indicated a rise in student engagement and involvement, student-centred teaching and learning, greater relevance and increased attention to individual needs in the classroom, and active, stimulating learning which was responsive to students' needs. In these respects the views of the students and teachers concurred. Comments indicated that students were learning more deeply rather than simply memorizing for a test.

Most of the teachers indicated that they felt they needed much more training and support in terms of active and interactive learning, with or without the tablet. Other comments from teachers indicated that the project had made no appreciable difference to the high-performing students, or, indeed, that some of them felt frustrated by the slowing down of their rate of learning, though other comments indicated that this was not the case, and that students were speeding up their rate of learning as a result of interactive teaching; some comments indicated that students liked this way of learning if they were proficient in ICT. Yet further comments indicated that the tablet was not making a real difference to teaching and learning, though it had improved student motivation.

A striking increase in the amount of ICT used by the teachers was reported, and with a range of different uses, particularly in terms of audio material, video/DVD, discussion boards/forums, real-time discussion boards/forums, uploading teaching materials for staff colleagues, uploading other teaching-related materials for students and students uploading and submitting homework online.

On the other hand, the teachers reported limited collaborative planning of curricula and teaching, increased marking, reliance on textbook material, a significant amount of teacher talk, and the need to ensure that there was sufficient variety of teaching and learning strategies, communication of requirements to students, application and demonstration of learning, higher-order thinking and student support. Indeed, the teachers indicated that there was no change in the amount of group work, suggesting that this aspect of the project was not having a noticeable effect here.

Further, the teachers' data suggested that the project was not fully achieving its intention of increasing parental involvement and communication, and the evaluators reported that: 'the teachers' data indicates that there is still a lot to be done in respect of parents and communication.'

Many comments from teachers indicated that they felt that the school had not done enough for the parents in respect of the project and the tablets, and, indeed, that many parents wished that their children were no longer part of the project and that they felt upset at this. Teachers complained, sometimes bitterly, that they were in the front line when receiving parents' complaints for problems and matters that were not of their making. It was reported that many parents were no longer 'on board', i.e. supportive of the project. Serious problems with the parental side of the project were widely and consistently reported.

In terms of the preparation for, and views on, the new ICT project, the teachers' data were mixed. On the one hand they indicated an increase in training and preparation for the project and an increase in comfort in using the tablet. On the other hand, the teachers harboured serious worries about the innovation, in terms of its consequences on students' performance, students' abilities to handle the innovation, how the new ICT project was being managed and led in the school and working with other teachers.

Further, the teachers articulated their need for more training on two key aspects of the innovation: ICT usage, and its connection with changing pedagogies to collaborative, active and interactive learning. Indeed, the evaluators reported thus:

> as an urgent priority, provide training on pedagogical practices, active learning, interactive and collaborative teaching and learning, and newer ways of assessment, both with and without ICT, so that the tablet usage is interactive and dynamic, not only to replace the whiteboard for didactic teaching. Provide specific, in-depth pedagogical and ICT-related training on how to plan a lesson using active and interactive pedagogies, and how ICT fits into and supports this, how to teach actively and interactively, on how to teach such-and-such (very specifically, e.g. specific lessons and specific content, concepts, skills, using active and interactive pedagogy and ICT-related pedagogies, i.e. where the ICT can help this). There could be discipline-specific or subject-specific nature in the deployment of ICT, whether it works well and how to do it. Encourage team-based planning and sharing by providing dedicated meeting times for this in the school day and school semester.

There was a note of optimism in the project, with the teachers seeing that the innovation could address challenges in the school, not least in terms of students' learning, motivation and engagement. For low-performing students, the innovation was reported to be bringing improvements to several areas, not least to the teachers' meeting the ability levels of the students and to the quality of their homework, though other data suggested that caution had to be exercised in expecting the innovation to be able to tackle the deep-seated problem of low-performing students' motivation. In terms of overall teaching and learning, the teachers' data indicated a reduction in traditional teaching methods, problems created by having large classes, passive learning, teacher direction and pressure of tests and examinations, together with an increase in student talk and teaching that was responsive to students' needs. The teachers reported a rise in student engagement and involvement, student-centred teaching and learning, greater relevance, an increased attention to individual needs in the classroom and active, stimulating learning which was responsive to students' needs.

The evaluators noted that the very senior officers of the school were typically more positive about the project than all the other participants and that some teachers felt as though they were in the 'firing line' for any complaints or hostility from parents and students about the project.

The evaluators reported that:

> the findings suggest that addressing these challenges is an immense task, and that it is perhaps unrealistic to expect all the school's wished-for changes to be realized by the project alone. The school's intention in the ICT project, including to change pedagogy, student motivation and relevance, and to increase parental involvement, will require a considerable amount of innovation and working on ingrained preferences and mentalities of students. How much these are happening due to the project is currently equivocal.

The significance of the time dimension of this multidimensional project was attested to by the evaluators in their reporting that:

> it is perhaps too early in the project to discern unequivocally whether, and to what extent, the project is working well in terms of student outcomes, attitudes and motivation. Once the novelty effect has worn off, it appears that there is a strong residual challenge presented by adherence to traditional mentalities and pedagogies by teachers, coupled with a lack of expertise in and experience of more active and dynamic ways of teaching and learning.

Lessons from the teachers' data for the leadership and management of multidimensional innovations

The lessons for leading and managing an innovation from this stage of the evaluation of the innovation in question are many and powerful. The teachers' data provides a rich source of formative data for the planning, leadership and management of complex innovations:

- Expect an innovation dip – the U-curve of innovation – after its initial launch;
- Take participants' workloads/overload seriously;
- Expect participants to have different needs, challenges, concerns, worries, commitments and agendas, and to require different degrees of support;
- Expect problems, setbacks and challenges: anticipate them;
- Expect different parts of the innovation to work to different levels of success and at different rates;
- Expect old habits to change only slowly, and expect participants to try to graft new practices onto old, rather than to replace old habits;

- Provide extensive and ongoing preparation, training and development in each of the areas of the innovation, i.e. plan for sustainable development;
- Plan and implement skills training and knowledge development in participants, i.e. capacity building;
- Expect change to be incremental rather than wholesale;
- Work on and with participants' real concerns, take heed of the problems identified by the participants and act swiftly to address them, i.e. take participants' views very seriously;
- Communicate, communicate, communicate;
- Identify areas of resistance and work on them;
- Ensure that training has immediate, practical and concrete impact and utility;
- Do not expect equal levels of success from all participants and all dimensions of the innovation;
- Provide immediate and direct support for 'front line' staff;
- Do not expect the innovation to work entirely in the ways expected or planned: change changes people and people change change;
- Have realistic expectations, but do not lose the overall vision of possible changes;
- Decide carefully the most suitable times to take stock and judge effectiveness.

These 'lessons' indicate the need to link ongoing leading, monitoring, reviewing, evaluating, planning and action.

The parents' views

At this stage of the innovation, parent-related matters surfaced as presenting significant challenges. The three groups of parents interviewed were very clear in their views. The evaluators noted that 'the parents want to help their child, yet they don't have access codes and they don't know how to use the tablet, and so they rely on their child'. They felt unable to help their child with the tablet, and they reported feeling helpless in trying to support their child or answer their child's questions about homework. Many parents – across all the age groups in the project – reported that their child's performance had gone down, their motivation and positive learning attitude had diminished, their child was spending more time on homework than before and their concentration had reduced. They reported that their child's courses were more difficult than before and their measured performance had gone down. They also reported that their child was irritable and in a bad mood more frequently, and was frustrated and angered because they saw their own performance and that of others reducing. Several comments indicated that their child could find material much more easily from textbooks and reference books than through the tablet.

Several parents indicated that they wished to switch their child to the non-pilot class, as they did not want their child to suffer and because they (the parents) were too worried about their child's learning and performance.

The evaluators reported that:

> to date the project has failed to live up to its promise of improving parental involvement, communication, information and benefit. Many parents are very angry and bitter about this, accusing the school of breaking its promise, and considering withdrawing their child from the project. They feel helpless and unable to help their child. The goodwill shown by the parents to the project at its inception has reduced very considerably. ... Parents were significantly excluded from the project. ... The strong and negative nature of the parents' comments suggest that the field of 'parents' is a major one, requiring urgent and significant attention.

These were very strong words indeed, deliberately reflecting the strength of critical feeling amongst the parents, and the school took immediate and strong action to address this, with meetings being held with parents and further communication being enhanced straight away.

In contrast to the views of teachers and students, which showed a range of views within each group, the parents were much more united in their views, regardless of the class to which their children belonged, and these views were critical or very critical of the school.

Lessons from the parents' data for the leadership and management of multidimensional innovations

One of the expressed intentions of the project was to involve parents more in their children's education. Though it was recognized that this was likely to be more of a concern for the parents of the younger rather than the older children, nevertheless the parents of older children involved in the innovation were concerned about real issues such as whether their son or daughter would pass the examinations or have to repeat a year at the school, whether their marks would drop, how they could help their child with homework (particularly in the case of the younger students) and how to use the tablet (many parents had little or no understanding of how to do this).

In terms of leadership and management of a multidimensional innovation, there are key lessons to be learned from the innovation at this stage. It is essential to provide suitable training and communication for parents, through many channels, to meet parents and discuss what is happening in the innovation, to give them feedback and data on its progress, to identify and handle parents concerns and anxieties directly and immediately and to keep parents 'in the loop' with information, particularly concerning matters about which they are anxious. It is important to anticipate and plan to handle parents' reactions and concerns and to communicate frequently and richly with parents.

The senior managers' views

At this round of the evaluation, 13 interviews were conducted with senior staff of the school. Very many comments indicated that the innovation was operating more fully and extensively at the secondary level than at the primary. Whilst several comments indicated that the project was going well, that staff and students were 'on board' more and that many participants were positive about the innovation and its effects on the students, many indicated reservations about, and problems with, the project and that staff were happy but anxious. It was widely voiced that teachers were working extremely hard on the project, giving of their private time freely and in abundance.

Many comments indicated that changes were happening and that people were hopeful for further positive developments. In general, most senior managers were appreciably more positive about the project than all the others interviewed, though they suggested that it might be unrealistic to expect the single innovation to deliver all the changes that were hoped for in the project.

Intangible areas were mentioned by all respondents, indicating that pilot group student motivation and self-motivation had improved perceptibly with the innovation, that the students liked the project and were positive about it. Comments also indicated that students were becoming more interested in their learning, being involved and engaged in class.

Very many respondents commented that students in the pilot groups had increased in class participation and active involvement, that they were more willing to speak out in class and to volunteer information.

Respondents noted that the innovation was benefiting the performance of the lower-performing students whilst having little effect on the highest performers, though, for many of the lower-performing students, improvement was in terms of behaviour rather than in learning and performance. Further, it was mentioned that, where the student performance had improved, this was not due so much to the pilot project and ICT as to the fact that the pilot group teachers were simply spending more time with the students, i.e. to teacher effects rather than innovation effects.

Very many comments indicated that there was increased active, interactive and student-centred learning in the pilot classes, with more group work, that students were learning by themselves more, that class discussion had increased, that the classroom atmosphere had improved, that there was a more positive working noise in classrooms, that students were paying more attention and were working harder and that teaching was becoming more flexible. Some comments indicated that teachers and students were becoming more connected with each other.

However, some respondents remarked that, in fact, there had been only a little or even no change to teaching method, that classrooms were still largely teacher dominated and traditional and that the ICT had been used to reinforce this. Indeed, several comments suggested that teachers needed strong, concrete and clear guidance on how to teach a particular concept, piece of knowledge, lesson, subject or activity in an interactive way, and with the software to support this, i.e. teachers needed to build up their expertise, extending to assessment as well as to curricula and pedagogy.

A major issue that was alluded to frequently was the teachers' experience of, and abilities and expertise in, active, collaborative and interactive learning. That this was a serious problem was voiced very many times, and it was supplemented by the comments that teachers needed considerable training, development and support here. It was widely recognized that too little emphasis had been placed on training staff for active, collaborative and interactive teaching and learning, and that this needed greater attention.

There was widespread criticism of the neglect of the parental aspects of the innovation. Several comments indicated that parents knew little about the project, and that they were more concerned about their child's performance than previously, that they were worried about their child's learning and whether their child would graduate. Many parents, it was reported, had little or no idea of what was happening on the project. On the other hand, some comments indicated that the school had run training workshops for parents but attendance was very poor, for various reasons outside the school's control.

Some respondents suggested that the ICT parts of the project were at risk of reinforcing traditional teaching – i.e. teacher dominated and with much teacher talk – and that the full potential of the software as a tool for interactive teaching and learning, for alternative pedagogies and for communication was not being fully utilized. Very many respondents noted that the ICT system was adding enormously to teachers' marking time, doubling it and even quadrupling it, because of the screen layout, marking on screen, the nature of the collation and presentation of the homework and assessment/examination items from students.

Whilst there was widespread agreement that the innovation was moving forward, several comments were received which indicated that not everyone was clear on who was in charge of which parts of the innovation, to whom different parties should turn for help and guidance, and that there was limited information circulating in the school and to the parents about the project. This was seen to be part of a larger issue that communication between all parties about the project was both insufficient and not well managed, and that holding in-depth meetings *all together* of key players to address developmental and practical, concrete matters was not happening.

It was widely mentioned that it was too early to tell what the outcomes of the innovation were, and that it might be too hasty either to come to judgements or for all the problems to surface. In passing, it was noted that the principal was considerably more optimistic and clear about the project than any other parties.

An important feature that emerged from the interviews with the senior teachers was that the innovation, given that it was a multidimensional change, required a change in organizational culture, from a culture of isolation to a culture of collaboration, and that this would take time to install in the school.

Lessons from the senior managers' data for the leadership and management of multidimensional innovations

Leaders of an innovation have the tasks not only of being the named person responsible for it but also of leading the people involved in it. Such leadership requires leaders to draw on profound reserves of character, perseverance, courage and clarity of vision that is not dimmed by setbacks. This was manifest in the innovation in question here, and many lessons can be drawn from it even at this early stage:

- Keep single-mindedly on the core purposes of the innovation;
- Handle distractions but do not be distracted from the core purposes;
- See setbacks as learning opportunities rather than failures;
- Acknowledge and reward staff workload;
- Keep positive but handle challenges;
- Identify and celebrate immediate, small successes as well as more sustained successes;
- Be ambitious but realistic in expectations;
- Acknowledge that deep innovations take time to become embedded in everyday practice;
- Provide training and staff development;
- Focus on setting the conditions for innovation as well as the innovation itself;
- Be ahead of your followers, but do not leave them behind;
- Recognize that innovation often concerns people more than content;
- Identify key emergent challenges and handle them immediately;
- Do not allow problems to fester;
- Recognize participants' limitations and work on reducing them;
- Ensure that links between the dimensions of the innovation are visible, clear and concrete;
- Ensure that the innovation is not distorted into buttressing up practices which it is supposed to be changing;
- Identify and communicate management responsibilities for the several elements of the innovation;
- Ensure that all parties know what is happening on the project and how it affects them;
- Communicate, communicate, communicate.

The logged data

The video playback facility was intended to enable students to re-watch the classroom sessions in order to review the lessons and to understand those parts that they had not understood or only partially understood in class. In particular, it was seen as a facility which lower-performing students would find helpful. However, when analyzing the data on video re-watching, logged automatically on the school server, overall, with outliers removed, there were no statistically significant differences found between the lowest-and highest-performing students ($p>0.05$) (defined in terms of the placement tests at the start of the school year) in terms of: (a) the total number of viewings; (b) the number of presentations watched; and (c) the amount of time spent watching. However, there were modest effect sizes of differences between the lowest and highest third of performers, in that the highest third of performers had more viewings, watched more presentations and spent longer overall on watching. Further, there were very high standard deviations for the amount of time spent watching, i.e. there was a great spread of time watching, from low to high amounts of time spent. Lower-performing students reported watching the video but still being unable to understand its contents. The evaluators reported that 'given that the project was designed to provide support for lower performing students, these students, whilst they do access the materials on the tablet, do so less than the high performing students'.

The innovation dip

At round two the evaluators reported that:

> In respect of students' attitude, motivation and interest at round two, there was no substantial difference: (a) between the low performing control and pilot groups; (b) between the high performing control and pilot groups, apart from maybe F1 students (though this is uncertain); (c) between the low and high performing groups from each class.

With respect to student performance, the results at round two were potentially dispiriting. The evaluators reported that:

> though there is some evidence that continual assessment is improving the marks of low-performing students, the overwhelming evidence is that in terms of academic performance, the project is not improving students' marks and, in very many cases, is leading to lower marks. Some findings indicate that the continual assessment is a device for improving students' marks without improving their academic learning or performance. The marks of the pilot groups go down much more than those of the control groups over time, and the *relative* drop in marks is higher for the pilot groups than the control groups, for each class or segments of each class.

... The effect sizes for marks at round two are often very large indeed, i.e. the intervention has had large (negative) effects in terms of students' marks.

Whereas, at the start of the innovation, there were no statistically significant differences between the marks of the control and pilot groups for each year (Primary 4, Form 1 and Form 4), six months into the project there were statistically significant differences between the marks of each pilot group and its corresponding control group (between group differences).

This posed a major challenge to the leader of the innovation: the school principal. After all, young lives were at stake here; should the school modify or abandon the innovation? The answer from the principal and the senior managers was an unequivocal and resounding 'no'. At interview, the principal indicated that he had been prepared for this to happen (in a double sense: (a) expecting it and (b) tolerating it) and that this would not deflect him or the innovation from its mission and core purposes, that this was a temporary setback and that the research evidence was on his side to support the innovation. Further, both he and the evaluators remarked that it was natural for a dip in student performance to occur, not only at that time in the school year anyway (and indeed the marks of the students in the control groups dipped at this time of the year), but in respect of that early stage of an innovation.

Despite these cautions, the principal's resolve was sorely tested, not least as parents were concerned about their children's marks (and, as noted in Chapter 3, repeating a year in Macau was a widespread phenomenon), and he was tenacious in his determination to continue unabated, and his determination was felt throughout the parties.

An inventory of positives and negatives

In drawing together the different views expressed by the several parties involved in the innovation, both positive and negative aspects emerged at the second round of the evaluation, and these are summarized below.

Positive aspects and benefits

The previous sections have found many emergent benefits from the innovation.

Students

- Many students liked having the tablet and their motivation and engagement had generally increased; they had a more positive attitude towards school and learning;

- Intangible benefits were more in evidence than tangible benefits (e.g. students' marks);
- Students liked school more, were more interested in reading for school subjects and found the lessons more interesting;
- Students appreciated the value of using ICT in everyday teaching and learning;
- There was evidence of increased student engagement and involvement in lessons, with active, interactive and collaborative pedagogies, together with encouragement and support for learning, increased teacher explanation and the setting of realistic challenges;
- The opportunity for poorer performing students to gain marks was welcomed by those students, and consequently they participated more in class;
- Students were beginning to tell the teacher if the work was too easy and if they had already learned the work before the lesson;
- Students were given the chance to apply learning in real-life situations;
- Students were finding it easier to find materials to help them to learn as soon as they needed to in the school, and they felt more supported by the school, outside lesson time, to help them to learn well.

Senior staff

- The senior staff were becoming more united in supporting the innovation;
- The principal-as-leader had enormous tenacity in holding fast to the project in the face of setbacks and negative feedback, and held to a very clear vision of the project and its benefits, which he adhered to unswervingly in the face of serious and radical challenges;
- The school acted immediately to rectify some key problems in the innovation.

Teachers

- Teachers continued to be optimistic about the project and appreciated the value of using ICT in everyday teaching and learning;
- Teachers were encouraging students to be active in the lessons, to discuss the contents of the lesson with classmates during lessons, to think hard in lessons, to enable the students to learn in their preferred ways and to have their own opinions about the contents of the lessons. They encouraged students to think of problems and how to solve them in lessons and stimulated students' interest in subject matter;
- Teachers were taking steps to find out during a lesson if students had understood the lesson, so that teachers could explain again if many students had made the same mistake in homework/had not understood a point during in the lesson.

The project in mid-stream 159

Setbacks and negative aspects

Many setbacks and challenges emerged as the innovation unfolded:

The innovation as a whole

- Not all of the parts of the innovation were working;
- The results were very mixed within and between groups – the extent of unanimity was limited overall, and only on a few points;
- It was unclear how much any observed changes were on account of the innovation and how much to other factors;
- Large differences were found between the three pilot classes, on many aspects of the innovation;
- Expectations of what the project could 'deliver' seemed to have been too high;
- Hardware and software problems were experienced with the tablets, by both teachers and students;
- The organizational culture of the school inhibited the development of the innovation;
- Perceptions and opinions of the innovation were not united, and they varied according to several factors;
- Links between some of the different elements of the innovation were weak;
- Communication within and outside the school was insufficient.

Students

- Student performance dropped or did not improve in terms of measured test scores;
- The extent of improvement to student motivation and attitude was patchy;
- The uptake of the video re-watching was limited and lower-performing students were making less use of the video playback than the higher-performing students;
- Some students were apathetic to, or unconvinced by, the value of the tablet and its intended related strategies;
- Some students felt that their learning was being impeded by the innovation and the tablet;
- The innovation did not have the hoped-for impact on raising the engagement of poorer performing students;
- Students noted a continuing lack of challenge in the tasks set by teachers;
- Student opinion was generally not much solicited or encouraged in lessons;
- Students tended not to speak out if they did not understand, or if the work was too easy or too difficult.

Parents

- Parents were disaffected with their limited involvement in, and limited communication from, the school;
- Parents reported many negative effects of the project on their children;
- Many parents felt that their children's learning was being impeded by the innovation and the tablet;
- Communication with, and involvement of, parents continued to be low.

Teachers

- Teachers did not have sufficient expertise or training in how to run collaborative, active, interactive and group-based learning, either with or without ICT;
- Teachers needed to learn more about maximizing the software being used;
- Teacher commitment to the project was high, though they had reservations about its efficacy to date;
- There was little collaborative planning by teachers;
- Teacher workload continued to be enormous, and they were spending huge amounts of time on on-screen marking;
- Teachers felt that they were having to face the parents with insufficient support;
- Capacity building was insufficient.

Senior staff

- The leaders were considerably ahead of the followers in the innovation;
- Not all the senior staff or the teachers were convinced of the efficacy of the innovation;
- Some management responsibilities and identification of persons responsible for different aspects of the innovation were unclear.

Pedagogy

- Cooperative, collaborative, active and interactive teaching and learning were much less extensive and consistent than intended;
- Traditional teaching continued to be extensive, using ICT to reinforce didactic strategies;
- There was limited group activity, limited student talk and limited discussion in lessons;
- There was still a moderate amount of learning by repetition and limited real-life application of knowledge;
- There was little student choice of materials, and students continued to have difficulty in finding materials to help them to learn;
- Teaching and learning had not improved much, if at all.

Here, then, is a multidimensional innovation which, in many of its dimensions, was encountering serious challenges and setbacks. Whilst some of these could have been anticipated, several of them were simply unknowns until they happened (e.g. student performance data, parental reactions). A simple tally of problems here indicates that they outweighed the expressed benefits being brought by the innovation. A major finding was that there was still a degree of disunity of opinion, outcome and practice within and between the several groups of participants.

The opening part of this chapter cited the work of Fullan and his advocation for identifying a limited number of priorities and pursuing them relentlessly; keeping a clear focus; sticking tenaciously to the main purposes of the innovation even in the face of challenges and distractions; and addressing problems rapidly as they emerge. In the situation reported here, the challenges and distractors were several, fundamental and large, and, indeed, some key dimensions of the innovation were faltering. What did not falter were the vision, determination and tenacity of the leader and his senior team. That the project continued is testimony to their conviction that the project would work, and that they would drive forward even when setbacks occurred.

Lessons learned

What lessons can we learn from the innovation at this stage of its progress? The school had embarked on a multidimensional innovation which intended to address many aspects of school life in a single innovation. The data at round two contained several important lessons; these are set out below in terms of key emergent fields of the innovation.

- Gather and use review and evaluation data.

Fullan (2001: 88–9) advocates 'After Action Reviews' of actions or events in which three questions are addressed: 'What was supposed to happen?'; 'What happened?'; and 'What accounts for the difference?'. Such reviews of events lead to lessons being learned, and these are presented below. Central to such reviews is an understanding of why matters went as intended and/or went well, and why they did not. In the innovation here, the success of the innovation was in terms of, for example, increasing the use of collaborative learning, ICT usage and facility, student motivation and improved attitude; these can be attributed to staff commitment and sheer hard work, leadership of the innovation and the content of the innovation itself, in other words to people and effort as well as to content.

On the other hand, the project at this stage did not bring the intended improvements to students' measured test performance; the intended improvements to the attitudes and performance of the lowest-achieving students did not materialize to any consistent degree; the staff workload continued to be immense and unsustainable; there continued to be hesitancy and reservations about the innovation in some quarters of the school; the impact on students was very mixed, within and between age groups and by subject; and parental opposition increased substantially. Why was this? There are many possible answers here:

1 The level of staff and student expertise in working with the new, collaborative pedagogy was limited and the capacity building that had taken place was inadequate, given the scope of the project, both in terms of pedagogy and ICT.
2 There was some small degree of misperception by the teachers on their preparation work, so they spent vast amounts of time in preparing resources that underlined a transmission model of teaching and learning rather than in planning for student-centred collaborative learning with and without the ICT tablets and software.
3 There was a lack of clarity in some management roles – to whom front line staff should turn when problems arose (e.g. when parents raised questions and concerns) – Fullan's (2011b: 91–2) advocacy of a 'guiding coalition' was not always clear to all participants.
4 There was increasing concern by parents, who felt excluded from the project, as they felt that the school had not provided them with sufficient information about the progress of the project.
5 Not all of the conditions conducive to the innovation had been laid; for example, collaborative planning, how to promote collaborative group work, how to conduct in-class assessments of class participation, how to conduct formative assessments – assessment for learning – and provide formative feedback to students, how to use the several functions of the software and the provision of sufficient e-resources for learning.
6 The organizational culture of the school supported the old style of operations, e.g. teachers working in isolation, textbook-driven transmission teaching, teachers as experts, a top-down management style, a lock-step curriculum in which all students moved through the material at the same pace, reinforced by frequent testing of lower-level recall), rather than the new style (open, collaborative, flexible, student-centred, teachers as learners).
7 The innovation was mandated and required of the teachers and students, rather than negotiated.
8 The workload on teachers was intense and heavy, as they were having to prepare at speed for new contents and methods of teaching, assessment, software usage and students' limited facility with the tablets, and all in the glare of spotlights on this new, high-profile project, with visitors coming to the school to see the project, not only from local schools, but also from across South-East Asia. They did not have time to internalize the innovation, as they were so busy surviving it: a drowning person does not suddenly learn to swim, (s)he does anything to stay afloat.

9 Not all the students were as enthusiastic about the innovation as the teachers and senior managers.
10 Whilst the school had excellent relations with parents, on this occasion the parents typically did not have sufficient expertise to be able to help their children in using the tablets.
11 As mentioned at the start of this chapter, there was a frequently observed cycle of performance during the school year, in which an initial increase at the start of the new year is followed by a dip in performance, followed – eventually – by an increase in performance; in other words, it is dangerous to assume that the innovation alone could account for the outcomes observed.
12 The hopes and expectations of the project were high, ambitious and characterized by challenging aspirations and goals, to stretch rather than to dislocate; hindsight indicated that perhaps some of these were too ambitious in terms of scope and timescale.

In the face of such challenges, the principal held fast to his determination that the innovation would continue, commenting that, at that stage, he was less concerned with students' marks (a preoccupation of many students and their parents) and that it would take time for the innovation to become embedded and more routine. He exemplified Fullan's (2011b: 35) point that leaders must keep being resolute, determined, relentless, persistent and unbowed by adverse emergent situations. Indeed, he argued that the leader of change at times must act with greater confidence than the situation might warrant (Fullan 2011b: 121). As he remarked, leaders have to recognize that change is a long-term affair and liable to face massive challenges, particularly in the early stages of an innovation (Fullan 2011b: 153); they need a strong ability to stay the course.

Key lessons to be learned for the leadership and management of multidimensional innovations are set out below.

- Progress, timing and timescales.

Rather than expecting a change to have immediate positive effect, it is wise to expect a U-curve in the innovation – achievement goes down before it goes up. Hence, innovators should expect problems, setbacks and challenges, anticipate them, and keep in mind that judging the success or failure of an innovation is time-sensitive, so it is essential to decide the most suitable times to take stock and judge effectiveness. Further, it is unwise to expect the outcomes of a multidimensional project to be unequivocal, uniform or singular. Rather, one should expect a range of degrees of change in participants, varying not only within each group of participants (e.g. teachers, students, parents), but at all levels of a school hierarchy (e.g. principal, senior officers, teachers). Indeed, the counsel here is to expect different parts of an innovation to work to different levels of success and at different rates, and to acknowledge that deep innovations take time to become embedded in everyday practice.

- The nature of change.

Some changes are immediately visible, tangible and, indeed, measurable. Others are less so; they may be qualitative, intangible and not susceptible to simple measurement. That said, it is important to ensure that links between the dimensions of the innovation are visible, clear and concrete. In the innovation reported here, those parts of the innovation which were more intrinsically related, such as the link between pedagogy and ICT, were more effective and those parts which were less intrinsically related, such as parental involvement, became marginalized and led to some serious problems with support for the project by parents. It is important to ensure that the core purposes of the project are logically and empirically linked with each other, that they cohere and are mutually supportive. Those parts of the innovation that cohered naturally were more effective than those parts where links between them were more strained and less easy to connect. Fullan (2005: 21–2) remarks on the need for coherence between the several parts of an innovation, making explicit and strongly connected its several components, and identifying and connecting the key priorities.

An important lesson that emerged very rapidly was for leaders to expect changes to be incremental rather than wholesale, and not to expect the innovation to work entirely in the ways expected or planned. In the face of this, the leaders – and indeed the other participants – had to 'keep the faith', believing in the value of the project, keeping positive whilst handling challenges immediately and decisively. This involved identifying key emergent challenges and handling them immediately so that they were not able to fester. Alongside this, it was important for all participants to hold fast to the overall core purposes and foci of the innovation, even when – particularly when – the going became rough. Leaders were ambitious but realistic in their expectations, and they did not lose the overall vision of possible changes; they aimed high in their expectations of what the innovation might be able to achieve, not only in terms of time but in terms of scope, and, indeed, they were prepared to modify some of their initial expectations (e.g. on the significance of parental changes), but not their aspirations for the project. They kept a single-minded focus on the core purposes of the innovation, handled distractions and did not allow them to distract them from the core purposes of the project. This involved an important mindset in which setbacks were regarded as learning opportunities rather than failures.

Whilst the leaders of the innovation were resolute and, indeed, relentless in holding on to their hopes for the innovation, they also reviewed their expectations of the innovation to 'deliver' wide-ranging improvements on its own, especially to the lower-performing students. This reflects the importance of maintaining momentum in the innovation (Fullan 2005: 88) and a positive, forward-looking atmosphere, demanding yet forgiving when things do not always go according to plan (2005: 58).

The effectiveness of an innovation is not simply the absence of negative forces but also the presence of positive ones. To simply have few negatives, alone risks inertia, whilst accompanying it with the presence of positive forces stimulates change and maintains momentum. In this respect, the perceptible changes in students' attitudes were a source of celebration and staff motivation.

For leaders of innovation, an important lesson to emerge from this stage of the innovation was to recognize the importance of focusing on the *conditions* for innovation as well as the innovation itself. Fullan (2001: 115) argues that, in working in cultures of change, leaders deliberately set up the conditions for innovation, and, as Gladwell (2000: 173) remarks, if we wish to change behaviour, values and beliefs, it is important to create a community around these so that they can be put into practice and nurtured. The context of innovation is as important as, if not more important than, the substance of the innovation itself. Fullan (2005: 14) remarks that all levels of an organization must be committed to the change in question and that this involves 'deep learning' in order to assure sustainability. Complexity theory tells us that leaders of change have to create the conditions for change, enabling positive and multiple interactions between parties in order for self-organized change to emerge, and this echoes a key feature of the innovation encountered here: a recognition that innovation often concerns people more than the specific contents of the change, and that changing people's behaviour is a critical element of change.

Whilst leaders of change should be ahead of followers, without leaving them behind, it is important for leaders to ensure that the innovation is not distorted into buttressing up practices which it is supposed to be changing, and that the changes are really happening. This involves reviewing management responsibilities to include far greater on-the-ground support (in the case of the innovation in question here, to ensure the development of student-centred, active, collaborative and interactive pedagogies, and how ICT fitted into these) and to conduct monitoring, reviews and evaluations to ascertain how far the project is being disseminated and understood through the school and outside, and to review those parts of the management of the project which are running well and less well, and the reasons for this.

- Clarity and communication.

As the innovation unfolded, an important lesson learned was to make the purposes of the innovation explicit to all parties. Communication, through many channels (not just written), is a critical element, critical in the sense that it can facilitate or obstruct an innovation. In the case here, the lack of communication with parents blew up a storm and the school had to move quickly and decisively to quell it. It is essential – of the essence – to keep all participants involved and informed, to ensure that all parties know what is happening on the project and how it affects them. Equally important is the provision of feedback to all relevant parties on the achievements, the ongoing developments, positive and negative aspects of the project, its rewards to students and staff, and its benefits and achievements. In the case reported here, this involved monitoring and disseminating improvements in performance and motivation across the ability range and motivation range of all students, holding regular meetings of all parties for in-depth sharing of information, problems and potential solutions, and disseminating more widely to relevant parties the risk assessment that the school had undertaken and the outcomes of that assessment. Indeed, the evaluators recommended increasing internal and external communication, e.g. installing a project newsletter, a dedicated website for the innovation, additional documentation, project handbook/manual for parents and outsiders and information-sharing sessions. Part of the substance of the communication is also to identify and communicate management responsibilities for the several elements of the innovation, so that all participants know to whom to turn when a particular situation presents itself.

It is crucial to ensure that all staff are 'on message' about what is to be achieved, where relevant and appropriate, with putative timelines and targets. Alongside this is the need to communcate and raise expectations for what counts as effective practice and success in the project, and to ensure that they are the already-stated purposes and success criteria for the project.

- Taking participants seriously.

Taking participants seriously means acting with, on and for them (cf. Holmes *et al.* 2013). It is important to accept – not simply to recognize – that different parties have different views of the innovation, its value, benefits and progress, some of them differing widely, and that it is only natural that there will be a mixed response to the innovation from its target groups. Leaders of the innovation should expect participants to have some reservations about the innovation and then work on and with participants' real concerns, taking heed of the problems identified by the participants, acting swiftly to address them and identifying areas of resistance and working on and with them.

The literature on expected resistances is vast. Morrison (1998: 122–9) indicates that resistances can come from practical, value, psychological and power barriers, lack of information, personal threat, de-skilling, lack of ownership, lack of clarity in the innovation, discontinuity with existing practices, changes to social relations, threats to self-esteem and security, fear of the unknown, heightened sense of vulnerability, reluctance to take risks, loss of control, conviction in the rectitude of existing practices, fear of failure, stress, and increased workload (see also Chapter 1). Indeed, Senge's (1990: 69) much quoted aphorism can be applied here: 'The harder you push, the harder the system pushes back.' Heifetz and Linsky (2002: 3) note that bringing about changes involves challenging the very things that people hold dear, and only on the strength of a possibility that the change will work, so they will push against it and against any disturbance to their existing, familiar equilibrium. Kampylis *et al.* (2012) remark that innovation is more than likely to meet resistance because of the complexity that inheres in it. Add to this the multidimensional nature of the innovation in question here, and it is hardly surprising that resistances and obstacles were encountered.

In taking participants seriously, it is essential to recognize the importance of listening to, and providing immediate and direct support for, the front-line staff, working on and with their concerns when managing a complex, multidimensional innovation. Expect different participants to have different needs, challenges and agendas. This also entails ensuring that concerns raised by all staff can be channelled by means other than face-to-face meetings (e.g. through a third party), so that staff can speak out without fear of recrimination. As reviews and feedback take place, it is important to discuss the results of evaluations with participants, to understand their difficulties and views, and to try to explain review, monitoring and evaluation findings in a spirit of sharing and mutual development (as happened in the school here).

Another aspect of taking participants seriously is to consider their workloads/overload. Innovation typically brings extra work, as old practices have to change, and overcoming de-skilling whilst simultaneously re-skilling takes time. Leaders have a duty to ensure that workloads are manageable and sustainable, and to intervene and take direct action when they are not. This may involve reviewing teachers' workloads and preparation-time allowances, what they should be preparing, and how, and giving greater guidance on these. Typically, it may mean providing much more time and more activities for the preparation and development of all parties, in initial and ongoing time frames. It is important to consider providing greater incentives and rewards for being involved in the innovation.

Concomitant with the workloads issue is the need for capacity building, providing such development and training as is essential for participants to undertake the innovation properly, and this involves all parties: teachers, students, parents, senior officers and so on. In the school in question here, training for teachers and students was provided, and training for parents was provided, albeit with minimal uptake of the latter. A central requirement is to provide extensive and ongoing preparation, training and development in each of the areas of the innovation, i.e. to plan for sustainable development and capacity building and to ensure that training has immediate, practical and concrete impact and utility.

Part of the provision of suitable capacity building is to identify participants' limitations and to work on reducing them (for example, in the case reported here there were many areas, including: ICT usage; collaborative, student-centred, active, engaged and interactive learning; new forms of assessment). Coupling capacity building with success involves acknowledging and rewarding staff workload, identifying and celebrating immediate, small successes as well as more sustained successes, and, indeed, recognizing that it is unrealistic to expect equal levels of success from all participants and all dimensions of the innovation. Short-term successes are a key element in maintaining momentum and a positive view of the innovation, together with ensuring that staff are really able to keep up with the speed of the innovation, e.g. by slowing down or speeding up as necessary. In the school here, it was important to ensure that preparation time was devoted to pedagogical as well as technical matters, to identify the minimum necessary requirements at each stage of the project, and to ensure that sufficient time was provided for these to happen.

The lessons learned here are simple yet profound: simple in the sense that they are straightforward to articulate and, in many cases, obvious; profound in the sense that they are system-disturbing, relationship-disturbing, practice-disturbing, power-disturbing, values-disturbing, people-disturbing, persona-disturbing and leadership-disturbing. They are fundamental rather than superficial. Schools, as complex adaptive systems, are interactive, dynamical systems, naturally prone to setback, inertia and challenge. Recognizing this is to accept that making multidimensional innovation work is a complex, adaptive act.

This chapter has argued that, whilst it may be expected that an innovation will not always unfold in the ways intended, nevertheless this should not obstruct the press to succeed; but that the press to succeed relies on people – leaders, followers and other parties involved – to learn rapidly from what is happening as the innovation rolls out, and to adjust expectations, practices and behaviours accordingly whilst keeping a clear eye on the overall intents of the innovation, i.e. thinking big and acting small, thinking longer term but very mindful of the present and the immediate. As mentioned at the start of this chapter, in short, it is the human side of an innovation that enables it to succeed, not simply the contents of the innovation itself.

Inside each person is a multidimensional view of the innovation; the task is to change people, and, in this, as the chapter has demonstrated, changing behaviour and practices often precedes changing values and beliefs. This is a simple yet profound conclusion, well rehearsed in the literature but nonetheless not losing any of its punch.

6 Turning the corner

This chapter reports, analyzes and draws implications from the latter stage of the pilot project (nine months into the project), teasing out key issues in, and lessons to be learned from, the leadership and management of multidimensional innovations in schools.

Nine months on, the innovation was emerging from its 'implementation dip'; it had turned the corner. This was when round three of the evaluation took place, and it painted a mixed picture of what was emerging, differing according to: (a) which party was giving its view (e.g. teachers, students, parents), with some parties being more positive than others, and with considerable variability *within* a single party; (b) which instrument was being used (e.g. the results varied according to the instrument used, in some cases the results from questionnaires contradicted results from interviews); (c) which class was being referred to (e.g. comments about Form 4 (F4) were much more positive than comments about Primary 4 (P4) and Form 1 (F1)).

The innovation had become much more 'bedded down', with far fewer unanticipated matters and setbacks arising, and there was strong evidence that all parties were much more positive about the innovation and that it was on course. Distributed leadership was working more effectively and roles were becoming more clearly defined. The strong leadership by the principal from the very beginning was bringing positive results in powering up the innovation through the other participants.

Data at round three indicated that all students had benefited from the project, including the poorest achievers and low-motivation students. Students reported widely that they liked the tablet and would not like to go back to the previous situation of books and recitation learning. Whilst all the students had benefited, some had done so much more than others.

By round three, the school had acted on several of the evaluation findings from round two, including, for example:

- Greater communication with parents;
- Stabilization of the ICT system;
- Appointment of staff with responsibility for pedagogy;

- Clarification of roles of different parties within the school, vis-à-vis the pilot;
- Preparation for the expansion of the project;
- Further attention to interactive pedagogies within classrooms;
- Addressing on-screen marking of homework;
- Rendering it easier for students to submit work online;
- Resolution of the situation with regard to government support for the project.

Adopting the 'Levels of Use' of an innovation from Hall and Hord (1987, 2011), the participants had moved rapidly from 'non-use' through 'orientation' (starting to find out about the innovation), through 'preparation' (planning for how the innovation would run), through the 'mechanical' stage (finding out about the practicalities of the innovation), through the 'routine' use of the innovation (being more comfortable with the innovation and using it as intended), and were approaching the stages of 'refinement' (working with others to continuously improve the innovation) and 'integration' (integrating the innovation into other aspects of the school), but had not yet reached the stage of 'renewal' (exploring new ways of implementing and working with the innovation). That they had moved so far in such a short time is testimony to the commitment of all parties to the innovation. It is a rare leader who can motivate participants to move so far so quickly.

Overall effects of the intervention

Generally, the intervention had made significant, and the greatest, benefit to F4 students. From the student questionnaires, overall, the project had had mixed outcomes at that point in time. There were positive and many negative outcomes for F1 and P4 students. Overall, the reported means of the pilot groups on many indicators of success were slightly higher overall than those of the control groups (66 out of 93 (71.0 per cent) means for the pilot group were higher than those of the control group), but several of these were on account of random fluctuations rather than being statistically significantly higher or having large effect sizes.

For the pilot groups, increases in means were observed between rounds one and three. On the positive side:

- Teachers gave more challenging tasks;
- Students' behaviour had improved;
- There was slightly more group work;
- There was more classroom talk;
- Students felt more confident in using ICT, finding it easier to use the tablet, and they understood the project more;
- Teachers were using ICT more in class, students were using ICT more to learn, including submitting homework using ICT;

- There was greater use of PowerPoint, software, downloaded and stored materials, discussion boards/forums, real-time discussion boards, uploaded materials, email, other electronic forms of communication and social networking.

Several of the purposes of the project were being realized, particularly in respect of ICT usage. The overall positive increased effects of the intervention on students were large (i.e. over 5 per cent increase in means) in respect of two questionnaire items: 'Generally, how well behaved are the students in your class?' (an overall increase by 5.6 per cent); and 'Generally, how much group-based work takes place in class?' (an overall increase by 5.0 per cent).

On the other hand, to the question 'Generally, how difficult do you find the subjects?' there was an overall increase by 8.4 per cent, and for the question 'How much pressure are you under from your parents/family to do well in school?' there was an overall increase of 8.3 per cent. Clearly, a multidimensional innovation will have multiple effects, some beneficial and others not so.

However, overall effects disguised some large differences between the effects of the project on the three different classes. For example:

1 For P4, 24 variables showed positive effects and 50 of the 74 variables showed negative effects. In respect of positive effects, eight 'positive' variables had improved by 5–10 per cent and five had improved by more than 10 per cent.
2 For F1, 28 variables showed positive effects and 46 variables showed negative effects. In respect of positive effects, 15 'positive' variables had improved by 5–10 per cent and eight had improved by more than 10 per cent.
3 For F4, 63 variables showed positive effects and 11 variables showed negative effects. In respect of positive effects, 36 'positive' variables had improved by 5–10 per cent and 21 had improved by more than 10 per cent.

The older the students, the fewer and lesser were the negative effects and the more and greater were the positive effects of the intervention.

The main differences between the pilot and control groups were in aspects of ICT usage rather than in other areas, and the differences were strongest and in more areas for F4, with the number of statistically significant differences found as the age of the students increased, and a very large increase in the number of these for F4 students. This suggested that the project was exerting an increasingly strong influence as the age of the student increased, with the major positive impact felt at the upper end of the secondary school.

From the student questionnaire data the intervention was bringing improvements in students' positive behaviour, increasing group work, active classrooms and ICT (where there were significant improvements). There had been a consistent increase in the amount of group work and in ICT usage across all three pilot classes in comparison to the control groups.

When combining the three pilot groups into a single group and the three control groups into a single group, effect size calculations (Cohen's *d*) indicated the following in respect of 75 variables on a comprehensive range of aspects of the innovation, in order from 'weak effect' to 'modest effect' to 'moderate effect and to 'strong effect':

- 51 had weak effects;
- 15 had modest effects;
- Seven had moderate effects;
- Two had a strong effect.

Modest *positive* effects (effect sizes of 0.21–0.50) were found for the following:

- How much do you like school?
- Generally, how much project work do you do in your subjects?
- Normally, do you tell the teacher if the work is too easy?
- Generally, how much do your teachers encourage you to discuss the contents of the lesson with your classmates during lessons?
- How much pressure are you under from your parents/family to do well in school?
- How much do you usually choose your own materials for learning in your class?
- How easily can you find materials to help you to learn as soon as you need them in the school?
- Generally, how good do you think the communication is between you and your teachers?
- Generally, how good do you think the communication is between your teachers and your parent(s)?
- Generally, how much do your teachers use IT in class?
- Generally, how much do you use online/real-time online Internet material in class?
- Generally, how much, for learning, do you share ideas with friends using social networking?
- Generally how much, for learning, do you use email?

Moderate (i.e. stronger than 'modest' effects) *positive* effects (effect sizes of 0.51–1.00) were found for the following:

- Generally, how much group-based work takes place in class?
- Generally, how much software/programs/IT-based materials are there in class?
- Generally, how much are discussion boards/forums used in class?

- Generally, how much are real-time discussion boards/forums used in class?
- Generally, how much do you use uploaded materials in class?
- Generally, how much do teachers use email out of class to help you with learning?
- Generally, how much do teachers use other electronic ways of communicating with you out of class to help you with learning?

Strong *positive* effects (effect sizes of >1.00) were found for the following:

- Generally, how much do you use ICT in your learning in class?
- How much do you hand in your work/homework electronically (e.g. by email or other ways of sending materials electronically to your teachers)?

The following trends were observed:

- The older the student, the fewer the number of weaker effects;
- The older the student, the greater the number of moderate effects;
- The older the student, the greater the number of strong effects;
- The older the student, the fewer the number of positive effects;
- The older the student, the fewer the number of weak negative effects.

The intervention at round three had made a very considerable and substantial positive effect on F4 students. All the large positive effects were in relation to ICT usage, and moderate positive effects included ICT and pedagogy, i.e. the intervention was having an effect on more than ICT usage.

For P4 students, effect sizes suggested that the intervention had moderate and strong effects on ICT usage, with some, but less, effect on matters of pedagogy (with only modest or weak positive effects). For F1 students, effect sizes suggested that the intervention had moderate and large effects in ICT-related aspects rather than in terms of pedagogy.

For F4 students, the effect sizes were very positive indeed. There was a total absence of modest, moderate or strong *negative* effect sizes, and there were only six weak negative effect sizes; by contrast there were very few weak *positive* effect sizes, several modest positive effect sizes, a very considerable number of moderate positive effect sizes and seven large positive effect sizes. In other words, the intervention had had a very considerable and substantial positive effect on F4 students. All the large positive effects were in relation to ICT usage, and moderate positive effects included ICT and pedagogy, i.e. the intervention was having an effect on more than ICT usage. The intervention, as perhaps could be expected, was exerting a stronger effect on ICT than other areas, suggesting that expecting the ICT intervention alone to bring in wholesale, multidimensional change was perhaps unrealistic, or at least in the short term.

Student attitude and motivation

The overwhelming number of responses from teachers/senior officers indicated that the project had improved motivation for very many students, including that of the weakest students, and in some cases particularly that of the weakest students. Many responses from staff indicated that increased and high student motivation was the biggest gain from the project. Student interest in learning had risen; they had a better attitude to learning; poor performers were more willing to study and to improve; and students enjoyed their classes more.

A very large number of responses from students indicated that they felt that their motivation had increased, as had their liking of school, learning and classes, though, in some cases this increase was small. Many students said that they found the lessons more interesting and less boring.

Students' liking of the project was strongly related to their confidence, knowledge and understanding of the project, preparation for the project, and ease of use of the tablet, as well as to pedagogical factors and interest, suggesting that significant aspects of the innovation were strongly within the power of the school to effect.

A mixed picture emerged from the parents. Many parents had seen an improvement in their child's attitude, motivation and interest, whilst some said that they saw no change in their child's attitude.

Teaching and learning

Nearly all the students indicated that there was more interactivity in the class with the project, that they welcomed this and that it helped them to learn. Many students commented that they liked the opportunity for out-of-class contact with their peers and teachers through email. Many students appreciated the hard work that their teachers had done to prepare materials for them and this had a positive effect on their learning. Teachers reported that the software was useful for indicating problems in the class and addressing them immediately and that this was an improvement on the previous situation. Many students liked not having to take notes in class; they reported that there was less recitation-style learning in the lessons, though lessons were still dominated by teacher talk. They indicated that there had been an increase in group work and group study, and that there was more classroom talk, class discussion and students choosing their own materials and finding them more easily.

ICT-related increases were high. Teachers were more confident about the innovation, less worried about their abilities in it and less worried about the consequences of the innovation on students' performance, though they continued to be worried about working with other teachers on the innovation. This conforms to the later Stages of Concern (Hall and Hord 1987, 2011) mentioned in Chapter 2, in which 'collaboration' is a typical late-stage concern of users of an innovation. In other words, the fact that the teacher expressed concerns about collaborating with their colleagues indicated that they had moved on considerably in their working with the innovation; it was a very positive sign.

In respect of using ICT in teaching, from the teachers' perspectives, 19 of the 23 means (82.6 per cent) had risen between rounds one and three, some quite significantly. The overall picture at round three was notably more positive than at rounds one and two. The use of ICT in teaching had increased considerably, and, in many cases, dramatically, between rounds one and three. Teachers felt that ICT problems in the school had been solved by round three, and they were using a range of ICT software and functions much more than at round one, including interactive functions. Both overall and in respect of using ICT generally in teaching, after a slight slump in the means at round two, the teachers were feeling better about the project at round three and were more comfortable with using ICT in their teaching.

From the teachers' view, the project had brought significant increases in classroom interactivity and student activity, participation, discussion, engagement and involvement. Several comments indicated that students' initiative was improving, not least as they had to research online instead of just taking notes or operating in recitation mode.

Teachers reported that student involvement had increased in classes, as they were all required to participate in class more, and this was reinforced by awarding marks for class participation. Students were less bored in class. Even the lazy students were becoming more involved, though it was reported that the project had not touched some of the very laziest students, particularly boys, as some had already given up. Teachers commented that the tablet had helped students to absorb material and learn, and that the classroom video playback facility was useful, particularly for weaker students. It was mentioned frequently that the materials for teaching and learning were more interesting and helped students to learn. The in-class software-based voting system made it easier for quiet and less confident students to join in the class by voting. Teachers said that they were more able to have a greater focus on students; they could monitor students more closely, particularly in their behaviour.

Large class size was reported by teachers to be an inhibitor of interactive teaching and learning in some cases. Further, some comments indicated that some students were still unwilling to cooperate with each other.

Student performance

Many comments from teachers and senior officers indicated that students' performance had improved, particularly that of the weaker students. A few comments were more guarded and unsure about such improvement, and yet others indicated that it was too soon to be able to comment on improved performance. Some comments indicated that increasing class participation was improving learning and that marking for class participation was working effectively here, in this marks-oriented culture. Many comments indicated that including marks for class participation and continuous assessment (CA) had improved student motivation and performance. Some comments were a little more cautious, indicating that, whilst the project had improved the performance, marks and motivation of some students, for others there had been little or no improvement, although it had done them no harm.

In terms of marks, the overall picture in terms of the effects of the intervention on marks was mixed, being positive and equivocal in some parts and differentiated in others. Analyses of marks were conducted by the evaluators overall, by class, and within classes by comparing the highest scoring and lowest-scoring thirds of the class. However, in all the comments that follow, it is difficult to attribute causality to the intervention here, apart from, perhaps, the effect of CA on marks, and caution has to be used in interpreting the results here, as the sub-samples were very small, the standard deviations were large and many differences were not statistically significant.

Primary 4

For P4, generally, the intervention without CA was not exerting a positive effect on marks, but CA was making a considerable difference in raising the pilot group students' mean marks in English and much less so in mathematics. Without the inclusion of CA, the marks of the pilot group were often lower than those of the control group, but with the inclusion of CA the scores of the pilot group lifted a lot, rendering several of them higher than those of the control group – on one item statistically significantly in English but never in mathematics. In other words, the picture is inconsistent across the two subjects but CA appeared to be having a positive effect on students' marks.

Given that part of the project was targeted towards improving the weaker students, the marks of the lowest third of the class were examined and compared to those of the lowest third of the control group. The P4 pilot group consistently had higher marks than the control group; in the case of the English and mathematics examinations, the inclusion of CA had made a statistically significant increase to the marks of the pilot group, suggesting that the innovation brought benefit to the low-performing students in P4.

The evaluators also examined the marks of the highest third of the class and compared them to those of the highest third of the control group. For high-performing P4 students, in contrast to the low performers, it was only the introduction of CA that lifted the scores of the pilot group in both mathematics and English, without which the gap between the marks of the two groups would have been greater. Even with the gains in marks afforded by CA, the scores of the high-performing pilot group students were often lower than those of the control group, though, importantly, these differences were not statistically significant (i.e. they could have been caused by random fluctuations). In comparing the highest-performing third in pilot and control groups at round three, though the mean marks of the control group were higher in all cases but one for English and mathematics, these differences found were largely not statistically significant.

For the high third of the pilot class, the intervention had had some negative impact on their mean daily marks overall, but there was a rise in mean English and mathematics examination scores because of CA's significant positive impact. For both low and high thirds, it appears that the main effect of the intervention was to improve their mean marks as a result of adding in CA.

In looking at improvements in marks between rounds two and three of the evaluation for the P4 pilot and control groups, several points emerged:

1. For P4 students in mathematics, for the pilot group, four sets of marks out of eight had increased;
2. For P4 students in mathematics, for the control group, two sets of marks out of two had increased;
3. For P4 students in English, for the pilot group, two sets of marks out of four had increased;
4. For P4 students in English, for the control group, three sets of marks out of four had increased.

Given the baseline trend (the control group's scores over time) it appears that the innovation had made little appreciable positive difference to the marks of the P4 students. (This was based on the formula $\{(E_2-E_1) - (C_2-C_1)\}$ where E_2 = the mean of the experimental group at round three; E_1 = the mean of the experimental group at round one; C_2 = the mean of the control group at round three; C_1 = the mean of the control group at round one.)

The results present a mixed picture. The addition of CA had made a very significant *relative* difference to the lowest third of the pilot class. For the lowest-performing third of P4 in round three, comparing the means of the pilot group marks with those of the control groups, the mean marks of the pilot group were higher than those of their peers in the control group, though in most cases these were not statistically significant except after adding the CA, in which case two of the differences were statistically significant. In terms of marks, the innovation brought more benefit to the low-performing students in P4 than to the high-performing students.

Form 1

For F1, the intervention, both with and without the CA, was making a positive difference in English, whereas for mathematics (divided into two sections: algebra and geometry) it was arguable whether the intervention was making a difference, as the results for algebra were quite different from those for geometry (i.e. the differences may have been on account of the subject area rather than the intervention). There was some slender evidence that CA was raising the mean marks a little in both the daily and examination marks for English, algebra and geometry.

For the lowest-performing third of the class, the inclusion of CA into their assessment had lifted their performance, and indeed in mathematics (rather than English), it had made a notable difference, suggesting that the innovation was making a difference to the low-performing students' scores, though some of the data were equivocal (i.e. differences observed were not always statistically significant).

For high-performing F1 students, the inclusion of CA had improved their mathematics scores considerably, but less so in English. Overall, with just two exceptions in aspects of mathematics, the high-performing pilot groups outperformed the control groups in English and mathematics, and in the case of English, two of these differences in scores were statistically significant.

Overall, with only two exceptions, the scores of the pilot group were higher than those of the control group, and, in many cases these differences were statistically significant. In this respect, it appears that the intervention made an appreciable difference to the students' marks in both English and mathematics. Whereas CA had made a noticeable improvement to the marks in mathematics, this difference was less pronounced in English.

In looking at improvements in marks between rounds two and three of the evaluation for the pilot and control groups, several points emerged:

1 For F1 students in mathematics, for the pilot group, six sets of marks out of 11 had increased;
2 For F1 students in mathematics, for the control group, one set of marks out of four had increased;
3 For F1 students in English, for the pilot group, all four sets of marks had increased;
4 For F1 students in English, for the control group, three sets of marks out of four had increased.

Given the baseline trends in marks over time (the control group), the innovation had made an appreciable difference to F1 more in mathematics than in English, using the same formula for calculating difference as for P4 (see earlier).

The picture that emerged for F1 students was quite different from that of P4 students; the innovation's inclusion of CA appeared to be having a positive effect, particularly for the low-performing students, and it was making some difference overall to students' marks, though many of these could have been on account of random fluctuations. The marks here suggested that the innovation had improved marks, though in a largely inconsistent way, across the two age groups.

Form 4

For F4 the intervention was having mixed effects. For the lowest third of this pilot class, the intervention had made little difference – either positive or negative – to their mean marks in both English and mathematics. In several cases the addition of CA had lifted their mark, but in other cases it made no appreciable difference. For the low-performing students, the innovation was having little, if any, effect on their English scores, and had it not been for the CA in mathematics, the scores for the low-performing students would have been lower than for the control group. None of the differences found were statistically significant, and this, too, suggests that the innovation, with or without CA, was not having much of an effect on the scores of the low-performing students though there was a consistent pattern of raised mathematics performance with CA in the pilot group here.

For English, for high-performing students, the pilot group consistently outperformed the control group, though the inclusion of CA had had a limited effect on marks. By contrast, for mathematics, the control group consistently outperformed the pilot group without CA, whereas the CA made an appreciable difference to the pilot group here, and, indeed, had turned the tables, giving the pilot group overall higher mathematics scores than the control group. For the high third of the pilot class, it appears that the intervention had made an appreciably positive difference to the mean marks in English but no real difference – either positive or negative – to the mean marks in mathematics.

Overall, with one exception in English and two exceptions in mathematics, the scores of the pilot groups were higher than those of the control groups, though in only two cases were these differences statistically significant. However, CA for English appeared to have made little difference to marks, whereas it had made a very clear difference in mathematics, suggesting that, whilst the innovation overall had improved scores, CA exerted an inconsistent effect.

In looking at improvements in marks between rounds two and three of the evaluation for the pilot and control groups, several points emerged:

1. For F4 students in mathematics, for the pilot group, only one set of marks out of four had increased;
2. For F4 students in mathematics, for the control group, two set of marks out of four had increased, both statistically significantly;
3. For F4 students in English, for the pilot group, no marks had increased;
4. For F4 students in English, for the control group, six sets of marks out of seven had increased, four of these statistically significantly.

Given the baseline trends in marks over time (the control group), the innovation had made little difference to F4 marks in mathematics and it appeared to have had some negative effect on marks in English, using the same formula for calculating difference as for P4 (see earlier).

In interpreting students' marks, great caution had to be exercised: the sample and the sub samples were small, the standard deviations were high, the timescales were short, and in many cases the differences in marks were not statistically significant. With these cautions in mind, the evaluators suggested that, in terms of marks (and only in terms of marks, i.e. not the whole 'story' of the innovation), the intervention seemed to be exerting several positive effects on P4 students, but also several negative effects on them, a possible positive effect in English for F1 and F4, and an unclear effect for F1 and F4 in mathematics. For the lowest third of students in each pilot class, the intervention had made no real difference to overall mean marks though there was evidence that CA had raised some mean marks. For the highest third of each pilot class, with the exception of English in F4 (where it had raised mean marks), the intervention had made no real difference to mean marks.

It seemed that CA was making a difference, though it was not uniform across age groups, ability groups or subjects, but was assisting the lowest third of the class in terms of marks.

That the intervention at round three had made only a few positive differences in marks could be taken two ways. Negatively, it might be said that the results in terms of marks were disappointing; on the other hand, positively, it could be said that the lack of negative effects (apart from mainly in P4) suggested that the innovation was causing little harm to student performance and that it would take longer for effects to manifest themselves.

An important message to come from the students' marks was that the innovation was not operating uniformly in terms of its effects, and that several other variables were clearly at work and were having an impact on the students' scores.

Students' marks were only one indicator of the effectiveness of the project, and, indeed, given the cautions introduced above, they may have had limited validity in demonstrating the effectiveness of the innovation. Put briefly, there was much more to the innovation than whatever might be revealed in students' marks, and, anyway, the cautions about how much to rely on the marks was sufficient to note that, even in a strong marks-oriented local culture of schooling generally, changes in marks were often more attributable to chance than to causality.

Students

Students felt that their performance had improved with the project and that their understanding in lessons had increased. Only a very few students were more negative, reporting that they felt that their performance had improved in other subjects in comparison to those that had used the tablet (English and mathematics). Some students reported that the project had made no difference to their performance; others commented that they felt that their performance had risen in English because of the tablet, particularly in oral English and in their confidence in speaking English, but not in mathematics. Nearly all the students said that they liked being able to gain marks for class participation.

None of the students interviewed said that their parents used the computer or helped them with their tablet-based homework. Several comments, from all age groups, indicated that students did not want their parents to help them or use their tablet anyway.

Overall, from the students' questionnaire data, there were very few differences between the lowest-and highest-performing third of each class: in only 9.8 per cent of the total number of items were there such differences, and whilst these were not patterned or consistent across the same items across the classes, the F1 highest-performing students stood out as being less positive than their lowest-performing counterparts, with the opposite being true for P4 and F4 students.

For P4, statistically significant differences were found between the high and low performers for only seven out of 102 questionnaire variables (6.9 per cent). The motivation level of the low performers was statistically significantly lower than that of the high performers, and the low performers found limited relevance to the lessons, did not tell the teacher if they did not understand a point and felt that communication between them and teachers, and between teachers and parents, was weak. No statistically significant differences were found between the low performers and high performers in P4 in respect of the innovation and the use of ICT in class.

For F1, statistically significant differences were found between the highest and lowest performers for only 12 out of 102 questionnaire variables (11.8 per cent). The high-performing F1 students were more negative about the pilot than were the low-performing F1 students. Only two statistically significant differences were found between the low performers and high performers in F1 in respect of the innovation and the use of ICT in class.

For F4, statistically significant differences were found between the high and low performers for only 11 out of 102 questionnaire variables (10.8 per cent). With only one exception, the high-performing F4 students were much more positive about the pilot than were the low-performing F4 students. Only three statistically significant differences were found between the low performers and high performers in F4 in respect of the innovation and the use of ICT in class.

Across the three classes, there were only 30 questionnaire variables out of a possible 306 (9.8 per cent) in which there were statistically significant differences between the low-performing and high-performing groups. This could be taken two ways: (a) positively speaking, the project had equalized the results of the questionnaire, with the results of the lowest third in each class no different from those of the highest third; (b) negatively speaking, the project may have suppressed the results of the highest-performing third in each class. The limited number of statistically significant differences found between high- and low-performing groups at round three was similar to the position at the start of the project.

In making comparisons on the means of the questionnaire items, very few statistically significant differences were found between the means of:

- The lowest-performing pilot students and highest-performing pilot students of each class at round three;
- The lowest-performing pilot students of each class at rounds one and three;
- The highest-performing pilot students of each class at rounds one and three;
- The lowest-performing students of the pilot groups and control groups at rounds one and three;
- The highest-performing students of the pilot groups and control groups of each class at rounds one and three.

However, caution must be exercised here, as the sub-sample sizes were very small and the timescale was only nine months.

The picture that emerges here suggests that a wide view of 'performance' needed to be adopted (i.e. not simply marks), and that, in taking a wider view, there was a mixed picture of student performance. Important, however, were: (a) the benefits of CA and awarding marks for class participation, raising the performance of the lowest third of each class; (b) differentiation of results by subject as well as by class; and (c) the expression of many parties in the school that appreciable improvements had been observed in student performance. In a local culture in which marks were given high significance (not least by students and parents), the findings augured well for the innovation in the school.

Teachers

Teacher enthusiasm was found to exert a very powerful influence on the innovation. Overall, teachers reported a positive increase in their views of the innovation; 98 out of their 134 means (73.1 per cent) for questionnaire items about the project had risen between rounds one and three. Teachers identified three key drivers of success in the project: students' motivation and interest in learning; the use of the tablet; and new ways of teaching and learning that were taking place in the classroom.

This suggested not only that it was essential for the school to prepare the teachers in respect of the tablet but also in respect of teaching and learning strategies, and to ensure that pedagogic practice actually changed in classrooms.

Teachers' responses indicated that the innovation was going well and according to plan, and that the staff and students were more 'on board' and comfortable with the innovation and were more positive about it, more accepting of it, and more open to it. Very many of their comments received indicated a noticeable shift towards a more positive and upbeat view of the innovation and its implementation. Teachers felt much more at home with the tablet and were using it extensively to promote interactive teaching and learning. They commented that, as their familiarity with the software and the innovation grew, so their planning had changed from planning content to planning pedagogy. They reported that they understood the innovation more now, and that this had made a positive difference to their willingness to be involved in it.

Several comments indicated that obtaining the support and approval for the innovation from the local government's education authority (the Direcção dos Serviços de Educação e Juventude (DSEJ)) was a 'breakthrough' moment, and this had persuaded teachers, students and parents that the innovation was important and positive; it gave teachers' motivation a boost, reduced attacks and negativity from several parties, and – to a very limited extent – eased some dealings with partners and publishers (e.g. publishers were more willing to have materials put onto the tablets at reduced cost).

Parents

With almost no exceptions, the parents were positive about the innovation overall, the hardware and the software. They felt that it was a good idea, in some cases at interview, unanimously so. Many comments indicated that the parents were happy with their child's performance and that the change had been for the better.

Comments from teachers and senior officers indicated that parents were becoming more positive as they saw positive changes in their children. Many comments suggested that the gravity of the communication challenges with parents at round two had receded somewhat, though there continued to be important areas on which the school should focus, providing information to the parents.

Many parents said that they saw an improvement in their child's performance, particularly in English. Several parents said that they saw a worsening and a drop in performance, particularly in examinations. Others said that they saw no change in their child's performance. Very many comments were received from all parent groups that they had seen a positive improvement in their child's computer use and skills.

Teacher workload

Many comments indicated that teacher workload continued to be a problem. Teachers were still spending much of their private time out of school in preparing and creating materials. Even though it had reduced slightly, it was still significantly too high and still a major concern for the school as it impacted on teacher motivation, enthusiasm and the sustainability of the innovation, which were critical factors in the success of the innovation.

Homework

Generally, the older the child, the more contented were the parents and the less the parents were concerned with monitoring homework or felt the need for training on the tablet. For P4 students, many parents were still concerned about the tablet use and its effects on their children's learning. Homework supervision was a problem with the tablet. Many parents commented on this, saying that they could not help their child with the tablet because they did not know how to use it, that their child would 'refuse' to let the parents near to the tablet, that their child (the parents of the older children in the school) was spending time on surfing the Internet and communicating with classmates, and they worried about losing control over their child's homework.

Students felt that it was easier to submit work with the computer and that the 'erase' function enabled them to rewrite answers to homework (though younger students reported that they sometimes erased material by accident). Some students indicated that homework had become easier and more interesting with the tablet; others indicated that the tablet had not made much difference to their homework. Many students commented that they could share homework, questions and online discussions in doing their homework, and that this was both helpful and useful, though it meant that a few lazy students could copy others' work.

Assessment and examinations

The school had made it clear that, in the early stages of the innovation, assessment would be addressed in detail in the second year of the innovation. Some challenges were reported in standardization and reducing variability of marking and marking criteria for class participation, CA, and the integration of assessment, examinations, ICT, teaching, learning and curriculum. Staff needed more preparation for CA and assessment of class participation.

Innovation management

Many comments received indicated that, though the management of the innovation had improved over the duration of the innovation, and there was greater cooperation, there were still problems of insufficient communication between all parties.

Several comments noted that the innovation required a change of culture and mentality in the school, whereby more parties were involved, sharing and working together, giving feedback to each other, anticipating and focusing on emergent problems together and taking on voluntary leadership roles; in short, greater teamwork needed to be developed. Even though this was a longer-term matter, it was voiced as a key issue by several respondents.

Teacher and student preparation

There was an ongoing serious matter of teacher preparation and training in pedagogy and the use of the tablet as a tool to support active and interactive pedagogies. There was a clear recognition by several parties that pedagogy and pedagogical training needed strengthening considerably in the school, and that the school had taken positive steps to address this. Very many comments indicated that teacher preparation in the hardware was acceptable but in terms of active, interactive and collaborative pedagogy and the use of the software for teaching there was still much room for development and greater provision, on an ongoing basis, including training the in-school trainers. Put simply, the teachers needed more guidance, guidelines and training on newer and unfamiliar forms of pedagogy in order to meet the aspirations of the project. Nor was this confined to the teachers: students needed more preparation on the use of the tablet and the teaching and active, interactive and collaborative pedagogies that it supported.

Video and video playback

From the automatically logged data on the school's servers, there was considerable variation by class in: (a) the number of students per class who viewed lessons (from five to 40); (b) the number of lessons viewed (from 11 to 58); (c) the total number of hours by subject and by class (from one to 98). For English and mathematics, the older the students, the lower the number of times lessons were viewed. P4 students made by far the greatest use of the video playback, both in terms of the number of times lessons were watched and the total number of hours spent on viewing lessons.

Several students indicated that they had not used the video playback very frequently. Students gave mixed reactions to the video facility, some finding it useful, particularly for examination revision or if they had missed something in class, others not using it very much, if at all, and others indicating that it made no difference, because re-watching material did not help them to understand it more and, anyway, sometimes the speed of the lesson was too fast so that, even with re-watching they could not keep up.

Several students reported that they disliked being videoed, and they felt that their parents (who could watch the videos) might feel that they were simply chatting when, in fact, they were discussing matters. Several comments indicated that students did not like what they felt was 'surveillance' on the computer.

P4 students spent many hours watching mathematics (98 hours) but only 23 hours watching English. Between rounds two and three for P4 students, in both mathematics and English, there was an increase in the number of *hours* spent viewing but a drop in the total number of *times* lessons were viewed and the number of students viewing. For P4 students, the highest third in terms of performance had more viewings, watched more presentations and spent longer in watching than the lowest third, in both English and mathematics. The innovation was having some impact for an important target of the innovation – the lowest-performing students – even if they used the video playback less than the highest-performing students.

F1 students recorded approximately equal amounts of viewing time on English and mathematics, but there was a very large difference between the number of hours spent on geometry (one hour) and algebra (36 hours). Between rounds two and three for F1 students there was a considerable decrease in the number of hours spent viewing both English and mathematics, and a considerable drop in the number of students viewing. The lowest third of students (in terms of performance) spent more time than the highest third in watching English, whilst for mathematics they had more viewings and watched more presentations than the highest third. It appeared that one intention of the intervention – to support the lowest performers – was working, but differentially by subject.

F4 students spent very little time viewing English lessons (seven hours) whereas for mathematics they spent 78 hours and with over twice as many viewings. There were more viewings of F4 mathematics at round three than at round two and more hours spent on mathematics at round three in comparison to round two. By contrast, at round three in English the number of viewings, hours of viewing and number of students viewing had dropped significantly. The lower third spent more time than the higher third watching English and mathematics. For English there was very little difference between the lowest and highest third of performers in terms of total views and number of presentations, whilst for mathematics the lowest third had more viewings and watched more presentations than the higher third. It appeared that, as for F1, one intention of the intervention – to support the lowest performers – was working, but differentially by subject.

In comparing the results of the total viewings by class and by lowest and highest performers, the intervention had made a difference to students, but these differences were very diverse with no clear patterning by age, apart from the observation that: (a) for English, the older the student, the fewer total viewings and presentations they watched in English; and (b) for mathematics, the older the student, the less time they spent in watching mathematics. It appeared that the lowest performers benefited from the viewings, particularly in mathematics. (The sub-samples were very small and so it was invidious to read too much into these general trends.)

Comparing rounds two and three

In terms of ICT, the system had stabilized much more since round two, and was working much better. In comparing rounds two and three, the evaluators noted that, whilst there had been little improvement in terms of students' marks (though CA had lifted the marks of the lowest third of the students at both rounds), there was a much more positive spirit about the project and the attitude to it amongst the teachers and senior officers than at round two. Further, from many staff data sources, student motivation was higher at round three than at round two.

There was evidence of more extensive use of active and interactive pedagogies at round three than at round two, and this paralleled teachers' increasing familiarity with the tablet. That said, there was still evidence of much teacher talk and directive teaching.

At round two the problem of communicating with parents and involving them was seen as a significant matter, requiring immediate and serious attention as parents were disaffected and angry. At round three, whilst the disaffection and anger had subsided, the problem of providing information about the innovation for the parents, and communicating with them still needed attention.

At round three, as with round two, English seemed to be faring better than mathematics in the innovation, and, as with round two, there was a clear trend: the older the students, the greater the benefits appeared to be. As with round two, at round three many students reported that they were positive about the innovation but many were either negative or indifferent, and whilst some comments indicated that improvement to motivation was notable in respect of low-performing students rather than the medium-performing or high-performing students, overwhelmingly, there was little substantial difference between the low-, medium- and high-performing students in this respect.

At round two, the problem of teachers' out-of-hours workload had been noted; it was still a significant issue at round three.

Controlling for variables

In order to separate out the possible effects of the intervention from other factors, partial correlations were conducted, in which factors which might have influenced the intervention were controlled out of the results. These were:

- How much of the success of the project depends on your teachers' motivation and interest in the project?
- How much of the success of the project depends on your motivation and interest in learning?
- How much of the success of the project depends on your teachers' enthusiasm when they are teaching you?
- How much of the success of the project depends on your parents' interest in the project?
- How much of the success of the project depends on whether you like English and mathematics?
- How much of the success of the project depends on the fact that you can now get marks for class participation in the project?
- How much of the success of the project depends on your ability to use ICT?

After controlling for these variables, how much the students liked the innovation correlated strongly with the following variables:

- Generally, how confident are you when working in the new ICT project?
- Generally, how worried/scared do you feel about the new ICT project?
- How easy do you think it will be to use the tablet?
- How well prepared do you think you are by the school for the new ICT project (how much do you know about the project)?
- Generally, how good is the teaching in the school?
- Generally, how good are you at learning?
- How much do you like school?
- Generally, how interested are you in reading for your school subjects?
- Generally, how much effort do you put into your homework?

This suggests that students' liking of the project was strongly related to their confidence, knowledge of the project, preparation for the project, and ease of use of the tablet, as well as to pedagogical factors and interest.

After controlling for the same variables indicated above, how confident the students felt about working in the new ICT project correlated strongly with the following variables:

- How much the school has explained to the students about the project and how much they understand about it;
- How well prepared do you think you and your parents are by the school for the new ICT project (how much do you know about the project)?
- Generally, how good is the teaching in the school?
- Generally, how good are you at learning?
- How much do you like school?
- Generally, how interested are you in reading for your school subjects?

After controlling for the same variables indicated above, how well prepared the students felt for the new ICT project correlated strongly with the following variables:

- How much the school has explained to the students about the project, its purposes, and how much they understand about it;
- How well prepared do you think your parents are by the school for the new ICT project (how much do they know about the project)?
- Generally, how good is the teaching in the school?
- Generally, how good are you at learning?
- Generally, how interested are you in reading for your school subjects?

The results suggest that students' confidence in working in the project and their liking for it were strongly related to their understanding of it, their preparation for it by the school, as well as to pedagogical factors and interest. This important finding suggested that significant aspects of the innovation were strongly within the power of the school to effect.

The students' questionnaire included questions designed to investigate how much of the project's success was dependent on a range of different factors (independent variables):

- In your opinion, how much of the success of the project depends on the tablet?
- In your opinion, how much of the success of the project depends on the new ways of teaching and learning that take place *in the classroom*?
- In your opinion, how much of the success of the project depends on the learning that you do *at home*?
- In your opinion, how much of the success of the project depends on your motivation and interest in learning?
- In your opinion, how much of the success of the project depends on your teachers' enthusiasm when they are teaching you?
- In your opinion, how much of the success of the project depends on your parents' interest in the project?
- In your opinion, how much of the success of the project depends on the fact that you can now get marks for class participation in the project?

A multiple regression was conducted in which these were regressed onto each of a set of dependent variables, in order to discover: (a) which of the independent variables were exerting a statistically significant effect ($p<0.05$) onto each of the following dependent variables; (b) how much the regression model explained, or accounted for, the dependent variable. The dependent variables were:

- Generally, how good is the teaching in the school?
- Generally, how good are you at learning?
- Generally, how motivated are you to learn at school?
- How much do you like school?
- Generally, how interested are you in reading for your school subjects?
- Generally, how much effort do you put into your homework?
- Generally, how interesting do you find the lessons?
- Generally, how difficult do you find the subjects?
- Generally, how easy do you find the subjects?
- Generally, how much do you use IT in your learning in class?
- Generally, how much do your teachers use IT in the class?
- Generally, how much do you use IT in your learning at home?

Table 6.1 reports the statistically significant independent variables that exerted an effect on the dependent variable in question. It suggests that the tablet exerted a strong influence. Besides this, teacher enthusiasm exerted a powerful influence in respect of 'Generally how good is the teaching in the school?' and 'Generally how interesting do you find the lessons?'. Further, student motivation exerted an important influence on 'Generally how good are you at learning?' and 'Generally how much do you use IT in your learning in class?', and new ways of teaching

Table 6.1 Statistically significant regressions onto dependent variables

	Standardized coefficients beta (ß)	Sig.
Generally, how good is the teaching in the school? Adjusted R square 0.226 Sig. of model 0.000	ß	Sig.
How much of the success of the project depends on the tablet?	0.265	0.013
How much of the success of the project depends on your teachers' enthusiasm when they are teaching you?	0.454	0.003
Generally, how good are you at learning? Adjusted R square 0.295 Sig. of model 0.000		Sig.
How much of the success of the project depends on the tablet?	0.284	0.005
How much of the success of the project depends on your motivation and interest in learning?	0.366	0.002
How much of the success of the project depends on the fact that you can now get marks for class participation in the project?	-0.289	0.008
Generally, how motivated are you to learn at school? Adjusted R square 0.391 Sig. of model 0.000		Sig.
How much of the success of the project depends on the new ways of teaching and learning that take place in the classroom?	0.455	0.000
How much do you like school? Adjusted R square 0.242 Sig. of model 0.000		Sig.
How much of the success of the project depends on the new ways of teaching and learning that take place in the classroom?	0.239	0.042
Generally, how interested are you in reading for your school subjects? Adjusted R Square 0.349 Sig. of model 0.000		Sig.
How much of the success of the project depends on the learning that you do at home?	0.229	0.008
Generally, how much effort do you put into your homework? Adjusted R Square 0.205 Sig. of model 0.000		Sig.
How much of the success of the project depends on the tablet?	0.279	0.010
Generally, how interesting do you find the lessons? Adjusted R Square 0.447 Sig. of model 0.000		Sig.
How much of the success of the project depends on the learning that you do at home?	0.219	0.006

(Continued)

Table 6.1 (Continued)

	Standardized coefficients beta (ß)	Sig.
How much of the success of the project depends on your teachers' enthusiasm when they are teaching you?	0.275	0.029
How much of the success of the project depends on the fact that you can now get marks for class participation in the project?	0.267	0.006

Generally, how easy do you find the subjects? Adjusted R Square 0.160 Sig. of model 0.002	ß	Sig.
How much of the success of the project depends on your parents' interest in the project?	0.249	0.026

Generally, how much do you use IT in your learning in class? Adjusted R Square 0.277 Sig. of model 0.000		Sig.
How much of the success of the project depends on the tablet?	0.289	0.006
How much of the success of the project depends on your motivation and interest in learning?	0.334	0.005
How much of the success of the project depends on your parents' interest in the project?	-0.249	0.017

Generally, how much do your teachers use IT in the class? Adjusted R Square 0.153 Sig. of model 0.002		Sig.
How much of the success of the project depends on your motivation and interest in learning?	0.253	0.047

Generally, how much do you use IT in your learning at home? Adjusted R Square 0.221 Sig. of model 0.000		Sig.
How much of the success of the project depends on the tablet?	0.323	0.003

and learning exerted an important influence on 'Generally how motivated are you to learn at school?' and 'How much do you like school?'.

These findings suggested that, if the school wished the project to be successful, in addition to working on the tablet it was important to focus on addressing new ways of teaching and learning, ensuring teacher enthusiasm for the project and working on student motivation and interest. These were clearly inter-related and confirmed data derived from other sources in the evaluation.

Lessons learned

What lessons can we learn from the innovation at this third round of its evaluation? At this stage the central purposes of the change were still on course, indeed had strengthened, whilst the innovation was unfolding non-uniformly. It was differentiating: not only were different dimensions unfolding to differing degrees and in different ways, and with differing levels and areas of success and setback, but they varied according to the age of the students, the subjects, the within-class differences, the aspects of the innovation itself and the impact on different parties. This yields some important lessons for managing multidimensional innovation, and these are explored below.

- The critical role of leadership.

At the third stage of the innovation, where both consolidation and further development were taking place, the leadership of the innovation had become clearer, with role articulation and devolution operating effectively. The principal was the overall leader of the change, with essential aspects of the leadership roles and tasks being distributed to senior staff in the school (e.g. the head of the curriculum, the head of ICT and the heads of subject departments). Adopting the terminology from Robbins and Finley (1998), the principal had taken on several roles:

- 'Pathmaker': being ahead of the others in time and vision in order to create a path for them to follow and be able to keep everything literally on track;
- 'Integrator': really understanding, reviewing what was happening, fitting it all together so that a big picture emerged (e.g. a culture change) and ensuring that the change was safe and secure;
- 'Negotiator': navigating a course through the challenges and solving different demands from different aspects of the innovation (including the people);
- 'Game player': ensuring that all parties worked together cooperatively rather than competitively, and reducing any sense of threat and defensiveness on the part of the participants.

Each of these roles would come to the fore at different times; in other words, the leader(s) of the change must be prepared to take on these roles as the occasion demands during the innovation, whilst still keeping firmly to a vision of where the innovation should be heading. Indeed Sharma (2001) argues that at the initiation phase of an innovation the leader must adopt a 'nurturing' role, whilst at the implementation stage more of a 'championing' role is undertaken. The point here is that multidimensional innovation requires multidimensional leadership, embracing fitness for purpose, people, dimensions and stages of an innovation, tasks and relationships.

An ongoing feature of the innovation, as at round two, was the firm and unswerving conviction of the school principal, not only of the rectitude of the innovation but also that it would proceed despite setbacks and distractions. In this he had the strong support of key senior staff in the school, and there was a determination that the innovation would move on (and, indeed, roll out to other classes, teachers and subjects over the ensuing years as part of the school's Empowering Students for an Open School project. This steadfastness of resolve, coupled with openness to feedback and a willingness to act on it, was a hallmark of the leadership behaviour in the school. A dogged single-mindedness to persevere and to hold to the central tenets of the innovation was a key characteristic of the leaders of the innovation, and this had brought the success to the innovation that has been noted in this chapter.

- Balance impatience with patience.

The identification of minimum acceptable levels of development in each dimension must be made clear to all parties, together with ensuring that nothing falls below these. However, whilst the leaders of the innovation, understandably, might be impatient to move the innovation forward, they must also exercise patience, perhaps setting the bar of achievement high but tolerating slightly less, providing that it does not fall below a minimum level. In other words, a 'push' strategy at times can combine with, and adopt, a 'pull' strategy – proaction with reaction – with the leader taking people along together rather than 'pummelling' them into submission (Robbins and Finley 1998). The leader has a clear vision, and this is a vision that illuminates and directs attention rather than blinds (Hargreaves 1994).

- Have realistic expectations.

One corollary of patience is the recognition that, whilst expectations will be high, they may not all be met immediately or by all parties at the same time (cf. Hall and Hord 2011). It is essential for the leaders of the innovation to identify where and what, if any, concessions can and cannot be made in respect of which expectations will be met by whom and by when, without any risk of the innovation not keeping on track, i.e. the issue may be one of timing rather than changing course. The partners to expectations are support and the responsibility of the leaders of the innovation to provide ongoing practical support for the innovation, for example in training and staff development.

- Ensure that all the ingredients of effective innovation are in place.

Whilst the innovation itself had many dimensions, the hallmarks of effective innovation lie in the several ingredients of the innovation being present. For example, the Connecticut Accountability for Learning Initiative (CALI) (2011) identifies essential ingredients as: vision, skills, incentives, resources and action plan (see Figure 6.1), and this affects change outcomes and processes. These ingredients impact on people's attitudes, and, as Hall and Hord (2011) remind us, attitudes can be pivotal in ensuring the effectiveness of an innovation.

The absence of any one of these required elements diminishes or, indeed, transforms the innovation and the goodwill and commitment of its participants. As the CALI (2011) remarks, it is essential to 'engage the heart as

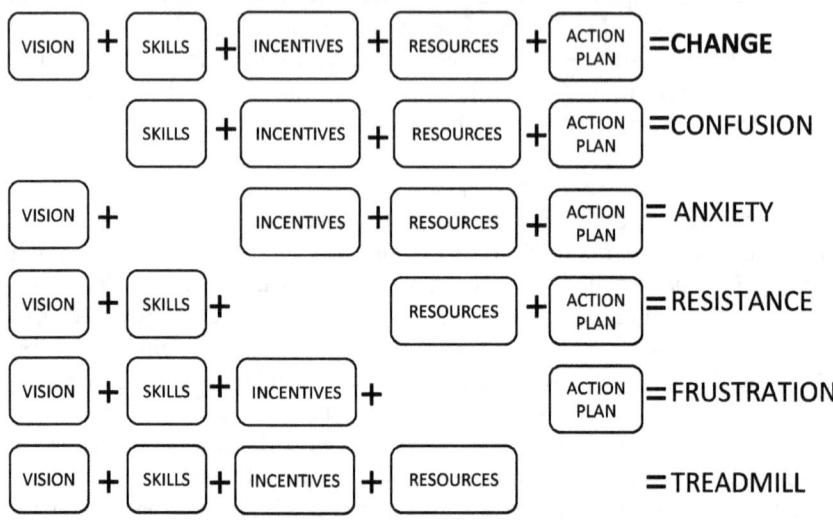

Figure 6.1 Managing complex change
Source: Reproduced with permission: Connecticut State Department of Education.

well as the head in the change'. In the school in question, whilst all of these elements obtained, their spread was uneven across and within the leaders, teachers and students so anxiety, confusion, some early resistance, some frustration and a sometime sense of a treadmill (e.g. in preparing lessons) were almost inevitable. To these ingredients can be added time, leadership, management, people, communication, support, capability, organizational culture, organizational climate and health.

- Attend to timing.

Timing is important in relation to all the stages and dimensions of the innovation, recognizing that not all dimensions of the innovation will proceed at the same rate (Hall and Hord 2011). It is important to plan the timing of different stages and dimensions of the innovation, and, as the innovation unfolds, to see how, where and why timings have or have not been able to be followed. It is also important to identify stress points: when time is going to become a significant issue and when it is likely to exert pressure on participants (Winsor 2012) (see below: Make workloads sustainable).

Knowing when to intervene in different elements of the innovation, and at which stages, requires the participants, particularly the leaders, to have their fingers on the pulse of what is happening, and this means having real data (see below: Act on feedback, evaluation and review). Extending the metaphor of the pulse, in Chinese medicine and its concern for the whole person (and the innovation took place in a Chinese school), there are 12 different pulses, each of which tells the doctor about different organs and functioning of the patient, with the intention of identifying which parts (e.g. ying and yang) are out of balance with each other. Further, the art of pulse taking and pulse reading in Chinese medicine requires much training; it is an art as much as a science. One can apply the analogy to innovations: different parts of the innovation operate in different ways, but each must balance with the other, and the art of timing concerns the divining of which parts are and are not out of step with the others, and when, where and how to intervene to move forward the whole system. This requires ongoing soundings, feedback and evidence (hence the three rounds of the evaluation). Timing also concerns setting appropriate deadlines for different parts of the innovation and decision making, and at what stages of the innovation (e.g. start-up/introduction; continuation; extension).

Timing also affects expectations: do not expect long term gains to manifest themselves immediately; do not expect too much too soon.

- Expect differentiated development.

Different parts of the innovation in question were developing at different rates, for example: (a) ICT work was moving faster than pedagogical change, which was moving faster than communication with parents; (b) teachers and students had different rates of uptake; (c) students were using the different functions of the software to different degrees (varying, for example, by age group, ability levels and subject); and (d) student achievement varied by progress in subjects, age group and ability levels. A key lesson from this is not to expect development to be uniform, linear and the same across all the dimensions of the innovation, and not to expect a single or consistent picture to emerge; that is unlikely to happen (Hall and Hord 2011). The corollary of this is that the participants in the innovation, particularly the leaders, should maintain a clear focus on the *key* features of the innovation, adhere to them with tenacity and without giving up on any of them. Further, it is essential to identify the key dimensions of the innovation and ensure as far as possible their integration and mutual potentiation: they intensify each others' benefits. Change is incremental, and the leadership and management of change are evolutionary and both piecemeal as well as wholesale, even if that is not intended. In the innovation here, the initial intervention (e.g. the tablets, the software and the pedagogical changes) was wholesale but was accompanied by an awareness that the consequences of these would not roll out in a single, uniform line.

- Ensure connectedness of the different dimensions of the innovation.

Complexity theory emphasizes connectedness. Whilst it is common to read of the value of synergy, establishing real rather than a contrived or paper-exercise of synergy is hard work. At the planning stage it involves seeing how the different dimensions really do link and how they can reinforce each other in theory and practice, with 'dimensions' having a wide embrace, for example: people; curricular, pedagogic and assessment components; support and development practices; content aspects of the innovation; process aspects of the innovation; leadership and management aspects of the innovation; attitudinal and motivational changes; interpersonal and intrapersonal changes; resource aspects; knowledge facilitation and transfer; expectations; action planning and success criteria; timing, and so on.

At the implementation stage it is important not only to ensure that the planned linkages come to fruition in practice, but that participants take stock, on an ongoing basis, of how these linkages are operating, with what challenges and effects, and how new linkages have arisen and how they can be brought into the frame of the innovation development and operations (see also below: Use action planning).

The *first* questions that can be asked here are: 'What is it that connects such-and-such a dimension of the innovation with such-and-such a dimension? Who, what and where is the node (or hub) in the innovation connecting which parts of the innovation?' Is it, for example, the cognate areas that bind the two (or more) dimensions together, the people who are working on these dimensions, the ways of proceeding in the development and implementation of these dimensions, the conceptual links between the dimensions and/or the practical links that can be made between the dimensions (and what are the 'practical links')? A node is a connection point: it receives, stores, sends and forwards signals to and from other parts of the innovation (people, content and process); in other words, it is the locus and the manager of communication.

The *second* question that can be asked here is: 'How many dimensions can be brought together/connected comprehensibly and straightforwardly, i.e. without conceptual or practical strain?'

The *third* question concerns people: 'Where and when is best to position which people as nodes/hubs in the innovation, connecting whom and what?' (For example, which people to have doing which tasks and connecting with whom.)

The planning of innovation in relation to these questions can be crucial. For example, a key connection in the innovation here was between collaborative, interactive learning and ICT: the three ran together, and the key 'people' nodes were the teachers, the head of curriculum and the head of ICT (and, subsequently, by round three, the new appointees to work with staff on developing pedagogies with ICT). Another key connection was between student motivation, attitude, interest, performance, assessment and pedagogy, which included ICT. In Figure 6.2 the connections are presented diagrammatically, with the teachers, students, heads of curriculum and ICT all included, and the nodes are the integrating points of contact.

Turning the corner 197

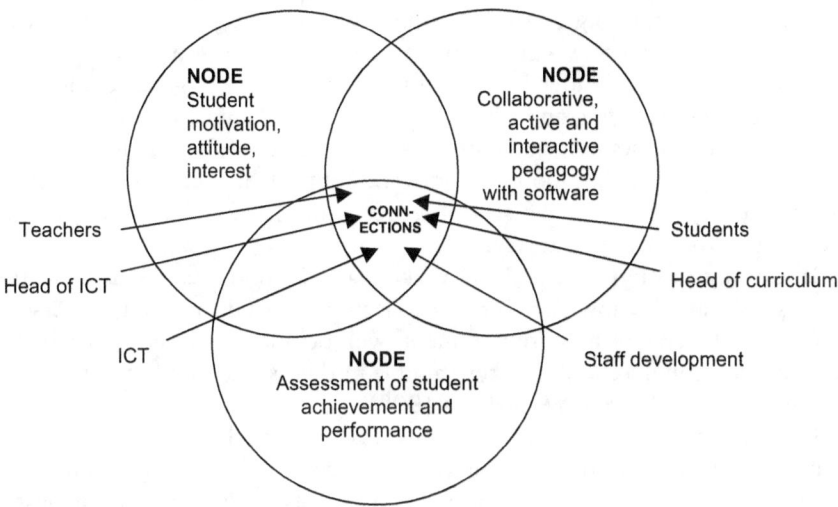

Figure 6.2 Nodes and connectors in the innovation

Connectedness, a key feature of complexity theory, exists everywhere. Connectedness through communication is vital. This requires a *distributed knowledge* system, in which knowledge is not centrally located in a command and control centre or the property of a limited set of agents (e.g. senior managers); rather, it is dispersed, shared and circulated throughout the organization and its members. Processing information and feedback for learning is not routed through a central control mechanism; it is *distributed* throughout the system, and information, knowledge and meanings, and their control, are also distributed throughout the system (Waldrop 1992: 145–7).

No individual leader possesses all the knowledge stored in an organization. The leader *relies* on distributed knowledge and being able to draw upon it. It is folly for leaders to believe that they have all the knowledge of the organization. The implication of this, as Wheatley (1996: 5) observes, is that self-organization through connectedness *requires* democratic processes; it is inevitable. As she says, 'you can't avoid including people' (1996: 5) (cf. Goldstein 2000: 15).

Connectedness also implies relationships, for example between individuals and teams, between teams, between subsystems and between the institution and its environment (Lewin and Regine 2000: 19). Further, these relationships are mutual, not one way. On an interpersonal level this suggests an increased need for trust between equal partners (cf. Hargreaves and Shirley 2009) – a collaborative rather than a competitive mentality. This creates a win-win situation, a 'both/and' rather than an 'either/or' (Hargreaves and Shirley 2009: 168) approach to inclusion.

The ramifications of connectedness are to suggest that leadership is not the preserve of the senior figure of the school; everyone everywhere can exercise leadership. The leader is simply the one who goes first and shows the way, not necessarily the boss. Leadership is no longer the activity of gatekeeping and directing but of enabling and empowering. Decentralizing control requires a flexible, adaptable system which, itself, is coordinated (cf. Youngblood 1997: 34). This argues against boundary-driven, controlled, inflexible, rigid systems and organizations. The school leader is the facilitator of information exchange rather than its gatekeeper.

If learning through feedback is to take place, if connectedness is to work successfully, and if knowledge is to be collected from a distributed, dispersed system, then an essential requirement will be effective communication. Communication in schools is a key variable in their success and their person-centredness (cf. Peters 1989; Cilliers 1998).

Communication is central to complexity theory and to the organizational and leadership theory that draws inspiration from complexity theory. Significant, open-ended and lateral communication must replace those vertical or bilateral forms of communication in which directions, decisions and instructions descend from on high in a hierarchical bureaucracy, and information ascends to the top of the hierarchy such that the nature or contents of the communication are different. Complexity theory suggests that, in a networked structure for self-organization, communication must take multiple forms, must be through multiple channels and must be open (Katz and Kahn 1978).

- Work with people's perceptions and emotions.

Managing innovation in school is as much an affective as a cognitive matter for all participants (cf. Hall and Hord 2011): leaders, teachers, students, parents and so on. Indeed, Hall and Hord indicate that people's feelings and attitudes may supersede the cognitive and practical aspects of the innovation (hence the emphasis on the Stages of Concern, which informed the three rounds of evaluation). Feelings of discouragement may not be far away when an innovation does not go according to plan, or when the workload is high and intense. For the leader of change, leadership can be a lonely occupation. For the teachers it is almost guaranteed to be stressful, and, despite delineations of stress being positive or negative – eustress or distress, respectively – that is small comfort for teachers who work tirelessly in their own time to ensure that innovation works without harming their students, indeed, to ensure that it has positive outcomes.

Affective states can be both positive and negative. Positively they can bring commitment to the innovation and a willingness to make sacrifices in order for it to work; negatively they can bring hostility, or, even worse, apathy (Egan 1993). Whilst participants may need to be pressed a little to change – the parent bird pushes the fledging out of the nest in order to teach it to fly – it is important for incentives to be installed (a 'pull' strategy) rather than relying on compulsion alone.

- Move cautiously with self-organization.

The nature of the innovation in the school here was premised on self-organization, with roots traceable to complexity theory. The innovation was not externally mandated but arose from within. However, self-organization comes at a price, which is that it may not bring about what was originally planned, as self-organizing, dynamical systems have their own impetus and are autocatalytic such that new situations and scenarios arise and evolve. As Morrison remarks, change changes people and people change change (1998: 145). In the school here, for example, the initial setbacks in the innovation (e.g. late delivery of the hardware) obstructed staff development, the delay in obtaining copyright clearance impeded the innovation, the U-curve of innovation displaced several of the project's aspirations and the need for more staff development in collaborative pedagogies narrowed the impact of the innovation to a smaller sphere than had originally been hoped.

Not everything went smoothly, and some of the hopes that the ICT might bring in a range of other pedagogical changes were not fully realized. Whether those aspirations were or were not realistic is not the point here; the point is that the innovation did not proceed as originally conceived. Some of the planning and implementation were frustrated by events that occurred during the innovation, and the emergent situation was different from the original plan. As Hall and Hord (2011) note, the *actual* 'innovation configuration' is not the same as the *intended* configuration of the innovation. Tolerance of such changes is important, with the leader acting as a careful helmsman/helmswoman, steering a passage that may change as events arise, but which keeps the ship on course overall.

Events arise that may indicate that the original intentions, whilst entirely worthy, might turn out to be more complex than originally foreseen. For example, in the project reported here, the intention had been to encourage student motivation, particularly of the lowest-performing students, not only through ICT but also through class participation, which, in a mark-oriented culture, included awarding marks for class participation. However, the assessment of class participation turned out to be different in each of the classes. This gave rise to the need for a clear marking criteria and moderation exercise. This, in turn, gave rise to the need for an updated assessment policy. This gave rise to the need for adjusting staff responsibilities and management to make a school appointment of a member of staff responsible for assessment. This, in turn, gave rise to the recognition that this was too serious a matter to be addressed rapidly in the first year of an innovation, and that it would be addressed in the second year. What started as a noble intention turned out to be opening up somewhat of a Pandora's box of important matters.

Similarly, it was recognized early on in the innovation that considerable staff development was required in collaborative, active and interactive learning, as, without these, there would be a danger that the ICT would be used to buttress up existing didactic pedagogy. By the third round of the evaluation it was recognized that this was actually a critical rather than a less significant feature, and it led to the school making two additional appointments of staff with responsibility for staff development in these areas, moving outstanding teachers in the school to these positions, and releasing them from some of their teaching commitments in order to work with and alongside other teachers in the school in furthering pedagogical developments.

The school was self-organizing in response to emergent needs and situations, whilst keeping a clear view of where the innovation was going and should be going. The school, as a learning organization, recognized that learning changes one's views and situations. The intention was that the innovation would bring in wide-ranging change, and it did. However, by the third round of the evaluation of the innovation, it had been realized that, whilst the vision had not dimmed, it had been unrealistic to place such store on the ICT to largely to bring about the hoped-for changes.

A key lesson here is that self-organization should keep sight of the long-term vision and direction, but that planning and implementation should be through a series of shorter, ever-changing steps, as some unanticipated matters arise and situations evolve. The plan is not a single blueprint, but a direction and an end point, with emerging horizons rather than a single horizon.

The lesson is not to expect self-organization to deliver necessarily what you want it to deliver, or in the way that you want it to be delivered, and not to expect things to go as planned. Indeed, Morrison (2010) argues that self-organization and emergent order may be unsafe in some situations and that control may be necessary (cf. Morrison (1998: 76–8) and Solow and Szmerekovsky (2006: 53)). Self organization is not the same as voluntarism, autonomy and an absence of coercion or directives, but it can be agentically *responsive* as well as agentically *initiating* (Stacey 2000, 2001). Self-organization is an inevitability, regardless of the form that it takes – responsive or active.

- Decide your indicators of success carefully.

As this was a multidimensional innovation, it was important to use a range of success criteria. For example, using the students' marks alone was limiting, because it was not clear what they were indicators of, or for what they were proxies. Indeed Hargreaves and Shirley (2009: 91) argue for 'multiple indicators' to move beyond simply test scores. It is important to select carefully the indicators of success, and not to exaggerate or over-infer what they do or do not show. This is a matter of validity: ensuring that the indicators genuinely indicate what they should be indicating.

In the example here, the innovation included a range of areas: collaborative, active and interactive teaching and learning; ICT usage and development; student motivation; improvements to students' behaviour and attitude; engaged learning; student achievement and performance; student assessment; and parental communication. To use students' marks solely or largely as an indicator of success here is to misrepresent the complexity and multidimensionality of the innovation. The school principal was very aware that parents and students would be concerned with outward signs of an innovation, not least the students' marks in this mark-oriented culture. However, he made it very clear to all parties that marks alone were insufficient indicators of success. Indeed, it became clear that a range of indicators was needed and that some of these would be more of a qualitative than a quantitative nature and more intangible than tangible (e.g. motivation, attitude, behaviour, enjoyment, interest).

Further, it became clear that timing of the use of the indicators of success was to be a significant issue, and that to expect too many significant changes in the first year alone, for example to students' marks, might be hasty and premature.

- Ensure true causality.

In a multiple innovation it is often difficult to separate out the causes of an effect or the effect of a cause (Morrison 2009). It is the same as if I were to take five different tablets to cure a headache: my headache goes but I am unsure which tablet(s) had brought about the cure, whether it was the interaction of these tablets, some or all of them acting together, or, indeed, whether the tablets had had no effect at all, and my cure was on account of other factors, not least, for example, the headache reducing of its own accord. This is the same criticism as has been advanced against some forms of Total Quality Management (e.g. Bank 1992); namely, that they instigated many new interventions but it was impossible to see which interventions had brought about which improvements.

It is important to be clear on whether changes are on account of the innovation itself or to other factors acting on the situation, and this means establishing controls in the data collection. For example, in the evaluation reported here, the evaluators had conducted an experiment with random allocation of students to pilot and control groups, and several controls had been put into place so that it would be possible to suggest with some certainty that changes were because of the intervention and not from other factors. Similarly, the statistics used in the data processing and analysis included controlling for several variables in the data analysis.

Attention to causality is also a matter of ensuring that correct inferences are made. For example, at round three it was found that high-performing students in F4, in English, had improved dramatically in comparison to their control-group counterparts. However, it is unclear what might have been the cause of this. Was it, for example, an enthusiastic teacher, classroom pedagogic practices, out-of-class work on English, attendance at a private tutorial centre, strong student motivation, parental pressure, sudden maturation in the students, the subject matter of the lessons, the ICT usage, a realization that English was important in the non-English speaking environment, peer pressure in that group of high performers, the looming examinations, or what? The familiar concern that correlation does not equal causation applies strongly here.

Similarly, at round three of the evaluation it was found that the motivation of some of the low-achieving students had not really improved, but this does not necessarily indicate that the innovation was not working well for them as their motivation might have been even worse without the innovation (and, indeed, for the control groups there was some evidence that the motivation of the lowest-performing students had reduced over the year). This is the counterfactual argument for causality (Morrison 2009).

For managing multidimensional innovation, careful attention must be paid to establishing clear success criteria: the indicators of different aspects of the innovation and their success, together with explicit statements of what evidence will be used to inform those indicators, how controls will be placed on the variables to ensure that inferences of causality are legitimate, how to rule out other possible causes, and how to establish the link between cause and effect, or, in reverse, between effects and cause.

It is all too easy to suggest that an innovation is or is not working, or to rely too heavily on perception and opinion alone, as opinions and human judgement can be biased and fallacious, even to the extent of ignoring evidence (Kahneman 2011).

- Act on feedback, evaluation and review.

Complexity theory places great store on *feedback*, which must occur between the interacting elements of the system (Waldrop 1992; Cilliers 1998). Feedback is essential if the system and an innovation are to be in step with themselves, each other and their environment (Marion 1999: 74–5).

Positive feedback uses information not merely to regulate but to change, grow and develop (Wheatley 1999: 78). It amplifies small changes (Stacey 1992: 53; Youngblood 1997: 54). Senge *et al.* (2000: 84) cite the example of a baby animal whose eating is voracious, and the more it eats, the faster it grows; its rate of growth accelerates. Once a child has begun to read she is gripped by reading, she reads more and learns at an exponential rate.

Not only can feedback be positive, it also needs to be rich. If I simply award a grade to a student's work then she cannot learn much from it except that she is a success or a failure, or somewhere in between. If, on the other hand, I provide rich feedback then she can learn more. If I only point out two matters in my feedback then the student might only learn those two matters, if I point out 10 matters then the student might learn 10 matters. We have to recall that the root of 'feedback' is 'food': nourishment rather than simply information.

Feedback must be evidence-based, with objective, neutral, unbiased, comprehensive and honest data (e.g. Goffin *et al.* 2010). In the case here, the school had brought in external evaluators to conduct an ongoing in-depth evaluation of the pilot innovation. The evaluators collected data in three rounds: at the start, the middle and the end of the pilot project. At three time points, the evaluators provided the school with oral and detailed written reports, reporting not only to the school but also to parents and the local government education authority, both formally and less formally. Such reporting ensured that the school could take immediate action to address setbacks and challenges, and, indeed, the school acted on the contents of the reports quickly and decisively.

The evaluators were neutral and disinterested, providing as accurate, honest and detailed a set of reports as possible, even if the some of their news did not make for easy reading. In an age of evidence-based education and pressure to know 'what works', the evaluators were able to feed into the school's ongoing decision-making on the innovation. This is particularly important, given that, as complexity theory tells us, complex adaptive systems such as schools are dynamical, with innovations operating often in unpredictable, non-linear ways.

At issue here is the need not only for detailed, accurate and unbiased data, but for these data to be timely and on an ongoing basis, to match the evolutionary nature of the innovation. Schools need to be continuously reviewing the innovation and updating themselves on what is happening, so that decisions are data-driven. Ongoing debriefing, sharing and review are essential elements of an ongoing innovation and these should be evidence-based.

As mentioned in earlier chapters, the Concerns Based Action Model of innovation from Hall *et al.* (1986) and Hall and Hord (1987, 2011) was used to inform some of the focus of the data collection. The progress of the innovation conformed to a common trajectory of measured concerns, from high concern in the earliest stages of the innovation being 'awareness', 'information' and 'personal' concerns, to high concerns in the middle stages of the innovation being 'management' and 'consequence' (to the students') issues, and on to a high concern for 'collaboration' in the later stages of the innovation. These also matched the Levels of Use of the innovation (Hall and Hord 1987, 2011), from 'non-use' to 'orientation' and 'preparation' in the early stages, to 'mechanical' use and 'routine' use in the middle stage, to 'integration' (into the everyday operations of the school/curriculum) and 'refinement' at the later stage.

At issue here is the importance of conducting reviews, monitoring and collecting data so that the innovation and its component parts are kept on track, and so that, if parts of it are veering too far off track, or if parts of it are proceeding out of step with other parts (e.g. some parts going too fast or too slow, or a lack of integration of the dimensions of the multidimensional innovation), then steps can be taken to intervene in a timely fashion.

- Make workloads sustainable.

A recurrent theme across all three rounds of the evaluation was the workload, or, often, overload on the teachers involved in the innovation. They spent hours in school and out of school on their school work, giving of their time plentifully and selflessly throughout the project. Indeed, the evaluators repeatedly indicated that, whilst there was massive goodwill on the part of the teachers here, their effort was not sustainable in the longer term. Further, the time that teachers were spending was on preparing materials and teaching sessions, rather than, for example, reflection, review and pedagogy. If reflective practice was required, then time for reflection and review was essential. Whilst innovation typically increases workload (Morrison 1998), the issue for leaders is to ensure that reasonable demands are made on participants and that there is time for review and reflection in order to promote personal learning and planning.

Winsor (2012) observes that workloads are closely related to time pressures and that timing matters can 'stifle' rather than 'enhance' an innovation; time pressure can be detrimental to an innovation. He argues that managers have to pay great attention to time issues: what time is available and what pressures time will bring on participants. He indicates that managers must take steps to reduce undue time pressures on people, including providing for some slack time ('down time') in pressured environments.

- The agenda is changing the school culture.

If the school is to be a learning organization, then it requires data, advice and an ability to learn, not only on the part of the students, but also on the part of all participants (e.g. Senge *et al*. 2000; Morrison 2002a; Senge 2012). A cultural change is needed, and, indeed, Tan (2010: 894) notes that cultural and structural features and characteristics of a school might exert an effect on the nature and level of ICT usage in classrooms.

In the school in question, the heart of the innovation was shifting the culture of the school from a hierarchical organization with teachers working in relative isolation from each other to a collaborative culture of openness, trust, sharing (including sharing of power), cooperation, distributed leadership and shared responsibility, and from a culture of the teacher as didact and expert to the culture of the teacher as facilitator and collaborator in learning. This involved changing practices, mindsets, values, norms and behaviours at institutional, departmental and individual levels: in short, becoming a 'professional learning community' (Hall and Hord 2011). Indeed, the long lever of change – the twin concerns for ICT and pedagogy – was a way of opening up the school to its participants, so that, at all levels and in all spheres, the school would be open to itself and its members (cf. Dalin *et al*. 1993; Hall and Hord 2011).

It is delusional to think that changes in one area of a school will not impact on another; in this instance, that changes in pedagogy would not impact on changes in personal practices, behaviour, attitudes and emotions, ways of working together, the tasks that teachers and students undertake, leadership tasks and roles, relations with parents, and so on. In a multidimensional innovation it is important to recognize that the dimensions of the innovation are linked, and that, together, they constitute an important contributor to the school culture. Organizational culture – be it at a superficial level of artefacts and practices, or a deeper level of espoused values and behaviours (see Figure 6.3), or the deepest levels of underlying assumptions (e.g. Deal and Kennedy

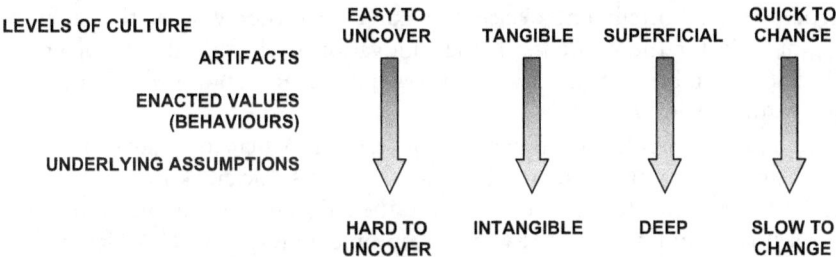

Figure 6.3 Levels of organizational culture

1982; Schein 1992; Ashkanasy *et al.* 2000) – is the real target of change, and, in the school in question here, this was frequently alluded to by the teachers and senior officers of the school.

Further, initiating and supporting the development of a changing school culture is a heavy responsibility for the leaders of the school (Dalin *et al.* 1993; Morrison 1998, 2002; Sharma 2001; Hall and Hord 2011), focusing on values, people, tasks, relationships, communication, roles and responsibilities, open and mutual accountability and fostering commitment and involvement of staff, leading the innovation by example, self-evaluation and self-involvement of the leaders (e.g. Menter *et al.* 2010).

- Ensure ongoing support and development.

A recurrent refrain of all parties in the school was the need for initial and ongoing training and professional development. Indeed, though the school provided some, and by the time round three of the evaluation had been completed it had made two appointments to provide staff development and support, the need for more support and development, particularly in pedagogical matters in the school, was repeatedly alluded to by many participants in the innovation. It is commonplace to read of the significance of capacity training, support and development (e.g. Bessant *et al.* 1996; Burnes 2005; Hall and Hord 2011; Senge 2012), and, indeed, Bessant *et al.* (1996) argue that the provision of support builds trustworthiness, benevolence and integrity.

In short, the provision of professional development is a 'game changer'; without it, the extent of innovation is under threat. In the school here, it was not only in terms of ICT training – and there is plentiful evidence to support the view that ICT training is a key requisite for effective usage in schools (e.g. Mumtaz 2000; O'Mahony 2003; Webb and Cox 2004; Zandvliet and Fraser 2004; ICT Cluster 2010; Light 2010; Tan 2010; Sang *et al.* 2011; Education, Audiovisual and Culture Executive Agency 2011) – but also in many other spheres, e.g. pedagogical change.

Barnes and Soken (2012) indicate that innovation capability focuses on leadership that enables people to focus, deep competency development within a facilitative culture and active learning, enabling structures and processes and intelligent decision making. In other words, the support is not only for the contents of the innovation itself, but also to promote the most suitable conditions, structures, people and contexts in which the innovation is embedded.

At a practical level, the immediate concerns of participants may be for 'survival' in the new world of the innovation, with sufficient knowledge, skills and competencies to be able to handle the substance of the innovation (in the school in question here it was, for example, in terms of ICT-related matters, pedagogical matters and assessment issues). What became clear was that capacity and capability training needed to both precede and continue in parallel with the innovation. Start-up training is necessary for innovation readiness, but on its own it is insufficient, as real needs emerge over time and they need to be handled both in advance of, and whilst, they are occurring.

- Use action planning.

Action planning concerns the more systematic approach to planning and implementation, identifying preparation, routes and destinations, but, importantly, how to evaluate the achievement of these (Hargreaves and Hopkins 1991: 54–5). In action planning, the authors state that it is important to commence by identifying *destinations, target* and *success criteria*, then *routes* and *tasks*, then *preparations*. These then roll out in reverse order: the implementation activities start with preparations (initial tasks), requiring 'checks for readiness', then move on to routes (tasks), requiring checks on progress, and then to destinations, checking for success against achievement of targets and in line with pre-specified success criteria. Action planning is useful for innovation planning, monitoring and evaluation. In planning an innovation, the ethics of education require schools to ensure that students and teachers are protected from any negative fallout from an innovation, and this requires evidence-based ongoing monitoring and review of the innovation. Importantly, at every stage (preparation, routes and destinations), evaluation and review are built into the process, ensuring that the innovation is kept on track. This requires schools to establish their *targets, tasks, indicators* of success, *success criteria* for making judgements based on their indicators, and the *evidence* needed to inform the success indicators and criteria.

In operating the action plan, the intention is to chart the congruence between what was intended to happen and what actually happens (Hall and Hord (2011) term this 'innovation configuration'). This echoes Stake's (1967) 'countenance' model of evaluation (see Figure 6.4) in which evaluators seek to find the distance or congruence between: intended and actual *antecedents* (what was planned to be and what was actually present at the start of the innovation); *transactions* (what was intended to happen and what actually happened); and *outcomes* (what were intended to be the outcomes and what actually turned out to be the outcomes); and the reasons for the congruence or its lack.

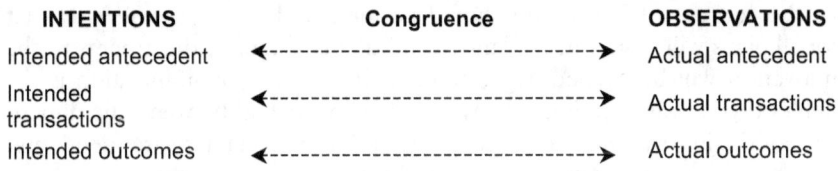

Figure 6.4 Stake's countenance model of evaluation

Action plans guide and steer. Given the unpredictable natures of many aspects of an innovation, they may be more helpful in indicating directions, end points and main routes, keeping an innovation on track, rather than prescribing closely detailed operations (as these may change as the innovation unfolds).

- Regard schools as complex adaptive systems.

Multidimensional innovation is complex and it is important to recognize that such innovation is set within a context of schools as complex adaptive systems (Morrison 2002, 2010) inasmuch as:

- They require organization and have distinguishing structures and features that change over time;
- They are dynamical and unpredictable organizations;
- They are non-linear, self-organizing organizations: causes do not always straightforwardly produce effects and it is difficult to infer causes from effects or outcomes;
- Small or large changes can have massive, large, little or no effect;
- They are complex, complicated and constantly changing;
- They are a human service and rely on people;
- Relationships are highly important in their work;
- They have to adapt in response to macro-and micro-societal change;
- The environments (external and internal) in which they operate are often changing and, indeed, unpredictable;
- They have to maintain 'relative autonomy' from the wider society, i.e. they have to position themselves in relation to the wider society, deciding where they wish to be in relation to the wider society (e.g. Cilliers 1998: 99);
- They have a range of methods of communication and rely on communication and effective networking;
- The synergy of their several parts is greater than any individual or combination of individuals;
- New properties emerge at every level of the organization (Lissack 2000: 8);
- They are learning organizations;
- They have a proclivity to instability and operate at the 'edge of chaos'.

The sequiturs to this for leading and managing innovation are that: (a) plans for the content of innovation should be tempered by the recognition that not all plans will work out as planned and that constant readjustments to the innovation will be needed; (b) internal and external communication is the lifeblood of the innovation – between participants and between the dimensions of the innovation; and (c) creativity and unpredictability are friends and opportunities, respectively, rather than threats and weaknesses.

Conclusion

Whilst many challenges that had presented themselves at round two of the innovation had been addressed by the time of round three, new and ongoing challenges emerged, and lessons from this have been drawn for the leadership and management of multidimensional innovation. The chapter has not only indicated the emergent complexity of the innovation, but has also indicated how these could not have been anticipated or prefigured. This, it was suggested, conforms closely to several canons of complexity theory, with its emphases on emergence through self-organization, unpredictability, connectedness and feedback. Further, the chapter indicated that, rather than proscribing leadership and authority within self-organization, the effectiveness of the innovation here fed from and, indeed, required strong leadership in order to navigate and hold the innovation on course despite storms and setbacks (e.g. Stacey 2000, 2001, 2012; Stacey *et al.* 2000). Schools as 'complex adaptive systems' require 'complex responsive processes' (Stacey 2000, 2012) in order to navigate change, and these are premised on the creativity, commitment, sheer hard work, and loyalty of the participants, supported by leadership and the provision of training and development.

The differentiated way in which the innovation was proceeding, with outcomes varying by subject, teacher, students, age and so on, suggests setting realistic expectations of what can be achieved, and, indeed, it has suggested that it is natural to expect a non-uniform, pluralistic and differentiated innovation to emerge. Imagine throwing a bucket of water: the water comes out of the bucket in a single sheet at first but then it disperses, breaking down into different drops and groups of drops and going in many slightly different directions before hitting the ground at different moments. So it is with multidimensional innovations. The innovation starts with the dimensions together, but they rapidly group, regroup and disperse in different ways and in different directions and touch the ground at different times. There is an overall direction and the same end point (like the water hitting the ground) but different ways of reaching it, at different speeds and following different trajectories.

The chapter has stressed the need for the provision of frequent impartial evidence and feedback in informing change and the need for review and tenacity in adhering to the central features of the innovation. In advocating the importance of evidence-based review and ongoing forward planning, the chapter has expressed the need to select appropriate indicators of the different dimensions of the innovation, the need to establish success criteria and to pay careful attention to establishing causal links between what is observed and what is attributable to the innovation. Action planning has been mentioned here as an instance of how to proceed in planning and review.

Further, the chapter has indicated the importance of establishing cognitive, people-related, task-related, content-related, concept-related and practice-related connections between different dimensions of the multidimensional innovation. These connections need to be built into the planning and implementation stages, ensuring congruence between what is intended to happen and what actually happens. When undertaken collaboratively, this builds schools as professional learning communities (Hargreaves and Shirley 2009; Hall and Hord 2011).

Critical factors in the innovation here were the importance of timing of different dimensions and stages of the innovation, workloads, ongoing support, capacity building and development activities. Whilst these are familiar matters in managing innovation, they are no less important for that. Further, the chapter emphasized that the real target of change was the culture of the school, but that, given that this was a deep-seated issue, it would require attention at several different levels and over time.

What emerges from the chapter is the ongoing central importance of effective leadership, in terms of both positional power and distributed leadership, and this requires leaders to have enormous reserves of single-mindedness, tenacity and a firm grip on the essentials of the innovation.

7 Postscript and lessons learned

By the time the pilot evaluation had been completed, the school was already preparing for the entire project to be rolled out over the course of the following three years to the entire school from P4 upwards, and across all the subjects of the school curriculum. In the first of these three years the project would be extended to all the subjects and all the new classes of P4, F1 and F4, which, when repeated in the second and third year, would mean that all the students from P4 upwards would be involved in the project. This would see the project grow from involving just over 100 students and six front-line teachers to over 1,500 students and some 60 teachers.

One year after the pilot evaluation had ended, the continuing story had unfolded in a way that, in many respects, mirrored the pilot evaluation. Even though the school had clearly learned a lot from the pilot, nevertheless when the full project was rolled out some similar challenges arose. For example, in the first semester of the new school year, the U-curve of innovation had been experienced across both primary and secondary school sections of the school, but particularly strongly in the secondary sector. Here, the staff had demonstrated some resistance to the extended use of ICT and the changing pedagogies required, and, indeed, had not been putting these into practice. At first, despite the best efforts of the school, many students had treated the tablet non-seriously, as a source of Internet games rather than as a tool for learning. Some students' marks had fallen and, perhaps naturally, in this marks-oriented culture, parents and students were very concerned. As in the pilot project, the senior staff of the school, very aware of this, took strong interventionist action, calling staff together and making it explicitly clear that not putting the project into action was not an option. Further, the school had put into practice a stringent policy to dissuade students from using the tablets for non-school-related matters in class. Further, the school convened more meetings with the parents to explain that the 'implementation dip' (Fullan 2013) was natural in a project of this kind and that it was expected that the project would improve and student performance would rise. Indeed, by the end of the second semester this had come true.

In other words, when threats to the project were posed, the senior staff intervened strongly, visibly and tenaciously. By this time the senior staff comprised not only the principal and vice-principals, but leadership was also distributed to the heads of curriculum and ICT, together with subject heads. This united front insisting that the project would proceed uninterrupted was sufficient to overcome the U-curve, and, indeed, served to reinforce the positional authority of these distributed leaders.

Further, following the whole staff meeting at which it was made clear that there could be and would be no opting out of the project, an additional extended programme of support and development was put into place with ongoing in-class support, external training in active and interactive pedagogies from an outside university (different from that of the evaluators), collaborative peer-group planning, review and sharing and more widespread involvement of the two teachers who had been appointed to develop the required pedagogies with and without ICT. In other words, an essential element of effective innovation, which had only been embryonic in the pilot project by virtue of its limited scope and number of teachers involved, was now firmly installed and working: the development of a professional learning community (Hall and Hord 2011) marked by collegiality and openness.

Alongside this, much clearer statements of required classroom processes had been put into place and were operating. These covered: guideline time allowances and proportions of each lesson for didactic/instructional sections and deliberate active, interactive and group work in class sessions, together with greater guidance on how to assess class participation.

In the pilot project, considerable time and effort had been spent on securing copyright agreements from reluctant, money-hungry publishers for materials, texts and resources to be stored on tablets. Now, the situation had changed and the publishers were much more cooperative and keen to support the project, offering discounts on materials. It was suggested that obtaining the formal, public support and imprimatur from the local government had been instrumental in this.

The students who came into the whole project liked using the tablets. Teething troubles with the hardware and software in the first semester had been resolved, and the scheduling of lessons which did and did not use the tablets had been planned carefully to provide variety in the lessons and to enable students to charge up their tablets at school during the day.

The high-profile intervention by the leaders to reinforce the non-optional requirements of the innovation indicates that the self-organization of complexity theory does not mean an abandonment of strong leadership or the promulgation of a laissez-faire, do-as-you-like school culture, or an anarchistic approach to decision making. Rather, self-organization can require tough, determined, resolute, persistent and staunch collective leadership to ensure adherence to the key principles and practices of an innovation, even in the face of resistance. Simply handing over responsibility to poorly prepared teachers can be a recipe for inertia. As Schein (1992: 15) remarked, if leaders do not manage the culture then the culture will manage them.

Further, the same intervention by the leaders signalled unequivocally that the school was setting the innovation as a key feature of its identity. This addresses a double key feature of complexity theory, which is that the organism is autocatalytic and develops identifying characteristics and identity to fit a niche in its environment through feedback and self-organization in response to such feedback. In other words, the school was a learning organization, and its learning led to change. As Hall and Hord (2011: 6) remark, 'change is learning'.

One year after the end of the pilot, and into the major part of the project, it was observed that student motivation had risen, their attitude to learning had improved and they were much more involved and engaged in the class lessons (not least because they knew that marks were awarded for class participation and, in this marks-driven culture outside the school (particularly by parents), this was harnessed to positive effect by the school). The dip in marks at the end of the first semester had given way to a clear rise in students' marks; parental negative concern had given way to positive support; teachers working in relative isolation had given way to teachers working together collegially and collaboratively in both planned and unplanned ways, sharing ideas, planning together, learning together and sharing resources and lesson ideas; and teachers were planning pedagogically rather than focusing only, or largely, on content (the change of heart by publishers was important here, as was the sharing of planning by teachers).

Teachers themselves were becoming the change agents, rather than relying on others. Clearly, the long lever of innovation had reached into the heart of the school culture and practice. Whilst it was recognized by the school that this was still 'early days' and that the full embeddedness of the project in the school could take another three or four years, nevertheless it was clear that the portents were very positive here.

Further, it had been noted at the end of the one-year pilot project that expectations of the extent of some of the changes to be wrought by the project had changed (e.g. that the school had been perhaps over-optimistic in expecting parents to use the tablets for communication and increased parental involvement, and the submission and marking of tests/exams online had given way to online submission for some rather than all tests/exams).

It became very clear that, by the end of the first year of the full implementation of the project, there was a close congruence between what had been planned to happen and what was actually happening. In terms of the Levels of Use and Stages of Concern of Hall and Hord (2011), the teachers, en masse, had moved quickly from the early 'informational', 'personal' and 'management' concerns to 'consequences' and 'collaboration' (2011: 73), and their levels of use had moved rapidly from preparation ('non-use' and 'orientation') to the levels of 'routine' (stable use) and 'refinement' (making changes to fit learners' needs) (2011: 94). The teachers had moved from 'assimilation' (specific pedagogical changes without interrupting the whole picture of the school) to 'transition' (ICT integrated with ongoing changes) to system-wide 'transformation' of practices and culture (Mioduser *et al.* 2004).

Lessons learned

This book has argued that innovation is multidimensional. Positively speaking, this renders it a fascinating and creative act; negatively speaking, innovation is the Hydra of Greek mythology. This section collates and summarizes the lessons learned throughout the book about planning and implementing complex innovation. In keeping with this, drawing together the several messages of the book is an essentially multidimensional task, and this is reflected in the different sections below.

Leadership

The critical factor in effective multidimensional innovation is leadership. Multidimensional innovation requires multidimensional leadership. Leadership is critical, it is the key here; it can unlock or lock innovation. The book has made repeated references to leadership, and from these can be drawn some key lessons for leadership. The book has identified several characteristics of effective leaders here, summarized in a list of powerful adjectives: leaders must be strong, confident, tenacious, single-minded, unwavering, informed, resolute, steadfast, unswerving, deliberative, deliberate, determined, dogged, proactive, decisive, resilient, clear-headed, personable, intelligent, empathic yet sometimes distant. Leaders must have a sense of balance, balancing hands-on and hands-off leadership (indeed developing and using distributed leadership) and balancing impatience with patience. Leaders must be ahead of followers, but not leave them behind, i.e. they must be connected to their followers rather than being out of sight of followers. Effective leaders combine authority and democracy in innovations, energize participants by their example and practice, have a clear vision – one that illuminates rather than blinds (Hargreaves 1994) – and develop people to meet that vision (a key feature of transformational leadership).

Leaders have a responsibility to address the 'people factor' of the innovation (discussed below) by recognizing that clear role articulation and devolution are important in an innovation, keeping up forward momentum and pressure, providing the infrastructure of support and setting and nurturing the conditions for change. They have a duty to make the innovation irresistible – attractive and unavoidable – and this may mean mandating change in order to break inertia and stagnation, whilst balancing pressure with support.

Leaders must 'practise what they preach': if they want ownership and commitment from staff then they must demonstrate their own visible and practical commitment to the innovation, supporting risk taking and experimentation (a culture of 'no blame' if genuine attempts have been made to implement the innovation) and learning from these. As trust and commitment are key elements of successful, sustainable innovations, so the leader must demonstrate these in her/his leadership. This involves having a view of leadership as not simply gatekeeping and directing but enabling and empowering.

Whilst a school principal is usually the named leader of the school, others, too, are leaders, and the task is to ensure the commitment and alignment of that commitment from the senior staff and leaders of the innovation. Leaders of the institution and of the innovation must be clear and united in their views and intentions of the innovation, and not easily swayed or put off by others. However, they must also be open to the views of others, and be prepared to modify their own views if persuaded by others and by evidence, and this means that leaders of the innovation must recognize that not everyone shares their views, and they need to decide how to handle this.

In their own behaviour, leaders of the institution and of the innovation must recognize that not only are they the ones to bring the dimensions of innovation into coherency, but so do participants, and they must work with, rather than against, participants. If they say that they value collegiality then they are part of it. In terms of working with colleagues, leaders must ensure the safety aspect of innovations – the cognitive, affective and psychological aspects of participants in the innovation – and they should consider the wisdom of not disclosing the full picture of the innovation at the start of the innovation in order to avoid overload and anxiety of participants, and they should avoid making promises that they cannot or might not be able to keep.

In terms of working with innovation, leaders' roles change at different times and stages of an innovation, and with reference to different dimensions of, parties involved in and emergent exigencies of the innovation. They must keep their fingers on the pulse of the innovation, working on all the dimensions of the innovation and the system (Hall and Hord 2011: 194), and, indeed, must expect the U-curve of innovation, and be prepared for how to handle it with different parties. When difficulties and setbacks occur, they must keep a firm eye on possibilities rather than be fixated on obstacles, be positive about the innovation and convey this to relevant parties, energizing all parties.

Learning from complexity theory, leaders of the innovation must keep sight of the long term vision and direction, but recognize that planning and implementation are better achieved through a series of shorter ever-changing steps as unanticipated matters arise and situations evolve.

Core purposes

It is essential to eliminate non-essentials in the innovation, to have clear goals and identifiable outcomes, to focus on a small number of ambitious goals and make them cohere and connect. These are the core purposes and priorities of the innovation, and it is vital to identify, expose and stick to these through thick and thin, making clear what will and will not be conceded as the change unfolds. Keeping to a small number of core, visible priorities, purposes and strategies, and combining these with managing the contents, people, capacity building, collaboration, processes, resources and dimensions of change contained within these simple purposes, is more effective than trying to change everything by a single innovation. Communication is critical, and it is essential to make the purposes of the innovation explicit to all parties, and constantly reinforce the messages of the innovation to key participants and relevant parties.

Innovation planning and preparation

There are several stages to an innovation, from its initial conception, to its planning, preparation, commencement, implementation, outcomes, renewal and refinement. A watchword for effective innovation is 'prepare, prepare, prepare, but be ready to change your plans once the innovation commences'. It is essential to plan how to identify the need for the innovation, how to introduce the innovation to all participants, how to prepare for its commencement, what the initial intervention will be to start the innovation in practice, what will happen at each stage of the innovation, how to know whether the innovation is working (success criteria) and on track, and how to be prepared for the innovation to change as needs arise. Further, it is important to accept that innovations typically do not go according to plan and that, whilst it is necessary to plan for the long term, participants must be prepared to change the short-term plans as different situations and exigencies of the moment arise.

In terms of planning and preparation, several features of multidimensional innovation come to the fore. Initially, there is a recognition that much change is incremental, evolutionary and piecemeal, as well as wholesale, even if that is not what is intended. It is important to ensure that the innovation addresses real needs, challenges and problems in the institution and that it brings demonstrable relative advantage over existing practice. If an innovation can identify a project that addresses the underlying causes of a need or a problem, in a single, multidimensional project, then this brings a sense of reality to the innovation, i.e. it is not simply innovation for innovation's sake. The corollary of this is the recognition that innovation is system-disturbing, relationship-disturbing, practice-disturbing, power-disturbing, values-disturbing, people-disturbing, persona-disturbing and leadership-disturbing, i.e. innovation is often fundamental rather than superficial. Hence, it is important to attend in detail to setting and sustaining the conditions for change; these are essential targets and requirements of an innovation.

A situational analysis and needs analysis are essential, yet different. The former is diagnostic and descriptive whilst the latter concerns turning a diagnosis into action: what are the needs in the school and what needs to be done to address them? Here action planning is helpful, clarifying the targets, routes to the targets, initial tasks and success criteria for each stage of the innovation. In planning the innovation, it is useful to identify levers of change, i.e. those specific interventions that can bring about large-scale change and which can have multiple, connected effects.

Focusing on 'chalk-face' problems can enhance teachers' motivation for involvement in an innovation, even in the face of apprehension, though it is important to recognize that 'chalk-face' problems may disguise central and deep-seated areas of school work and that it is these that require change. As argued below, changing the school culture is often the real agenda.

In planning the innovation, clarity and communication are essential. It is obvious to the point of being a platitude to note the importance of ensuring that all the ingredients for the success of the innovation are in place and that all the resources are in place to support the innovation, e.g. human expertise, equipment, finance, time, space, materials, administration, leadership and management. Nevertheless, this might not always be the case in practice, for reasons outside the control of the school (as in the school here), so it is important to have a back-up plan for when some of the ingredients are not assured. It is crucial to plan steps to take to prevent failure or negative aspects of key parts of the innovation and its consequences.

People are often the central ingredients of the innovation, and several sections below reinforce this. In planning for an innovation, it is wise to identify and clarify the roles, tasks and responsibilities of all parties in the innovation (including the leaders) to identify where and on whom the innovation is likely to make the most impact; to consider the workloads and how to keep increased workloads reasonable and manageable; to identify where overload might occur and to plan how to avoid or reduce it. Appreciation of staff is not enough; they need concrete support and steps must be taken to avoid placing an unsustainable workload on their shoulders. Further, whilst innovation requires information from multiple sources, both internal and external, a judicious balance has to be struck between necessary information and information overload.

Not all staff will necessarily agree with the innovation, for a variety of reasons (discussed below), and there is a difference between alignment of, and support from, staff. Hence, it is important to attend to their views, being realistic in identifying problems and the limits of support in introducing an innovation. It is also crucial to plan how to prepare the ground for those coming into the project later (e.g. after a pilot or as the innovation unfolds over time, involving more and more people).

Innovation success is not only due to people but also to the organizational features of the institution. Here is it necessary for innovation planners to consider how the structure of the school promotes, enables, inhibits and, indeed, obstructs the innovation, and this is addressed below (see: Organizational culture, climate and collegiality).

Multidimensional innovation

In planning, implementing and evaluating the innovation, this book has underlined the multidimensionality of innovation. Innovation is inherently multidimensional and it is essential to identify the key dimensions of the innovation and their key characteristics, e.g. size, scope, depth, scale, process, timing, participants, structure, networks, connections, leadership, management, capacity, etc.). Further, in planning the innovation, it is imperative to ensure that multidimensional innovations are fit for purpose.

Given the multidimensional nature of innovations, it should be regarded as requisite to ensure: (a) that links between the dimensions of the innovation are visible, clear and concrete; (b) coherence and coordination between the different dimensions of the innovation (cf. Hall and Hord 2011: 198); (c) connectedness of the different dimensions of the innovation, both internal and external; (d) suitable alignment between the dimensions; (e) that each dimension of the innovation receives adequate initial preparation before being joined with another dimension. This means that innovation planners must establish what the links are between an innovation's different dimensions, how they are understood and addressed in the minds and practices of the participants and how they will be developed and addressed in practice: 'joined-up thinking'. Then comes the task of planning how to establish and make clear, visible and practical the connections between the different dimensions of the innovation – contents, people, processes, resources – and work with their synergistic power. Interconnectedness of the dimensions of an innovation – participants, people, internal and external environments (however defined) – are central features of effective innovation. Hence, it is useful to plan for synergies between the different parts of the innovation, so that they support and potentiate each other. It is dangerous to focus on some dimensions to the neglect of others; rather, planners should work on them all simultaneously and as priorities dictate.

As dimensions of innovation become integrated, so greater preparation and staff development have to be provided in how to integrate these, with concrete examples and support. Further, inside each person is a multidimensional view of the innovation, and so it is essential that the integration and connectedness of the dimension of an innovation is not simply that which is written down in a plan but also that which is actually taking place in the minds of the participants – they must be able to see and embody the links.

Links may be in terms of content, people, power and responsibility, strategies for implementation, and so on. Indeed, one task of planners is to identify the nature of the links, identifying the nodes (what and who) connecting the different dimensions of the innovation and the strongest and weakest links in connecting the dimensions. From there, a strategy can be developed for introducing the different dimensions of the innovation over time.

Starting, continuing and seeing the outcomes of the innovation

Having developed an overall plan of the multidimensional innovation, it is crucial to ensure adequate start-up development and resources, to set the conditions for the start of the innovation, to make the innovation visible, clear and concrete. This means having a deliberate, clear, visible intervention, event or activity to start the innovation moving. It is also important to recognize that there is no perfect time to start an innovation, but let not the perfect stand in the way of the good, and so a propitious time – 'good enough' – rather than a perfect time might be the order of the day. Further, it is wise to expect the innovation not to commence as intended, as a range of unanticipated factors might suddenly come into play which affect the start of the intervention.

It is critical that solid foundations for the innovation are in place before moving on. These include, for example: core purposes, roles, tasks and responsibilities; planning and preparation; resources (many kinds); conditions and contexts of the innovation; organizational culture, climate and health; people and expertise; professional development; leadership and management matters; alignment of all parties and aspects of the innovation, and so on. It is important to ensure that the intended outcomes and tangible benefits of the project are made explicit to all parties.

Then, as the innovation proceeds, the lessons from this book are perhaps unsettling, as they suggest that it is unwise to expect the innovation to unfold as intended or to go to plan. The playwright, Harold Pinter, when asked what his plays were about, jokingly remarked that they concerned 'the weasel under the cocktail cabinet', i.e. that underneath routine everyday behaviour lurks menace, threat, strong feelings and the unexpected. Though he was dismissive of his own remark, nevertheless it has some truth in considering innovation: things happen which throw plans off course, upset participants, arise unexpectedly and threaten the innovation. This may be, for example, because of unanticipated events arising, or because original intentions may turn out to be more complex than originally foreseen, or because the innovation is affected by many other variables operating on the situation at the same time.

The argument in the preceding chapters has underlined the wisdom of identifying a few simple rules that can keep the innovation on track, sticking to them and recognizing that being both proactive and reactive are key processes of an innovation. Innovation is a constant negotiation rather than the simple putting into practice of a blueprint for what has been planned to happen.

Just as the central message of innovation processes is not to expect things to work out as initially planned, the same is true for outcomes of an innovation: it is unwise to expect the outcomes of the innovation to be the same as those intended. Gap analysis to identify the distance or congruence between what was intended and what actually happened was argued to be central in 'innovation configurations' (Hall and Hord 2011) and Stake's (1967) countenance model of evaluation, both introduced in Chapter 6. As complexity theory tells us, the self-organized, autocatalytic, emergent situation is usually different from the original plan.

Outcomes of innovation can be both positive and negative. In a multidimensional project they may not to be unequivocal and uniform, and results in some dimensions may not be consistent across or within target groups in an innovation and its several dimensions. This message is perhaps as uncomfortable as it is true.

Timing and the rate of change

The innovation that was reported in the preceding chapters of this book noted that the evaluators commented to the school that it was perhaps too soon for all the effects of the innovation to have manifested themselves. This teaches an important lesson: to be realistic in considering the time dimension and not to expect all the benefits of the project to reveal themselves immediately. Rather, it is important to consolidate, and allow time for, the innovation to 'sink in' to the minds and practices of participants, to expect change to be incremental rather than wholesale, and to expect differentiated development and at different rates. Judging the success or failure of an innovation is time-sensitive, so it is essential to pay careful attention to the timing of judgements made.

Further, practices often change before values and beliefs, hence it is good counsel to assume that old habits will change only slowly; indeed, participants may wish to, or try to, graft new practices onto old rather than to replace old habits. The recognition that time (years rather than months) may be required for an innovation to really become bedded down in a school raises the need to maintain momentum in the innovation, i.e. to sustain innovation in the face of stagnation. Hargreaves and Shirley (2009) and Hall and Hord (2011) suggest that developing professional communities is one means for this, which promotes collegiality and the learning organization. These authors accord great significance to the culture of the school, and the next section turns to this.

Organizational culture, climate and collegiality

Earlier chapters have discussed organizational culture, health and climate. Here the intention is to underline their significance in ensuring the success of the innovation. Indeed, Chapter 6 remarked that the real agenda is often changing the school culture (cf. Hargreaves 1994), setting and supporting the appropriate conditions, environment and people as well as the particulars of the innovation itself. If the conditions, context and culture of the school are weak, closed, divisive, Balkanized, paternalistic, over-hierarchical, over-directive, over-restrictive, over-controlled, over-pressurized or over-bureaucratized, if the principal is aloof, over-concerned with products and marks to the neglect of processes and learning, if the staff are disengaged from their work, their students and from each other, and if morale is low, then the innovation is under threat (Hoy et al. 1991; Holmes et al. 2013).

Positive organizational health, climate and collegiality are crucial, and they are the input, process and outcomes of the innovation; the innovation must work on and with them, promoting their positive features in supporting an innovation. Indeed, it was argued above that such development is a major responsibility of leadership, with trust and commitment as key elements of successful, sustainable innovations.

For innovation to be effective, it is important to harness the power of connecting people with each other and with the connected dimensions of the innovation, to ensure high morale, to identify, encourage and share different practices in reaching the goals of the innovation. In short, pride of place must be given to the people in the school, and it is to this vast area that the chapter turns.

People and perceptions

People are both the problem and the solution to effective multidimensional innovation. In managing 'simplexity' (Kluger 2007), Chapter 1 argued that the simple part was the content of the innovation whilst the complex part was the people. Indeed, primacy often had to be accorded to people over content. The task is to change people, but, as mentioned earlier, change changes people and people change change. In managing multidimensional innovation, this argues for sustained, in-depth attention to be given to the participants. Innovation, like engagement, is an affective, behavioural and cognitive matter, and this entails taking participants seriously, attending to their cognitive and affective side, e.g. concerns and anxieties about themselves, their students, their colleagues as well as the contents of the innovation (sections below address issues of their expectations, perceptions and development). Taking people seriously – all participants – entails working on and with them, not ignoring or overriding their concerns but working hard and continuously to bring and keep all parties 'on board', supportive and positive. Innovation is hard work, often with few guarantees of success.

The management of innovation is often largely about the management of perception and opinion. As the famous quotation from Thomas (1928) noted in Chapter 1, 'if men [*sic*] define their situations as real, they are real in their consequences'; if I think that there is a mouse under the table then I will behave as though there is, whether or not in fact there is a mouse. People act on the basis of perceptions, be those perceptions correct or not (Kahneman 2011), and declared perceptions may deliberately not be true, as people may have their own agenda in telling or withholding the truth. It is sensible for innovators to expect differentiated views, values, practices and opinions of participants from the very beginning onwards and to expect multiple and very different perceptions of the innovation. Indeed, there are multiple truths in the innovation, not a single version of the truth.

Innovators need to understand people's perceptions of the innovation and work with, and on, them as appropriate, not in a manipulative way but in an interpersonally sensitive and human-centred way. Relationships are important in managing complex innovations, and it is essential to listen to the frontline staff; listening is respecting. Innovation is stressful, creating positive and negative stress, and how to respond to participants' stress is an important leadership task. This involves identifying initial perceptions of different dimensions of an innovation, and looking for commonalities and differences in perceptions, concerns and practices between participant groups, in order to give a differentiated response to the challenges faced. It also involves working on areas where differences of perception and of positive and negative feelings are found to exist between participants, identifying common areas of agreement on perceptions of situations so that the innovation has potential for impact, together with planning how to handle different perceptions of a situation by different participants.

This book argues for the utility of finding out participants' concerns (with reference to Stages of Concern (Hall and Hord 1987, 2011) and by other means), recognizing that concerns and Levels of Use themselves change over time. The corollary of this is the need to ascertain participants' concerns at different points in the innovation and with relation to different dimensions of the innovation and its participants. Participants may have worries, anxieties as well as positive concerns about how to make the innovation go well. It is essential to identify these and to handle them; not to do so is to send a powerful message that they do not matter, which, in turn, is demotivating. A key message here is not to sacrifice or lose teacher motivation, as motivation and commitment are essential ingredients of effective innovation, and, indeed, the school in question here demonstrated this very fully. Teacher enthusiasm exerts a very powerful influence on the success of the innovation, and it is important to work on, and with, their intrinsic motivation. Participants are motivated by different factors; it is important find out what these are.

Harnessing and working with the enthusiasm of participants is crucial. In turn, commitment has many manifestations and may operate in many areas, and high priority has to be given to not losing staff motivation early on by inadequate preparation and training for an innovation and its contents. It is essential, indeed, inevitable perhaps, to start where the participants are but move them quickly.

Similarly, it is inadvisable to expect all the participants to be entirely enthusiastic about the innovation or all its dimensions, even though they may 'go along' with the innovation – practices often change before values and beliefs. Some participants may be hostile; some may need to be convinced; some may suspend judgement until they know more about the innovation and until it has unfolded; some may disagree with it; some may be apathetic or indifferent; some may worry about how it affects them, how it affects students, how it will be managed, how they will work with others, how it will unfold; some may be cautious in revealing their thoughts; some may be apprehensive of whether they can handle the innovation; some will need to be convinced with evidence that it is working. The point is that, for the best of motives rather than simple hostility, some participants may suspend their judgement. Hence, it is imperative to be prepared for resistance and criticism from participants, and stakeholders, and to plan how to address these. Innovation often requires a paradigm shift in the minds of participants, and they may be reluctant to let go of tried and tested practices, and so it is incumbent on the leaders of the innovation to persuade participants of the worthwhileness and benefits of changing paradigms and practices. It may be necessary to work on deep-seated preferences and mentalities of participants.

Participants in an innovation are both similar and different in their values and practices. Whilst it is useful to identify common concerns amongst different groups and different concerns between groups, it is also misguided to expect everyone to agree with everything in the innovation or, indeed, for everyone to reveal how they really feel about the innovation. It is important to listen to all participants, and consider why there may be silence as well as voice. Uniformity is but a distant companion of innovation. It is much wiser to expect different participants to have different needs, challenges, interests and agendas, different degrees of support, concern, worry and commitment, and the task is to engage, align and connect different people, groups, processes, contents and dimensions of the innovation and to make their commitment worthwhile. For some participants the innovation is a boon; for others it is doomed to succeed.

Engaging participants, really engaging them, not simply coercing them into submission, means adopting a comprehensive view of 'involvement' and 'engagement': cognitively, affectively, socially, interpersonally, behaviourally, psychologically; build trust in and between all parties, ensuring that all parties have a voice, and that it is heard, listened to and acted upon, and that the innovation is empowering rather than subjugating participants. Participants have a lot to offer an innovation, so building them in – inclusion rather than exclusion – is vital. This means providing safe conditions for creativity and change and recognizing that creativity is essential in order to sustain commitment and to make the innovation work in a non-mechanical way. Leaders of innovation must encourage and build on participants' creativity, even dissent, as this makes for a learning organization.

Expectations and anticipation

One of the lessons of the innovation in the school was that all the initial hopes and aspirations for the innovation did not materialize fully, or not in the ways expected. This is not uncommon in innovations. It is essential for leaders of the innovation to be ambitious but realistic in their expectations and to be prepared to modify expectations of what the innovation will 'deliver', to have high but realistic expectations of what the innovation will do and what its outcomes will be and to be prepared to modify these expectations as the innovation unfolds. Indeed, it is advisable to expect a range of levels of change, from a lot to nothing, from superficial to deep, and to expect different parts of the innovation to work to different levels of success and, indeed, at different rates.

It is misguided to expect all the dimensions of an innovation to show effects at the same rates, or to expect equal levels of success from all participants and all dimensions of the innovation. Some parts of an innovation go smoothly and without a hitch; others face obstacles at every turn. Innovation leaders can anticipate what might backfire or not work in the early stages of an innovation and how regression to more intensified forms of earlier practice might occur, and then intervene to prevent these.

Different parties in an innovation may have different agendas and expectations. Some or none of these may or may not come to fruition in the transacted innovation or its outcomes, so it is advisable to be prepared for some parts to have less success than others. However, there is a 'bottom line': the leaders must identify which parts of an innovation must not fail and which parts might be allowed to be less successful than others.

Support, development and capacity building

A recurrent theme across the innovation reported in this book, and, indeed, in the literature cited, is the crucial, critical centrality of support, development and capacity building. These are the *sine qua non* of effective innovation and leaders have an obligation to provide it. Staff development and building capacity are essential for the start of the innovation and its sustainability, and innovation capability requires capacity building, as innovations de-skill and require re-skilling. Capacity building must be built in from the beginning, but initial capacity building is not enough: capacity sustaining is the goal. Innovation leaders must plan not only for sustainable development but also for the ongoing professional development that is required to accompany this. This echoes the work of Dalin *et al.* (1993) and Hall and Hord (2011), one of whose principles of change is that change is learning.

Whether capacity building and development are realized in professional learning communities (and Hall and Hord (2011) are more enthusiastic about this than Hargreaves and Shirley (2009) even though professional learning communities serve the collegiality mentioned above as an important factor in effective change), or arranged through other means, it is critical (in the sense that without it an innovation might fail) to provide copious and sufficient advance, initial and ongoing training that is timely and relevant, together with support and development for all parties, in order to prepare for, to launch and to sustain all aspects of the innovation.

In arranging for professional development, it is important to recognize participants' limitations, and work on reducing them, to support teachers who may feel exposed and vulnerable, to identify what is the minimum level of expertise, training, development and preparation required for each dimension of the innovation to commence, and to ensure that it is present and has immediate, practical and concrete impact and utility.

Experiencing success

An innovation may take time for success to manifest itself, not least as the U-curve of innovation might bring a downturn before an upswing. This might be dispiriting for participants who are doing their best to make the innovation work, so it is important to identify and celebrate short-term successes as well as longer term, sustained success in order to strengthen morale and to maintain momentum. This means that it is important for leaders of the innovation to include in their planning the opportunity for staff to experience success right from the beginning of an innovation, particularly in the key dimensions of the innovation.

Addressing resistance and facilitation

The preceding chapters indicated the presence of facilitating and inhibiting factors in change and indicated what these might be, and, indeed, the evaluators drew attention to this. For an innovation to proceed effectively, it is important to identify facilitating and inhibiting factors, working with the former and on the latter. An inhibiting factor might not be as acute as overt resistance, but there might be factors in the institution which are causing 'drag' in the innovation (Morrison *et al.* 1989), from participants being reluctant to let go of tried and tested practices to participants not understanding what the innovation entails. If resistance to the innovation is observed, then it is essential to move quickly to identify reasons for it and work to overcome these, for example identifying the kinds of barriers (values, resources, practical, psychological, power, administrative, competence) and addressing them. In some institutions this means drawing a 'bottom line', whereby if staff are not prepared to move with the innovation then there is no place for them in the school.

By contrast, it is useful to identify facilitating factors and work with them. This might mean creating facilitating factors (e.g. incentives) for increased workloads working with the innovation; it might mean taking steps to create positive feelings towards the innovation, making workloads sustainable and giving public and concrete rewards for staff (e.g. promotion prospects). For example, a vastly trimmed-down picture of the facilitating and inhibiting factors in the school in question is presented in Figure 7.1.

The point of this present section is not to list inhibiting and facilitating factors, as this has been done in earlier chapters, but to draw attention to the need to identify these and to create and harness the facilitating factors and reduce barriers to, and inhibitors of, change.

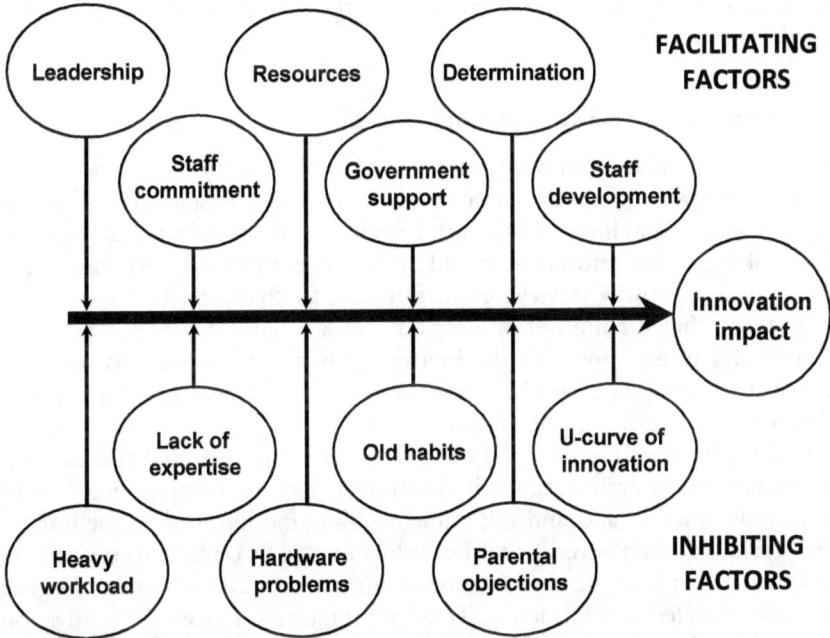

Figure 7.1 Facilitating and inhibiting factors in the school innovation

Setbacks and challenges

It is to be expected that there will be setbacks and challenges. That is one key message from both innovation research and complexity theory, and, indeed, in the school in question this was the case. Change the mindset: regard problems as opportunities for learning and development rather than as failures (though this is perhaps to take a kindly view when teachers are in the forefront of a mass of students whose computers decide not to work!).

The leaders of, and participants in, the innovation should anticipate what can go wrong, and plan for how to avoid or handle this, as well as to expect difficulties, setbacks and challenges, and try to anticipate where they may arise. In particular, they must not allow problems to fester but must solve them immediately, for example (as in the school) installing on-hand staff to address in-class problems immediately.

It is when setbacks occur that the affective aspect of innovation comes to the fore. Resilience and optimism are hard to sustain in the face of serious challenges, and the advice to remain positive and to tolerate setbacks and maintain optimism, confidence and determination is perhaps insulting to participants experiencing massive stress levels. However, the message about keeping positive should emanate from the leaders of the innovation and must be reflected in their practice. Further, it is incumbent on leaders and participants to anticipate possible setbacks and how to handle them, for example, the downturn (the U-curve) after the possible euphoria of launching the innovation.

Monitoring, review, evaluation and feedback

A key feature of the innovation in the school in question was the collection, interrogation and use of evaluation data (in this instance from external evaluators as well as internal sharing). Effective innovation and ongoing decision making in the innovation should be evidence-informed, with innovators acting on monitoring, review, evaluation and feedback. Such data are vital in ensuring that the innovation keeps on track, even if variance in practices occurs, and in ensuring that the innovation is not distorted into buttressing up the very practices which it is supposed to be changing (which was observed at one point in the school).

In the school in question, the evaluation data were provided and used on an ongoing basis, evaluating the innovation at all stages from its inception to its routine practice, and, indeed, refinement and modification in the institution, really sharing the results of the evaluation widely on the progress of the innovation and learning from them. In turn, this meant that the feedback was rich, detailed and formative. These are important lessons for innovation more widely, and, as was indicated in Chapter 1, feedback is a central element of complexity theory. Communication is a critical feature of innovation, and this includes evaluation data.

Further, a mixed methodology was employed in the evaluation, using both 'soft' data (perception-based data from interviews and questionnaires) and 'hard' data (test scores and logged data on computer use). This recognized that some benefits might be tangible and observable whilst others might be intangible and less easily observed.

One of the issues that arose in the school was the need to select carefully the indicators of success in order to ensure validity and reliability. This ensured that the causes of effects and effects of causes were really addressed, that causes were multiple and linked, and that it was known whether it was the innovation that was causing changes, or, indeed, other factors. Further, this identified success criteria for each stage and dimension of the innovation.

One characteristic of the school was its openness to all data, even bad news, regarding bad news as helpful in identifying what priorities needed to be addressed (and the school acted on these immediately).

Communication

Repeatedly in this study, the evaluators used the phrase 'communicate, communicate, communicate' to underline the significance of this core feature of successful innovation. Communication is not only essential for innovation, but it must be multi-channelled and through multimedia, both formal and informal. It cannot be stressed too strongly that the success of an innovation hinges in part on the provision of plentiful information, repeatedly and multi-channelled, to key parties involved in, or affected by, the innovation. They all have to be kept fully informed of what is happening in the innovation, at every stage. Leaders must be effective communicators and must have effective communicators in key positions (nodes) in the school and as link persons between the different dimensions of the innovation.

For example, the school showed the importance of anticipating and planning to handle parents' reactions, concerns and anxieties directly and immediately. It realized the dangers of not keeping parents 'in the loop', particularly concerning matters about which they were anxious. It accepted the significance of keeping parents informed, involved and 'on board', and it responded rapidly to an emerging negative situation by meeting parents to discuss what was happening in the innovation, and to give them feedback and data on its progress.

Utilizing complexity theory

One of the features of this book has been the appeal to one reading of complexity theory as indicating key features of effective innovation. As indicated in Chapter 1, complexity theory, as a theory of change and evolution, can make a significant contribution to an understanding of innovation in schools. Throughout this study some of the central tenets and lessons from complexity theory revealed themselves repeatedly, not least in the exhortation to regard schools as 'complex adaptive systems', dynamical, ever-changing, often in unpredictable and non-linear ways. Evidence was provided in the school in question to indicate the strength of these central tenets and lessons; over and over again key features of complexity theory manifested themselves.

For example, complexity theory argues that: (a) we should not expect innovation to be linear, as small interventions can lead to big change; (b) some change is predictable but much change is not, so it is important to plan for increasing returns; (c) detailed blueprints look nice but typically do not work, or not in the ways expected; (d) making multidimensional innovation work is a complex, adaptive act, and this was instanced in the school here.

Further, connectedness (e.g. of dimensions of innovation, people, internal and external environments) is central, be the dimensions loosely coupled or tightly coupled (Weick 1976). It is important to identify the strongest and weakest links in connecting the dimensions, and multidimensional feedback to and from the dimensions is essential for development. Barabási (2002), Buchanan (2002) and Watts (2003) argue that having multiple links within a network protects the network from system failure and ensures effective communication of the innovation: in an innovation, having links between the several dimensions of the innovation gives it resilience. Interconnectedness implies interrelationships; connectedness can be planned but its success depends on how it happens and how it is transacted, and that is a matter of people and their interactions.

Complexity theory is a theory of self-organization. Effective innovations take self-organization seriously, recognizing that self-organization has to be handled cautiously (with effective leadership) and is not 'do as you please', anarchy or laissez-faire.

Finally, emergence through self-organization is a central issue in innovation, and what emerges may not be the same as what was intended to emerge. The emergent situation is usually different from the original plan. Indeed, some aspects of innovation only emerge as the innovation unfolds.

All of these lessons were present and learned in the school in question. Complexity theory contains powerful lessons for planners, leaders, implementers and evaluators of innovations. As Morrison (2002a) argues, complexity theory is a theory whose time has come.

Piloting and scalability

It has long been recognized that 'trialability' and divisibility of change are important, i.e. whether it is possible to try out the innovation or a representative part of it before launching the entire innovation (Morrison 1998: 17; Hall and Hord 2011: 226). This is exactly what happened in the school, and it yielded several important lessons for the school, as indicated in the preceding chapters. In this instance it was important to use two high-profile subjects (English and mathematics) in the pilot, as this sent a clear signal as to the importance of the innovation and its centrality in the school and the intended high visibility of the innovation inside and outside the school (cf. Morrison 1998: 16–17).

By including in the pilot as many central features of the full innovation as possible, it was intended that the pilot would be scalable to the new innovation. The pilot project in many respects was a scaled-down version of the entire project, both quantitatively and qualitatively. A few teachers in a few classrooms teaching two subjects were the pilot for a massive, wholesale change affecting some 60 teachers and thousands of students across all subjects. Many of the issues that had been encountered in the pilot were subsequently being played out on a larger scale in the main project, for example: the U-curve of implementation; workload; the need for ongoing support and development; the critical role of tenacious leadership; the identification of a few key priorities and watchful adherence to these; attending to differentiated processes and outcomes; the need for communication and feedback; the need to work on several dimensions of innovation simultaneously and connectedly; the need to address the personal as well as the substantive aspects of the innovation; the need to address the school culture.

However, the school recognized that, when it came to the whole school innovation rather than the pilot, additional features would present themselves as the school-wide innovation was not just 'more pilot' but was qualitatively different from the pilot. As complexity theory tells us, an organization (a school) and an innovation within the context of the organization have to be studied at the level of the whole as well as the level of its component parts (Davis and Sumara 2005: 313). Moreover, complexity theory suggests that these component elements should be strongly, intimately and intrinsically connected. In the case of the school-wide innovation, however, the dimensions of the innovation were process factors and could be scaled-up. Innovation is input, process and outcome, with intervention as the starting mechanism (cf. Hall and Hord's (2011) comment that interventions are not the same as innovation, but are required to kick-start the innovation).

However, scalability engages several additional features, as the pilot was not just a pilot innovation but a microcosm of several features of the school, i.e. a matter of both the substance of the innovation and the context of the school (cf. Clarke et al. 2006). Scalability, therefore engages not only the innovation on a larger scale, but also the conditions within the school. Together, these contribute to an extended view of scalability which includes many elements (Blumenfeld et al. 2000; Mioduser et al. 2004; Clarke et al. 2006; Cohen and Ball 2007; Dede and Rockman 2007; Towndrow et al. 2010; Hall and Hord 2011; Law et al. 2011; European Commission 2013):

- Human capacity, capital and capability (knowledge, competencies and skills) for sustaining and sustainable innovation;
- Resources: human; material; temporal; financial; administrative; expertise (including connecting with external experts and providers);
- External support (e.g. academic, pedagogic; funding);
- Similarity of vision, aims, goals and objectives of the innovation;
- Degree of interconnectedness of the elements of the innovation and of the school more widely;
- Infrastructure together with support and developments (e.g. technological, organizational, curricular), i.e. an 'architecture for learning' (Law et al. 2011: 155);
- Support and ongoing development;
- Leadership and management;
- Innovator–adopter relations;
- Organizational structure of the institution;
- Participants;
- Communication;
- Feedback and evaluation;
- Internal school culture;
- Internal and external school environment;
- The principal maintaining good communication with parents about the innovation;
- Participants' 'buy in' to the innovation;
- The principal as an initiator of the innovation;

- Leaders who support team building and pedagogical development in teams;
- A clear, shared educational vision and goal;
- An evolutionary view of innovation as an ongoing process as teachers change over time, together with changes in the school ecology, both of which influence each other;
- The size of the 'adopting units' (Cohen and Ball 2007), e.g. teachers, classes, departments, school;
- The development of the school and teachers as a professional learning community.

Clarke et al. (2006) identify several features of effective scalability, differentiating the intervention's design from its 'conditions for success', in which a design for scalability requires the identification of which conditions are important and essential. These include teacher preparation (e.g. on ICT, on pedagogy), class size (as this affects how much individualization and interaction is possible and how much help and support there is for individual students), learners' academic achievement and self-efficacy (affecting the level of challenge to be appropriate for the learners) and learner engagement (including motivation and behaviour).

If scalability is to be effective, then holism and the fractal attributes of complexity theory tell us that, where possible, the pilot innovation must possess the central features of the scaled-up innovation, and in the school in question it largely did this. Apart from the scope of the professional learning community in the pilot, which was limited to a few teachers, students and managers, the key features of the scaled-up version of the innovation were present in the pilot. This meant that many lessons learned from the pilot could be applied usefully to the wider, cross-school innovation. In many respects the pilot was planned as a scaled down version or instance of the wider project, a homunculus, embodying many features of the wider innovation, rather than being a slice of one part of the innovation. The pilot was multidimensional, just as the wider project was multidimensional (see Figure 7.2). Figure 7.2 indicates the difference between an 'embedded' pilot (the first circle, which touches all key aspects of the wider innovation) and a 'non-embedded pilot' (the second circle, which excludes some key aspects of the wider innovation). In the embedded pilot, as Towndrow et al. (2010: 442) remark, scalability can be built into the innovation design, wherein each main dimension of the wider innovation is included in the pilot and there is space to address the additional specific features of the wider innovation and its environment (2010: 443). In the school here, the wider project had many additional features, but the initial planning of the pilot, to carry many of the features of the larger project, was useful to the school through the evaluation.

Further, if scalability is to be effective, particularly scaling up rather than scaling down, then it is essential to identify and set in motion the mechanisms by which this will happen (cf. Towndrow et al. 2010: 448) in the school.

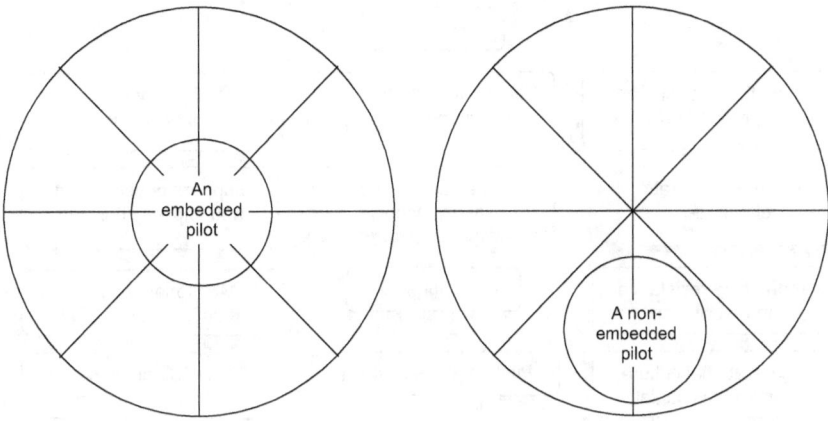

Figure 7.2 Embedded and non-embedded pilot innovations

Here the issues of staff development, collegial planning and implementation, acute awareness of roles and responsibilities of all parties in the innovation and clear roles of senior staff in the innovation, ensuring that the practical resources are in place, and staff capability and sustainability, all have to be addressed. 'Embeddedness' here takes on an additional feature: it is not only that the pilot innovation is embedded within the wider project, but also that the players recognize the essential embeddedness of the players in the innovation, wherein teachers are embedded within their social and working groups, working groups are embedded within their subject departments and subject departments within the overall structure of the school.

The important lesson for scalability is that it operates in more than one dimension:

- Size (scaling up and scaling down);
- Participants (scaling from the outside in and the inside out, e.g. individual to group, group to individual);
- Volume (scalability bringing exponential rather than arithmetical changes);
- Nature (quantitative and qualitative change, recognizing that sufficient quantitative change brings about qualitative change (a phase-state transition, in complexity theory)).

Scalability is a key feature in establishing the relations between a pilot and a wider innovation. Just as sampling theory tells us that a useful sample represents the wider population, so with the pilot: it must catch as many of the dimensions of the wider innovation as possible, recognizing that, as an innovation scales up or down, as it is affected by internal and external factors, as

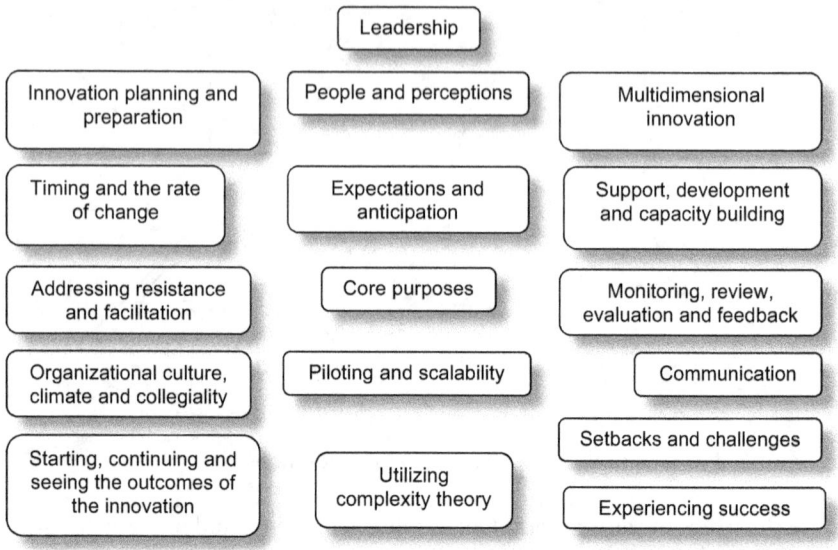

Figure 7.3 Key features in managing multidimensional innovation for engaged learning

it entails quantitative and qualitative change, so the mechanisms must be in place for scalability to work.

Hall and Hord (2011: 9–16) set some of their key principles of change: (a) individuals are the implementers of change (2011: 9), and they may not all progress at the same rate or develop in the same ways; (b) leadership is a key factor in sustaining innovation; (c) facilitating change is a whole team enterprise (2011: 14); (d) mandated change can be effective (as in the school here); and (e) context influences the processes of change. Importantly, they regard capacity building as central to change, be it at a limited or scaled-up level, building professional learning communities with positive supportive conditions, shared, collective learning, and shared, supportive leadership. Leaders create, nurture and support the conditions for effective innovation, at individual and scaled-up levels; they are both central and critical in the process.

The several elements of leading and managing multidimensional innovation for engaged learning are summarized in Figure 7.3.

Closing remarks

This book has taken a worked example of the effective management of a multidimensional, complex innovation in one school to raise questions of wider interest for those educators who are engaged in the never-ending task of configuring and reconfiguring schools, their moral purpose, and what happens in them as the external environment undergoes non-stop change. Complexity theory tells us that the internal and external environments of the school change each other, producing a new whole through the interactions of its members. That presents leaders of innovation in school with a daunting, yet exciting, task.

This book has drawn from the example of one school trying to embrace innovation. It has indicated a range of key lessons in planning, leading, managing, implementing, reviewing and evaluating a multiply linked, closely interconnected and intraconnected innovation. Some of its lessons are not new, but many are. Whilst is it commonplace to read of the centrality of leadership in managing effective change and the cultural changes that it brings, whilst there are legions of papers on how to plan and 'do' innovation, whilst the research on the dimensions of change advances exponentially, this book has argued that the alchemy which transforms these diverse elements into education for effective learning turns on people. Though this book has focused in part on new technologies, this is not the entire story of the innovation; we have to divest ourselves of the trappings of superficial innovation and their substantive contents and focus on people, engaging all parties. Inside innovations are real people. Innovation is not just a matter of technology. It is a human act.

References

Ager, R. (1998) *Information and Communications Technology in Primary Schools*. London: David Fulton Publishers.

Ager, R. (2000) *The Art of Information and Communications Technology for Teachers*. London: David Fulton Publishers.

Amis, J., Slack, T. and Hinings, C. R. (2004) The Pace, Sequence, and Linearity of Radical Change. *Academy of Management Journal*, 47 (1): 15–39.

Andriani, P. and Passiante, G. (2004) Complexity Theory and the Management of Networks. In P. Andriani and G. Passiante (Eds) *Complexity Theory and the Management of Networks* (pp. 3–19). London: Imperial College Press.

Aronson, N., Mastorovich, M. J. and Arsht, B. (2002) Letting Go . . . of Control Requires Bold Leadership. *The Journal for Quality and Participation*, Summer: 36–9.

Ashkanasy, N. M., Wilderom, C. P. M. and Peterson, M. F. (Eds) (2000) *Handbook of Organizational Culture and Climate*. Thousand Oaks, CA: SAGE Publications Inc.

Attard, A., Lorio, E. D., Geven, K. and Santa, R. (2010) *Student-Centered Learning SCL Toolkit*. European Students' Union, funded by the European Commission. Retrieved 2 April 2013 from www.esu-online.org/pageassets/projects/projectarchive/100814-SCL.pdf.

Bailey, R. (2000) *Education in the Open Society: Karl Popper and Schooling*. Aldershot, UK: Ashgate Publishing Ltd.

Bak, P. (1996) *How Nature Works*. New York: Copernicus.

Bank, J. (1992) *The Essence of Total Quality Management*. London: Prentice-Hall.

Barabási, A. L. (2002) *Linked: The New Science of Networks*. Cambridge, MA: Perseus Publishing Ltd.

Barbour, M. K. and Reeves, T. C. (2009). The Reality of Virtual Schools: A Review of the Literature. *Computers and Education*, 52 (2): 402–16.

Barnes, K. and Soken, N. (2012) *Managing Innovation: A Journey Toward Organizational Change*. Paper presented at the ASTD 2008 International Conference and Exposition Session Number: SU212. Copyright 2008 Barnes & Conti Associates, Inc. All Rights Reserved. Retrieved 25 April 2013 from http://astd2008.astd.org/PDF/Speaker%20Handouts/ice08%20handout%20SU212.pdf.

Bar-Yam, Y. (1997) *Dynamics of Complex Systems*. New York: Perseus Press.

Battram, A. (1999) *Navigating Complexity*. London: The Industrial Society.

Bennis, W. (1993) *An Invented Life: Reflections on Leadership and Change*. Reading, MA: Addison-Wesley.

Bessant, J., Caffyn, S. and Gilbert, J. (1996) Learning to Manage Innovation. *Technology Analysis & Strategic Management*, 8 (1): 59–70.

Blumenfeld, P., Fishman, B. J., Krajcik, J., Marx, R. W. and Soloway, E. (2000) Creating Usable Innovations in Systemic Reform: Scaling Up Technology-Embedded Project-Based Science in Urban Schools. *Educational Psychologist*, 35 (3): 149–64.

Bond, M. H. (1991) *Beyond the Chinese Face: Insights from Psychology*. Oxford: Oxford University Press.

Bond, M. H. and Hwang K. H. (1986) The Social Psychology of the Chinese People. In M. H. Bond (Ed.) *The Psychology of the Chinese People* (pp. 213–66). Oxford: Oxford University Press.

Bouffard, S. (2008) *Tapping into Technology: The Role of the Internet in Family-School Communications*. Cambridge, MA: Harvard Family Research Project. Retrieved 10 February 2011 from www.hfrp.org/publications-resources/browse-our-publications/tapping-into-technology-the-role-of-the-internet-in-family-school-communication.

Brandes, D. and Ginnis, P. (1986) *A Guide to Student Centred Learning*. Oxford: Blackwell.

Bray, M. and Koo, R. (Eds) (2004) *Education and Society in Hong Kong and Macau: Comparative Perspective on Continuity and Change* (second edition). Hong Kong: CER and Kluwer Academic Publishers.

Brinkerhoff, R., Brethower, D. M., Hluchyj, T. and Nowakowski, J. R. (1983) *Program Evaluation: A Practitioner's Guide for Trainers and Educators*. Boston: Kluwer-Nijhoff.

British Educational Communications and Technology Agency (BECTA) (October 2002) *Information Sheet: Parents, ICT and Education*. Retrieved 3 March 2006 from www.becta.org.uk/technology/infosheets/html/parents/html.

Brodbeck, P. W. (2002) Complexity Theory and Organization Procedure Design. *Business Process Management*, 8 (4): 377–402.

Brown, S. L. and Eisenhardt, K. M. (1998) *Competing on the Edge: Strategy as Structured Chaos*. Boston, MA: Harvard University Business School Press.

Buchanan, M. (2002) *Nexus: Small Worlds and the Groundbreaking Theory of Networks*. New York: W. W. Norton and Co. Inc.

Burnes, B. (2005) Complexity Theories and Organizational Change. *International Journal of Management Reviews*, 7 (2): 73–90.

Cairney, T. (2000) *The Knowledge Based Economy: Implications for Vocational Education and Training: A Review of the Literature*. Australia: Centre for Regional Research & Innovation (CRRI), University of Western Sydney and the Centre for Research and Learning in Regional Australia (CRLRA), University of Tasmania.

Capra, F. (1996) *The Web of Life: A New Understanding of Living Systems*. New York: Doubleday.

Capra, F. (2007) Complexity and Life. In F. Capra, A. Juarerro, P. Sotolongo and J. van Uden (Eds) *Reframing Complexity: Perspectives from North and South* (pp. 1–25). Mansfield, MA: ISCE Publishing.

Capra, F., Juarerro, A, Sotolongo, P. and van Uden, J. (2007) Reframing Complexity: Perspectives from the North and South. In F. Capra, A. Juarerro, P. Sotolongo and

J. van Uden (Eds) *Reframing Complexity: Perspectives from North and South* (pp. vii–xix). Mansfield, MA: ISCE Publishing.

Carley, K. M. and Hill, V. (2001) Structural Change and Learning Within Organizations. In A. Lomi and E. R. Larsen (Eds) *Dynamics of Organizations: Computational Modeling and Organizational Theories* (pp. 63–92). Menlo Park, CA: Association for the Advancement of Artificial Intelligence (AAAI) Press/Massachusetts Institute of Technology (MIT) Press.

Castro, C. D. M. (1999) Education in the Information Age: Promises and Frustrations. *TechKnowLogia*, November/December: 39–42.

Chaika, G. (1999) Technology in the Schools: It Does make a Difference! *Education World*. Retrieved 2 February 2001 from www.education-world.com/a_admin/admin122.shtml.

Chu, D., Strand, R. and Fjelland, R. (2003) Theories of Complexity: Common Denominators of Complex Systems. *Complexity*, 8 (3): 19–30.

Chu, H. (1999) In Macao, A Culture on the Cusp. *Los Angeles Times*, 17 December. Retrieved January 2014 from http://articles.latimes.com/1999/dec/17/news/mn-44796.

Cicco, E. D., Farmer, M. and Hargrave, J. (2000) *Using the Internet in Secondary Schools* (second edition). London: Kogan Page.

Cilliers, P. (1998) *Complexity and Postmodernism*. London: Routledge.

Clarke, J., Dede, C. and Jass Ketelhut, D. (2006) A Design-Based Research Strategy to Promote Scalability for Educational Innovations. *Educational Technology*, 46 (3): 27–36.

Cohen, D. K. and Ball, D. L. (2007) Educational Innovation and the Problem of Scale. In B. L. Schneider and S. K. McDonald (Eds) *Scale-up in Education: Ideas in Principle* (Vol. 1) (pp. 19–36). Plymouth: Rowman & Littlefield.

Cohen, J. and Stewart, I. (1995) *The Collapse of Chaos*. Harmondsworth, UK: Penguin.

Cohen, L., Manion, L. and Morrison, K. R. B. (2010) *A Guide to Teaching Practice* (revised fifth edition). London: Routledge.

Collis, B., de Boer, W. and van der Veen, J. (2001) Building on Learner Contributions: A Web-Supported Pedagogic Strategy. *Educational Media International*, 38 (4): 229–40.

Connecticut Accountability and Learning Initiative (CALI) (2011) *Leading Change … AND Getting Everyone on Board!* Connecticut State Department of Education. Retrieved 24 April 2013 from www.sde.ct.gov/sde/lib/sde/pdf/curriculum/cali/day2.pdf.

Cooper, J. R. (1998) A Multidimensional Approach to the Adoption of Innovation. *Management Decision*, 36 (8): 493–502.

Coriden, J. A., Green, T. J. and Heintschel, D. E. (1985) *The Code of Canon Law: A Text and Commentary*. New York: Paulist Press.

Coveney, P. and Highfield, R. (1995) *Frontiers of Complexity*. New York: Fawcett Columbine.

Covington, M. V. and Mueller, K. J. (2001) Intrinsic Versus Extrinsic Motivation: An Approach/Avoidance Reformulation. *Educational Psychology Review*, 13 (2): 157–76.

Cox, M. (1997) *The Effects of Information Technology on Students' Motivation*. London: National Council for Educational Technology and King's College London.

Cradler, J. (1994) *Summary of Current Research and Evaluation Findings on Technology and Education*. San Francisco, CA: Far West Laboratory, WestEd. Retrieved 3 February 2001 from www.wested.org/techpolicy/refind.html.

Craft, A. (2005) *Creativity in Schools: Tensions and Dilemmas*. London: Routledge.

Crook, C. (1994) *Computers and the Collaborative Experience of Learning*. London: Routledge.

Crossan, M. M. and Apaydin, M. (2010) A Multi-dimensional Framework of Organizational Innovation: A Systematic Review of the Literature. *Journal of Management Studies*, 47 (6): 1154–91.

Dalin, P., Rolff, H. G. and Kottkamp, R. (1993) *Changing the School Culture*. London: Cassell.

Davis, B. and Sumara, D. J. (2005) Challenging Images of Knowing: Complexity Science and Educational Research. *International Journal of Qualitative Studies in Education*, 18 (3): 305–21.

Davis, N., Desforges, C., Jessel, J., Somekh, B., Taylor, C. and Vaughan, G. (1997) Can Quality in Learning be Enhanced Through the Use of IT? In B. Somekh and N. Davis (Eds) *Using Information Technology Effectively in Teaching and Learning* (pp. 14–27). London: Routledge.

Day, C., Sammons, P., Hopkins, D., Harris, A., Leithwood, K., Qing Gu and Brown, C. (2010) *Ten Strong Claims about Successful School Leadership*. Nottingham, UK: National College for School Leadership.

Deal, T. E. and Kennedy, A. A. (1982) *Corporate Cultures: The Rites and Rituals of Corporate Life*. Reading, MA: Addison-Wesley.

Dede, C. and Rockman, S. (2007) Lessons Learned From Studying How Innovations Can Achieve Scale. *Threshold*, Spring: 4–10. Retrieved 15 May 2013 from www.ciconline.org/threshold.

Deighton, N. and Hocking, A. (1999) *Switching on Learners in the Middle Years: A Pedagogy of Engagement Through Learning Technologies*. Paper presented at the National Middle Years of Schooling Conference, Redesigning the Middle Years. State of Victoria (Department of Education, Employment and Training) Initiative of the Learning Technologies Programs Section. Retrieved 3 February 2002 from www.sofweb.vic.edu.au/lt/myos.htm.

Department for Education and Skills (2002) *Transforming the Way We Learn: A Vision for the Future of ICT in Schools*. London: Department for Education and Skills/National Grid for Learning.

De Robertis, C. and Morrison, K. R. B. (2009) Catholic Schooling, Identity and Social Justice in Macau. *International Studies in Catholic Education*, 1 (2): 152–69.

Dillenbourg P. (1999) What Do You Mean By Collaborative Learning? In P. Dillenbourg (Ed.) *Collaborative Learning: Cognitive and Computational Approaches* (pp. 1–19). Oxford: Elsevier.

Direcção dos Serviços de Estatística e Juventude (DSEJ) (2012) *School and Students in Macau*. Macau: DSEJ.

Direcção dos Serviços de Estatística e Census (DSEC) (2013) *Macau in Figures*. Macau: DSEC.

Dumont, H., Istance, D. and Benavides, F. (2010) *The Nature of Learning: Using Research to Inspire Practice*. Paris: OECD.

Dykes, M. (2001) *Assessment and Evaluation of Peer Interaction Using Computer-mediated Communication in Post-secondary Academic Education*. Occasional

Paper: Department of Educational Communications and Technology, University of Saskatchewan.

Dziuban, C., Hartman, J. and Moskal, P. (2004) Blended Learning. *EDUCAUSE Center for Applied Research, Research Bulletin*, (7): 1–12. Retrieved 30 March 2013 from http://net.educause.edu/ir/library/pdf/ERB0407.pdf.

Education, Audiovisual and Culture Executive Agency (2011) *Key Data on Learning and Innovation through ICT at School in Europe 2011.* Brussels: Education, Audiovisual and Culture Executive Agency of the European Commission.

Egan, G. (1993) *Adding Value.* San Francisco, CA: Jossey Bass.

Englert, C. S., Zhao, Y., Dunsmore, K., Collings, N. Y. and Wolbers, K. (2007) Scaffolding the Writing of Students with Disabilities through Procedural Facilitation: Using an Internet Based Technology to Improve Performance. *Learning Disability Quarterly*, 30 (1): 9–29.

Espinosa, A., Harnden, R. and Walker, J. (2007) Beyond Hierarchy: A Complexity Management Perspective. *Kybernetes*, 36 (3/4): 333–47.

European Commission (2013) *ICT-enabled Innovation for Learning in Europe and Asia: Exploring Conditions for Sustainability, Scalability and Impact at System Level.* Seville, Spain: European Commission, Joint Research Centre, Institute for Prospective Technological Studies.

Fairholm, M. R. and Fairholm, G. (2000) Leadership amid the Constraints of Trust. *Leadership and Development Journal*, 21 (2): 102–9.

Falconer, J. (2007) Emergence Happens! Misguided Paradigms Regarding Organizational Change and the Role of Complexity and Patterns in the Change Landscape. In F. Capra, A. Juarrero, P. Sotolongo and J. van Uden (Eds) *Reframing Complexity: Perspectives from the North and South* (pp. 135–50). Mansfield, MA: Institute for the Study of Coherence and Emergence Publishing.

Faure, G. O. and Ding, Y. F. (2003) Chinese Culture and Negotiation: Strategies for Handling Stalemates. In I. Alon (Ed.) *Chinese Culture, Organizational Behaviour and International Business Management* (pp. 85–98). Westport, Connecticut: Praeger.

Fetherston, T. (2001) Pedagogical Challenges for the World Wide Web. *Educational Technology Review*, 9 (1): 4.

Fullan, M. (1991) *The New Meaning of Educational Change.* London: Cassell.

Fullan, M. (2001) *Leading in a Culture of Change.* San Francisco, CA: Jossey-Bass.

Fullan, M. (2003) *The Moral Imperative of School Leadership.* Newbury Park, CA: Corwin.

Fullan, M. (2005) *Leadership and Sustainability: Systems Thinking in Action.* Newbury Park, CA: Corwin.

Fullan, M. (2011a) *The Moral Imperative Realized.* Newbury Park, CA: Corwin.

Fullan, M. (2011b) *Change Leader: Learning to Do what Matters Most.* New York: Jossey-Bass.

Fullan, M. (2013) *Stratosphere: Integrating Technology, Pedagogy and Change Knowledge.* Toronto: Pearson.

Fullan, M. and Hargreaves, A. (2008) *Change Wars.* Bloomington, IN: Solution Tree.

Gee, J. P. (2005) Learning by Design: Good Video Games as Learning Machines. *E-Learning and Digital Media*, 2 (1): 5–16.

Gell-Mann, M. (1994) *The Quark and the Jaguar.* London: Abacus.

Gibbs, G. (1995) *Assessing Student Centred Courses*. Oxford: Oxford Centre for Staff Learning and Development.

Gilmer, B. (1966) *Industrial Psychology* (second edition). New York: McGraw-Hill.

Gladwell, M. (2000) *The Tipping Point: How Little Things Can Make a Big Difference*. Boston, MA: Little Brown and Co.

Glazer, C. (2000) *The Emergence of a New Digital Divide: A Critical Look at Integrated Learning Systems*. Occasional Paper: University of Texas at Austin. EDC 385G: Literacy and Culture.

Goffin, K., Koners, U., Baxter, D. van der Hoven, C. (2010) Managing Lessons Learned and Tacit Knowledge in New Product Development. *Research Technology Management*, 53 (4): 39–51.

Goldstein, J. A. (2000) Emergence: A Construct Amid a Thicket of Conceptual Snares. *Emergence*, 2 (1): 5–22.

Goldstein, J. A. and Hazy, J. K. (2006) Editorial Introduction to the Special Issue: From Complexity to Leadership and Back to Complexity. *Emergence: Complexity and Organization*, 8 (4): v–vii.

Goodwin, B. (2000) Out of Control into Participation. *Emergence*, 2 (4): 40–9.

Grabe, M. and Grabe, C. (2001) *Integrating Technology for Meaningful Learning*. Boston, MA: Houghton Mifflin & Co.

Groff, J. (2012) *The Nature of Learning: Using Research to Inspire Practice: Practitioner Guide*. Paris: UNESCO.

Gronn, P. (2000) Distributed Properties: A New Architecture for Leadership. *Educational Management and Administration*, 28 (3): 317–38.

Gronn, P. (2002) Distributed Leadership as a Unit of Analysis. *The Leadership Quarterly*, 13 (4): 423–52.

Gronn, P. (2003) *The New Work of Educational Leaders: Changing Leadership Practice in an Era of School Reform*. London: Paul Chapman Publishing.

Guastello, S. J., Craven, J., Zygowicz, K. M. and Bock, B. R. (2005) A Rugged Landscape Model for Self-Organization and Emergent Leadership in Creative Problem Solving and Production Groups. *Nonlinear Dynamics, Psychology and Life Sciences*, 9 (3): 297–334.

Gunter, H. (2003) Introduction: The Challenge of Distributed Leadership. *School Leadership and Management*, 23 (3): 261–5.

Hall, G., George, A. and Rutherford, W. (1986) *Measuring Stages of Concern about the Innovation: A Manual for the Use of the SOC Questionnaire*. Austin, TX: Southwest Educational Development Laboratory.

Hall, G. E. (2010) Technology's Achilles Heel: Achieving High-Quality Implementation. *Journal of Research on Technology in Education*, 42 (3): 231–53.

Hall, G. E. and Hord, S. M. (1987) *Change in Schools*. New York: State University of New York Press.

Hall, G. E. and Hord, S. M. (2011) *Implementing Change: Patterns, Principles and Potholes* (third edition). Upper Saddle River, NJ: Pearson.

Hallinger, P. (2010) *Leadership for Learning: What We Have Learned From 30 Years of Empirical Research*. Seminar Series Paper No. 196, July 2010. Melbourne, Victoria: Centre for Strategic Education.

Halpin, W. (1966) *Theory and Research in Administration*. New York: Macmillan.

Hannon, V. (2009) *'Only Connect!' A New Paradigm for Learning Innovation in the 21st Century*. Retrieved 12 January 2013 from www.innovationunit.org/our-people/our-staff/valerie-hannon.

Hargreaves, A. (1994) *Changing Teachers, Changing Times: Teachers' Work and Culture in the Postmodern Age*. New York: Teachers College Press.

Hargreaves, A. and Shirley, D. (2009) *The Fourth Way*. Thousand Oaks, CA: Corwin.

Hargreaves, A. and Fullan, M. (2012) *Professional Capital: Transforming Teaching in Every School*. London: Routledge.

Hargreaves, D. and Hopkins, D. (1991) *The Empowered School*. London: Cassell.

Harris, A. (2003) Teacher Leadership as Distributed Leadership: Heresy, Fantasy or Possibility? *School Leadership and Management*, 23 (3): 313–24.

Hartley, S., Gerhardt-Powals, J., Jones, D., McCormack, C., Medley, D., Price, B., Reek, M. and Summers, M. (1996) Enhancing Teaching Using the Internet. Report of the Working Group on the World Wide Web as an Interactive Teaching Resource. Proceedings of the Conference on Integrating Technology into Computer Science Education. *SIGCSE Bulletin*, 28 (SI): 218–28. Barcelona, Spain: Association for Computing Machinery (ACM). Retrieved 3 February 2002 from http://portal.acm.org/citation.cfm?doid=237466.237649.

Hartwell, A. (1995) *Scientific Ideas and Education in the 21st Century*. Institute for International Research. Retrieved 2 February 2001 from http://www.newhorizons.org/ofc_21cliash.html.

Hattie, J. (2009) *Visible Learning: A Synthesis of Over 800 Meta-analyses Relating to Achievement*. London: Routledge.

Hattie, J. (2012) *Visible Learning for Teachers: Maximizing Impact on Learning*. London: Routledge.

Hawkins, R. J. (2002) Ten Lessons for ICT and Education in the Developing World. *The Global Information Technology Report 2001-2002: Readiness for the Networked World*. The World Bank Institute, World Links for Development Program. Oxford: Oxford University Press.

Heifetz, R. and Linsky, M. (2002) *Leadership on the Line: Staying Alive through the Dangers of Leading*. Boston, MA: Harvard Business School Press.

Hennessy, S. (2006) Integrating Technology into the Teaching and Learning of School Science: A Situated Perspective on Pedagogical Issues in Research. *Studies in Science Education*, 42 (1): 1–48.

Herron, J. D. (1996) *The Chemistry Classroom: Formulas for Successful Teaching*. Washington, DC: American Chemical Society.

Higgins, S. (2001) ICT and Teaching for Understanding. *Evaluation and Research in Education*, 15 (3): 164–71.

Holmes, K., Clement, J. and Albright, J. (2013) The Complex Task of Leading Educational Change in Schools. *School Leadership and Management*, 33 (3): 270–83.

Hopkins, D., Harris, A., Stoll, L. and Mackay, T. (2011) *School and System Improvement: State of the Art Review*. Keynote presentation prepared for the 24th International Congress of School Effectiveness and School Improvement, Limassol, Cyprus, 6 January 2011. Retrieved 16 January 2013 from www.icsei.net/icsei2011/State_of_the_art/State_of_the_art_Session_C.pdf.

Houchin, K. and MacLean, D. (2005) Complexity Theory and Strategic Change: An Empirically Informed Critique. *British Journal of Management*, 16 (2): 149–66.

Hoy, W. K., Tarter, C. J. and Kottkamp, R. B. (1991) *Open Schools, Healthy Schools*. London: SAGE Publications.

Hoyle, E. (1975) The Creativity of the School in Britain. In A. Harris, M. Lawn and W. Prescott (Eds) *Curriculum Innovation* (pp 329–46). London: Croom Helm and the Open University Press.

Hübler, A. W. (2007) Understanding Complex Systems: Defining an Abstract Concept. *Complexity*, 12 (5): 9–11.

ICT Cluster (2010) *Learning, Innovation and ICT: Key Lessons Learned by the ICT Cluster.* Report prepared for the ICT Cluster of the European Commission Education & Training 2010 Programme. Retrieved 1 May 2013 from www.crie.min-edu.pt/files/@crie/1269620361_Key_lessons_ICT_Cluster_final_report.pdf.

Jones, B. F., Valdez, G., Nowakowski, J. and Rasmussen, C. (1995) *Plugging In: Choosing and Using Educational Technology.* Washington, DC: Council for Educational Development and Research, North Regional Educational Laboratory.

Kahneman, D. (2011) *Thinking Fast and Slow*. London: Penguin Books Ltd.

Kampylis, P. G., Bocconi, S. and Punie, Y. (2012) *Towards a Mapping Framework of ICT-enabled Innovation for Learning.* European Commission Joint Research Centre, Luxembourg; Institute for Prospective Technological Studies. Luxembourg: Publications Office of the European Union.

Katz, D. and Kahn, R. L. (1978) *The Social Psychology of Organizations* (second edition). New York: John Wiley and Sons.

Kauffman, S. A. (1995) *At Home in the Universe: The Search for the Laws of Self-Organization and Complexity.* Harmondsworth, UK: Penguin.

Kearsley, G. and Shneiderman, B. (1999) *Engagement Theory: A Framework for Technology-Based Teaching and Learning.* Retrieved 21 March 2013 from http://home.sprynet.com/~gkearsley/engage.htm.

Kelly, S. and Allison, M. A. (1999) *The Complexity Advantage: How the Science of Complexity Can Help Your Business Achieve Peak Performance.* New York: McGraw-Hill.

Kluger, J. (2007) *Simplexity*. London: John Murray Publishers.

Kowch, E. G. and Schwier, R. A. (1997) *Characteristics of Technology-based Virtual Learning Communities.* Occasional Paper: College of Education, University of Saskatchewan.

Kramarski, B. and Feldman, Y. (2000) Internet in the Classroom: Effects on Reading Comprehension, Motivation and Metacognitive Awareness. *Education Media International*, 37 (3): 149–55.

LaJoie, S. P. (1993) Computer Environments as Cognitive Tools for Enhancing Learning. In S. P. LaJoie and S. J. Derry (Eds) *Computers as Cognitive Tools* (pp. 261–88). Hillsdale, NJ: Lawrence Erlbaum Associates.

Lakomski, G. (2000) *Leadership: How to Manage Without it.* Paper prepared for the Centre for Educational Leadership, University of Hong Kong, 27 September 2000. Retrieved 4 April 2001 from www.hku.hk/educel/Handout-ProfLakomski.pdf.

Law, N., Yuen, A. and Fox, R. (2011) *Educational Innovations beyond Technology: Nurturing Leadership and Establishing Learning Organizations.* New York: Springer Science+Business Media.

Lea, S. J., Stephenson, D. and Troy, J. (2003) Higher Education Students' Attitudes to Student Centred Learning: Beyond 'Educational Bulimia'. *Studies in Higher Education*, 28 (3): 321–34.

Leithwood, K. A. and Riehl, C. (2003) *What We Know About Successful School Leadership*. Nottingham, UK: National College for School Leadership. Retrieved 24 November 2012 from www.principals.in/uploads/pdf/leadership/1_NCLP.pdf.

Leithwood, K. and Seashore-Louis, K. (2011) *Linking Leadership to School Learning*. New York: Jossey-Bass.

Leithwood, K., Seashore-Louis, K., Anderson, S. and Wahlstrom, K. (2004) *How Leadership Influences Student Learning*. Center for Applied Research and Educational Improvement, University of Minnesota; Ontario Institute for Studies in Education; and the Wallace Foundation. Retrieved 2 November 2012 from www.sisd.net/cms/lib/TX01001452/Centricity/Domain/33/ReviewofResearch-LearningFromLeadership.pdf.

Leithwood, K., Day, C., Sammons, P., Hopkins, D. and Harris, A. (2006) *Seven Strong Claims about Successful School Leadership*. Nottingham, UK: National College for School Leadership.

Leithwood, K., Patten, S. and Jantzi, D. (2010) Testing a Conception of How School Leadership Influences Student Learning. *Educational Administration Quarterly*, 46 (5): 671–706.

Leo, E. and Galloway, D. (1996) Evaluating Research on Motivation: Generating More Heat than Light? *Evaluation and Research in Education*, 20 (1): 35–48.

Lepper, M. R., Sethi, S., Dialdin, D. and Drake, M. (1997) Intrinsic and Extrinsic Motivation: A Developmental Perspective. In S. S. Luthar, J. A. Burack, D. Cicchetti and J. R. Weisz (Eds) *Developmental Psychopathology: Perspectives on Adjustment, Risk and Disorder* (pp. 23–50). New York: Cambridge University Press.

Lewin, R. (1993) *Complexity: Life on the Edge*. London: Phoenix.

Lewin, R. and Regine, B. (2000) *The Soul at Work: Listen, Respond, Let Go: Embracing Complexity Science for Business Success*. New York: Simon & Schuster.

Lichtenstein, B. M. B. (2000) Emergence as a Process of Self-Organizing: New Assumptions and Insights from the Study of Non-Linear Dynamic Systems. *Journal of Organizational Change Management*, 13 (6): 526–44.

Lichtenstein, B. M. B., Uhl-Bien, M., Marion, R., Seers, A., Orton, J. D. and Schreiber, C. (2006) Complexity Leadership Theory: An Interactive Perspective on Leading in Complex Adaptive Systems. *Emergence: Complexity and Organization*, 8 (4): 2–12.

Light, D. (2010) Multiple Factors Supporting the Transition to ICT-rich Learning Environments in India, Turkey, and Chile. *International Journal of Education and Development Using Information and Communication Technology (IJEDICT)*, 6 (4): 39–51.

Lissack, M. R. (2000) *Complexity Metaphors and the Management of a Knowledge Based Enterprise: An Exploration of Discovery*. Retrieved 3 February 2002 from http://lissack.com/writings/proposal.htm.

Litwin, G. H. and Stringer, R. A. (1968) *Motivational and Organizational Climate*. Boston, MA: Harvard University Graduate School of Business Administration.

Liu, Z. F. E., Lin, S. J. S. and Yuan, S. M. (2001) Design of a Networked Portfolio System. *British Journal of Educational Technology*, 32 (4): 492–4.

Long, M. and Jennings, H. (2005) *Does it Work? The Impact of Technology and Professional Development on Student Achievement*. Calverton, MD: Marco International.

Louis, K. S., Leithwood, K., Wahlstrom, K. L and Anderson, S. E. (2010) *Investigating the Links to Improved Student Learning. Final Report of Research Findings.* Learning from Leadership Project commissioned by The Wallace Foundation. University of Minnesota and Ontario Institute for Studies in Education, University of Toronto. Retrieved 27 January 2014 from www.wallacefoundation.org/knowledge-center/school-leadership/key-research/Documents/Investigating-the-Links-to-Improved-Student-Learning.pdf.

Loveless, A. (2007) Creativity, Technology and Learning: A Review of Recent Literature (No. 4 update). *Futurlab*. Retrieved 20 June 2010 from www.futurelab.org.uk/litreviews.

Loveless, A. (2008). Creative Learning and New Technology? A Provocation Paper. In J. Sefton-Green (Ed.) *Creative Learning* (pp. 61–72). London: Creative Partnerships.

Loveless, A. (2011) Didactic Analysis as a Creative Process: Pedagogy for Creativity with Digital Tools. In B. Hudson and M. A. Meyer (Eds) *Beyond Fragmentation: Didactics, Learning and Teaching in Europe* (pp. 239–51). Opladen and Farmington Hills, MI: Verlag Barbara Budrich.

Loveless, A. and Ellis V. (2001) *ICT, Pedagogy and the Curriculum*. London: RoutledgeFalmer.

Luke, J. S. (1998) *Catalytic Leadership: Strategies for an Interconnected World*. San Francisco, CA: Jossey Bass.

Lumpkin, A. (2007) Caring Teachers: The Key to Student Learning. *Kappa Delta Pi*, 43 (4): 158–60.

McClintock, R. (1992) *Power and Pedagogy: Transforming Education through Information Technology*. New York: Institute of Learning Technologies.

McElroy, M. W. (2000) Integrating Complexity Theory, Knowledge Management and Organizational Learning. *Journal of Knowledge Management*, 4 (3): 195–203.

MacIntosh, R. and MacLean, D. (1999) Conditioned Emergence: A Dissipative Structures Approach to Transformation. *Strategic Management Journal*, 20 (4): 297–316.

McKelvey, W. (2004) Simple Rules for Improving Corporate IQ: Basic Lessons from Complexity Science. In P. Andriani and G. Assiante (Eds) *Complexity Theory and the Management of Networks* (pp. 39–52). London: Imperial College Press.

McMaster, M. D. (1996) *The Intelligence Advantage: Organizing for Complexity*. Boston, MA: Butterworth Heinemann.

Majchrzak, A., Logan, D., McCurdy, R. and Kirchmer, M. (2006) Four Keys to Managing Emergence. *MIT Sloan Management Review*, 47 (2): 14–18.

Marion, R. (1999) *The Edge of Organization: Chaos and Complexity Theories of Formal Social Systems*. London: SAGE Publications.

Marion, R. and Bacon, J. (2000) Organizational Extinction and Complex Systems. *Emergence*, 1 (4): 71–94.

Marion, R. and Uhl-Bien, M. (2001) Leadership in Complex Organizations. *The Leadership Quarterly*, 12 (4): 389–418.

Marsick, V. (2000) Learning Organizations. Cited in V. Marsick, J. Bitterman and R. Van Der Veen (2000) *From the Learning Organization to Learning Communities toward a Learning Society*. Information series no. 382. ERIC Clearinghouse on Adult, Career and Vocational Education. ED-99-CO-0013. Ohio State University, Columbus: Ohio. Retrieved 3 May 2001 from http://ericacve.org/docs/marsick/marsick3.pdf.

Menter, I., Hulme, M., Lowden, K. and Hall, S. (2010) *Learning from Innovation and Change Management in Glasgow Secondary Schools*. Report produced for the Scottish Government by APS Group Scotland (DPPAS 05/10). Edinburgh: Scottish Government. Retrieved 26 April 2013 from www.scotland.gov.uk/Resource/Doc/311860/0098439.pdf.

Miles, M. (1975) Planned Change and Organizational Health. In A. Harris, M. Lawn and W. Prescott (Eds) *Curriculum Innovation* (pp. 192–203). London: Croom Helm and the Open University Press.

Miller, J. H. and Page, S. E. (2007) *Complex Adaptive Systems*. Princeton, NJ: Princeton University Press.

Mioduser, D., Nachmias, R., Forkosh-Baruch, A. and Tubin, D. (2004) Sustainability, Scalability and Transferability of ICT-based Pedagogical Innovations in Israeli Schools. *Education, Communication and Information*, 4 (1): 71–82.

Mitchell, M. (2009) *Complexity: A Guided Tour*. New York: Oxford University Press.

Moeller, B. and Reitzes, T. (2011) *Integrating Technology with Student-Centered Learning*. Report to the Nellie Mae Education Foundation. Quincy, MA: The Nellie Mae Education Foundation. Retrieved 30 March 2013 from www.nmefoundation.org/getmedia/befa9751-d8ad-47e9-949d-bd649f7c0044/Integrating-Technology-with-Student-Centered-Learning?ext=.pdf.

Morrison, K. R. B. (1998) *Management Theories for Educational Change*. London: Paul Chapman Publishing Ltd.

Morrison, K. R. B. (2001) *The Open Society and Education in Macau. Public sapientia* lecture presented at the Inter-University Institute of Macau in October 2001.

Morrison, K. R. B. (2002a) *Complexity Theory and School Leadership*. London: Routledge.

Morrison, K. R. B. (2002b) *Education for the Open, Democratic Society in Macau*. Paper presented to the Catholic Teachers' Association, Macau, April 2002.

Morrison, K. R. B. (2004) *Breaking the Homogenisation of Early Childhood Education in Macau*. Keynote address to the Association for Childhood Education International. Hong Kong, October 2004.

Morrison, K. R. B. (2006) Sensitive Educational Research in Small States and Territories: The Case of Macau. *Compare*, 36 (2): 249–64.

Morrison, K. R. B. (2008) Educational Philosophy and the Challenge of Complexity Theory. *Educational Philosophy and Theory*, 40 (1): 19–34. Reprinted in M. Mason (Ed.) (2008) *Complexity Theory and the Philosophy of Education* (pp. 16–31). Chichester: Wiley-Blackwell.

Morrison, K. R. B. (2009) *Causation in Educational Research*. London: Routledge.

Morrison, K. R. B. (2010) Complexity Theory, School Leadership and Management: Questions for Theory and Practice. *Educational Management, Administration and Leadership*, 38 (3): 374–93.

Morrison, K. R. B. (2013) Interviewing Children in Uncomfortable Settings: Ten Lessons for Effective Practice. *Educational Studies*, 39 (3): 320–37.

Morrison, K. R. B. and Tang, F. H. (2002) Testing to Destruction: A Problem in a Small State. *Assessment in Education*, 9 (3): 298–317.

Morrison, K. R. B. and Ieong, O. N. A. (2007) Does Repeating a Year Improve Performance? The Case of Teaching English. *Educational Studies*, 33 (3): 353–71.

Morrison, K. R. B., Gott, R. and Ashman, T. (1989) A Cascade Model of Curriculum Innovation. *British Journal of In-Service Education*, 15 (3): 159–69.

Moseley, D., Higgins, S., Bramald, R., Hardman, F., Miller, J., Mroz, M., Tse, H., Newton, D., Thompson, I., Williamson, J., Halligan, J., Bramald, S. and Newton, L. (1999) *Ways Forward with ICT: Effective Pedagogy Using Information and Communications Technology for Literacy and Numeracy in Primary Schools*. Durham, UK: University of Newcastle upon Tyne and CEM Centre, University of Durham.

Mulgan, G., with Wilkie, N., Tucker, S., Ali, R., Davis, F. and Liptrot, T. (2006) *Social Silicon Valleys – A Manifesto for Social Innovation: What It Is, Why It Matters, How It Can Be Accelerated*. London: The Young Foundation.

Mumtaz, S. (2000) Factors Affecting Teachers' Use of Information and Communications Technology: A Review of the Literature. *Journal of Information Technology for Teacher Education*, 9 (3): 319–42.

Napoli, R. D. (2004) *What Is Student Centred Learning?* London: Educational Initiative Centre, University of Westminster. Retrieved 14 March 2014 from www.westminster.ac.uk/__data/assets/pdf_file/0004/41782/StudentCentredLearning.pdf.

National Council for Educational Technology (1994) *Technology Works! Stimulate to Educate*. Coventry, UK: National Council for Educational Technology.

Noss, R. and Pachler, N. (1999) The Challenge of New Technologies: Doing Old Things in a New Way, or Doing New Things? In P. Mortimore (Ed.) *Understanding Pedagogy and Its Impact on Learning* (pp. 194–211). London: Paul Chapman Publishing.

OECD (2011) *PISA 2009 Results: Students on Line: Digital Technologies and Performance* (Vol. VI). Paris: OECD.

OECD and Eurostat (2005) *Oslo Manual – Guidelines for Collecting and Interpreting Innovation Data*. Paris: OECD.

Olson, J. L. (2008) *A Literary Review of Engaged Learning and Strategies That Can Be Used in Planning and Implementing Instruction That Engages Students in the Learning Process*. Research paper for the Master of Science Degree in Education. The Graduate School, University of Wisconsin-Stout. Retrieved 29 March 2013 from www2.uwstout.edu/content/lib/thesis/2008/2008olsonj.pdf.

O'Mahony, C. (2003) Getting the Information and Communications Technology Formula Right: Access + Ability = Confident Use. *Technology, Pedagogy and Education*, 12 (2): 295–311.

O'Neill, G. and McMahon, T. (2005) *Student-Centred Learning: What Does it Mean for Students and Lecturers?* Dublin: All Ireland Society for Higher Education (AISHE). Retrieved 2 April 2013 from www.aishe.org/readings/2005-1/oneill-mcmahon-Tues_19th_Oct_SCL.html#XLea2003#XLea2003.

Osberg, K. M. (1997) *Constructivism in Practice: The Case for Meaning-Making in the Virtual World*. PhD dissertation. University of Washington. Retrieved 2 February 2001 from www.hitl.washington.edu/publications/r-97-47/.

Pachler, N. and Byrom, J. (1999) Assessment of and through ICT. In M. Leask and N. Pachler (Eds) *Learning to Teach Using ICT in the Secondary School* (pp. 125–46). London: Routledge.

Paivio, A. (1986) *Mental Representations: A Dual Coding Approach* (Vol. 9). New York: Oxford University Press.

Pankuch, B. (2000) *Why Use Animations and Simulations?* Paper presented at the Summer 2000 Chemistry Conference, Retrieved 3 February 2002 from www.chem.vt.edu/confchem/2000/b/pankuch/uses.htm.

Papert S. (1989) *Constructionism: A New Opportunity for Elementary Science Education.* A Proposal to the National Science Foundation. Cambridge, MA: Massachusetts Institute of Technology, Media Laboratory, Epistemology and Learning Group.

Parellada, R. J. F. (2007) Modeling of Social Organizations: Necessity and Possibility. In F. Capra, A. Juarrero, P. Sotolongo and J. van Uden (Eds) *Reframing Complexity: Perspectives from the North and South* (pp. 151–68). Mansfield, MA: Institute for the Study of Coherence and Emergence Publishing.

Parmenter, L., Lam, C., Seto, F. and Tomita, Y. (2000) Locating Self in the World – Elementary School Children in Japan, Macau and Hong Kong. *Compare*, 30 (2): 133–44.

Parperis, I. (2002) Lifelong Education in Cyprus. In G. Baldacchino and C. J. Farrugia (Eds) *Educational Planning and Management in Small States: Concepts and Experiences* (pp. 269–82). London: Commonwealth Secretariat.

Peak, D. and Frame, M. (1994) *Chaos under Control: The Art and Science of Complexity.* New York: W. H. Freeman.

Perifanou, M. (2010) *Collaborative Blended Learning Methodology (CBLM) ver. 2. WebQuest for HRM project.* European Commission under the Lifelong Learning Programme. Retrieved 2 April 2013 from www.adam-europe.eu/prj/7398/prd/18/1/Methodology_ENG_v2.0_23_10.pdf.

Peters, T. (1989) *Thriving on Chaos.* London: Pan.

Pont, B., Nusche, D. and Moorman, H. (2011) *Improving School Leadership, Volume 1: Policy and practice.* Paris: OECD. Retrieved 29 March 2013 from http://www.schoolleadership.eu/sites/default/files/oecd_pointers_52.pdf.

Prensky, M. (2011) *The Reformers Are Leaving Our Schools in the 20th Century.* Retrieved 30 March 2013 from www.marcprensky.com/writing/+Prensky-The_Reformers_Are_Leaving_Our_Schools_in_the_20th_Century-please_distribute_freely.pdf.

Prensky, M. (2012) *Teaching the Right Stuff.* Retrieved 30 March 2013 from http://marcprensky.com/writing/Prensky-TheRightStuff-EdTech-May-Jun2012.pdf.

Prigogine, L. and Stengers, I. (1985) *Order Out of Chaos.* London: Flamingo.

Programme for International Student Assessment (PISA) (2003) *Database – Pisa 2003. Interactive Data Selection.* Retrieved 10 February 2006 from http://pisa2003.acer.edu.au/interactive.php.

Programme for International Student Assessment (PISA) (2006) *Database – Pisa 2006. Interactive Data Selection.* Retrieved 15 March 2009 from http://pisa2006.acer.edu.au/interactive.php.

Programme for International Student Assessment (PISA) (2009) *Database – Pisa 2009. Interactive Data Selection.* Retrieved 2 January 2012 from http://pisa2009.acer.edu.au/interactive.php.

Puniani, A. S. (2002) Issues in Human Resource Management for Small States: A Tonga Perspective. In G. Baldacchino and C. J. Farrugia (Eds) *Educational Planning and Management in Small States: Concepts and Experiences* (pp. 25–38). London: Commonwealth Secretariat.

Renzulli, J. S. (2003) The Three-ring Conception of Giftedness: Its Implications for Understanding the Nature of Innovation. In L. Shavinina (Ed.) *The International Handbook on Innovation* (first edition) (pp. 79–96). Boston: Elsevier Science.

Robbins, H. and Finley, M. (1998) *Why Change Doesn't Work*. London: Orion Business.

Robinson, B. (2001) Innovation in Open and Distance Learning: Some Lessons from Experience and Research. In F. Lockwood and A. Gooley (Eds) *Innovation in Open and Distance Learning: Successful Development of Online and Web-Based Learning* (pp. 15–26). London: Kogan Page.

Robinson, V., Hohepa, M. and Lloyd, C. (2009) *School Leadership and Student Outcomes: Identifying What Works and Why. Best Evidence Synthesis Programme*. Wellington: New Zealand Ministry of Education.

Roschelle, J. and Teasley, S. D. (1995) The Construction of Shared Knowledge in Collaborative Problem Solving. In C. E. O'Malley (Ed.) *Computer-Supported Collaborative Learning* (pp. 69–197). Berlin: Springer Verlag.

Roschelle, J. M., Pea, R. D., Hoadley, C. M., Gordin, D. N. and Means, B. M. (2000) Changing How and What Children Learn in School with Computer-Based Technologies. *Children and Computer Technology*, 10 (2): 76–101.

Salcedo, A. (2008) Teacher Stress in the Macau Workplace. Unpublished PhD thesis: Macau Inter-University Institute, Macau.

Sandholtz, J. H., Ringstaff, C. and Dwyer, D. C. (1997) *Teaching with Technology: Creating Student-Centered Classrooms*. Teachers College, Columbia: Teachers College Press.

Sang, G.Y., Valcke, M., van Braak, J., Tondeur, J. and Zhu, C. (2011) Predicting ICT Integration into Classroom Teaching in Chinese Primary Schools: Exploring the Complex Interplay of Teacher-Related Variables. *Journal of Computer Assisted Learning*, 27 (2): 160–72.

Santonus, M. (1998) *Simple, yet Complex*. Retrieved 4 May 2001 from www.cio.com/archive/enterprise/041598_qanda_content.html.

Sawyer, R. K. (2005) *Social Emergence: Societies as Complex Systems*. New York: Cambridge University Press.

Scardamalia, M. and Bereiter, C. (1994) Computer Support for Knowledge-Building Communities. *The Journal of the Learning Sciences*, 3 (3): 265–83.

Schein, E. H. (1992) *Organizational Culture and Leadership* (second edition). San Francisco, CA: Jossey Bass.

Schreiber, C. and Carley, K. M. (2006) Leadership Style as an Enabler of Organizational Complex Functioning. *Emergence: Complexity and Organization*, 8 (4): 61–76.

Senge, P. (1990) *The Fifth Discipline: The Art and Practice of the Learning Organization*. London: Century Business.

Senge, P. (2012) Creating the Schools of the Future: Education for a Sustainable Society. *Solutions*, 3 (2): 1–5. Retrieved 2 May 2013 from www.thesolutionsjournal.com.node/1116.

Senge, P., Cambron-McCabe, N., Lucas, T., Smith, B., Dutton, J. and Kleiner, A. (2000) *Schools that Learn*. London: Nicholas Brealey Publishing.

Sergiovanni, T. J. (1998) Leadership as Pedagogy, Capital Development and School Effectiveness. *International Journal of Leadership in Education*, 1 (1): 37–46.

Sharma, R. (2001) *Innovation in Schools: Identifying a Framework for Initiating, Sustaining and Managing Them*. Paper presented at the Eighty-second Annual meeting of the American Educational Research Association, Seattle, USA. Retrieved 20 April 2013 from www.eric.ed.gov/PDFS/ED453598.pdf.

Siggelkow, N. and Rivkin, J. W. (2005) Speed and Search: Designing Organizations for Turbulence and Complexity. *Organization Science*, 16 (2): 101–22.

Siggelkow, N. and Rivkin, J. W. (2006) When Exploration Backfires: Unintended Consequences of Multilevel Organizational Search. *Academy of Management Journal*, 49 (4): 779–96.

Simonson, M., Smaldino, S., Albright, M. and Zvacek, S. (2000) *Teaching and Learning at a Distance: Foundations of Distance Education*. Upper Saddle River, NJ: Prentice-Hall.

Sivin-Kachala, J. (1998) *Report on the Effectiveness of Technology in Schools, 1990–1997*. Washington, DC: Software Publishers Association.

Smeets, E. and Mooij. T. (2001) Pupil-centred Learning, ICT and Teacher Behaviour: Observations in Educational Practice. *British Journal of Educational Technology*, 32 (4): 403–17.

Smith, A. C. T. and Humphries, C. E. (2004) Complexity Theory as a Practical Management Tool: A Critical Evaluation. *Organization Management Journal*, 1 (2): 91–106.

Smith, F. (1971) *Understanding Reading*. New York: Holt, Rinehart and Winston.

Smith, F. (1982) *Writing and the Writer*. London: Heinemann.

Smits, R. (2002) Innovation Studies in the 21st Century: Questions from a User's Perspective. *Technological Forecasting & Social Change*, 69 (9): 861–83.

Solow, D. and Szmerekovsky, J. G. (2006) The Role of Leadership: What Management Science Can Give Back to the Study of Complex Systems. *Emergence: Complexity and Organization*, 8 (4): 52–60.

Sringam, C. and Geer, R. (2000) *An Investigation of an Instrument for Analysis of Student-Led Electronic Discussions* Australian Society for Computers in Learning in Tertiary Education. Retrieved 14 December 2012 from www.ascilite.org.au/conferences/coffs00/papers/chinawong_sringam.pdf.

Stacey, R. D. (1992) *Managing the Unknowable*. San Francisco, CA: Jossey-Bass.

Stacey, R. D. (1995) The Science of Complexity: An Alternative Perspective for Strategic Change Processes. *Strategic Management Journal*, 16 (6): 477–95.

Stacey, R. D. (1996) *Complexity and Creativity in Organizations*. San Francisco, CA: Berrett-Koehler Publishers.

Stacey, R. D. (2000) *Strategic Management and Organisational Dynamics* (third edition). Harlow, England: Pearson Education Limited.

Stacey, R. D. (2001) *Complex Response Processes in Organizations: Learning and Knowledge Creation*. London: Routledge.

Stacey, R. D. (2012) *Tools and Techniques of Leadership and Management: Meeting the Challenge of Complexity*. London: Routledge.

Stacey, R. D., Griffin, D. and Shaw, P. (2000) *Complexity and Management: Fad or Radical Challenge to Systems Thinking?* London: Routledge.

Stake, R. (1967) The Countenance of Educational Evaluation. *Teachers College Record*, 68 (7): 523–46.

Stewart, M. (2001) *The Co-evolving Organization*. Rutland, UK: Decomplexity Associates Ltd. Retrieved 27 August 2001 from www.decomplexity.com/Coevolving%20Organization%20US.pdf.

Stoney, S. and Oliver, R. (1999) Can Higher Order Thinking and Cognitive Engagement be Enhanced with Multimedia? *Interactive Multimedia Electronic*

Journal of Computer-enhanced Learning, 1 (2). Retrieved 2 February 2001 from http://imej.wfu.edu/articles/1999/2/07/printver.asp.

Strobel, J. and van Barneveld, A. (2009) When Is PBL More Effective? A Meta-Synthesis of Meta-Analyses Comparing PBL to Conventional Classrooms. *Interdisciplinary Journal of Problem-based Learning*, 3 (1). Retrieved 30 March 2013 from http://docs.lib.purdue.edu/ijpbl/vol3/iss1/4.

Stufflebeam, D. L. (1971) *Educational Evaluation and Decision Making*. Itasca, IL: F. E. Peacock.

Sun, K., Lin, Y. and Yu, C. (2008) A Study on Learning Effect among Different Learning Styles in a Web-Based Lab of Science for Elementary School Students. *Computers and Education*, 50 (4): 1411–22.

Sundarasaradula, D., Hasan, H., Walker, D. S. and Tobias, A. M. (2005) Self-Organization, Evolutionary and Revolutionary Change in Organizations. *Strategic Change*, 14 (7): 367–80.

Surie, G. and Hazy, J. K. (2006) Generative Leadership: Nurturing Innovation in Complex Systems. *Emergence: Complexity and Organization*, 8 (4): 13–26.

Swieringa, J. and Wierdsma, A. F. M. (1992) *Becoming a Learning Organization: Beyond the Learning Curve*. Wokingham, UK: Addison-Wesley.

Tabar (2013) *What Is Simplexity?* Retrieved 12 January 2013 from www.tabar.com.au/insight/item/35-what-is-simplexity.

Tagiuri, R. (1968) The Concept of Organizational Climate. In R. Tagiuri and G. W. Litwin (Eds) *Organizational Climate: Exploration of a Concept* (pp. 11–32). Boston, MA: Harvard University Graduate School of Business Administration.

Tam, W. M. and Cheng, Y. C. (1996) A Typology of Primary School Environments. *Educational Management and Administration*, 24 (3): 237–52.

Tan, S. C. (2010) Technology Leadership: Lessons from Empirical Research. In C. H. Steel, M. J. Keppell, P. Gerbic and S. Housego (Eds) *Curriculum, Technology & Transformation for an Unknown Future. Proceedings ASCILITE Sydney 2010* (pp. 891–5). Retrieved 20 April 2013 from http://ascilite.org.au/conferences/sydney10/procs/Seng_chee_tan-concise.pdf.

Tang, F. H. and Morrison, K. R. B. (1998) When Marketization Doesn't Work: The Case of Macau. *Compare*, 28 (3): 245–63.

Teddlie, C. and Tashakkori, A. (2009) *Foundations of Mixed Methods Research*. Thousand Oaks, CA: SAGE Publications.

Tetenbaum, T. (1998) Shifting Paradigms: From Newton to Chaos. *Organizational Dynamics*, 26 (4): 21–32.

Thomas, W. (1928) *The Child in America*. New York: Knopf.

Tolmie, A. and Boyle, J. (2000) Factors Influencing the Success of Computer Mediated Communication (CMC) Environments in University Teaching: A Review and Case Study. *Computers and Education*, 34 (2): 119–40.

Towndrow, P. A., Silver, R. E. and Albright, J. (2010) Setting Expectations for Educational Innovations. *Journal of Educational Change*, 11 (4): 425–55.

Tschannen-Moran, M. (2000) Collaboration and the Need for Trust. *Journal of Educational Administration*, 39 (4): 308–31.

Underwood, J. and Brown, J. (Eds) (1997) *Integrated Learning Systems: Potential into Practice*. Oxford: Heinemann.

Valdez, G., McNabb, M., Foertsch, M., Anderson, M., Hawkes, M. and Lenaya R. L. (2000) *Computer-Based Technology and Learning: Evolving Uses and Expectations*.

Washington, DC: North Central Regional Educational Laboratory. Retrieved 2 February 2001 from www.ncrel.org/tplan/cbtl/toc.htm.

Vygotsky, L. S. (1978) *Mind in Society: The Development of Higher Psychological Processes* (M. Cole, Ed.). Cambridge, MA: Harvard University Press.

Vygotsky, L. S. (1981) The Development of Higher Mental Functions. In J. V. Wertsch (Ed.) *The Concept of Activity in Soviet Psychology* (pp. 189–240). New York: Sharpe.

Wagner, T. (2012) *Creating Innovation: The Making of Young People Who Will Change the World*. New York: Simon & Schuster.

Waldrop, M. M. (1992) *Complexity: The Emerging Science at the Edge of Order and Chaos*. Harmondsworth, UK: Penguin.

Watkin, C. (2000) The Leadership Program for Serving Headteachers: Probably the World's Largest Leadership Development Initiative. *Leadership and Organization Development Journal*, 21 (1): 13–19.

Watts, D. J. (2003) *Six Degrees: The Science of a Connected Age*. New York: W. W. Norton and Company.

Webb, M. and Cox, M. (2004) A Review of Pedagogy Related to Information and Communications Technology. *Technology, Pedagogy and Education*, 13 (3): 235–96.

Wegerif, R. (2002) *Thinking Skills, Technology and Learning*. Bristol, UK: Futurelab Report 2.

Weick, K. E. (1976) Educational Organizations as Loosely Coupled Systems. *Administrative Science Quarterly*, 21 (1): 1–19.

Weiner, B. (1992) *Human Motivation: Metaphors, Theories, Research*. Thousand Oaks, CA: SAGE Publications Inc.

Wheatley, M. (1996) The New Science of Leadership: An Interview with Meg Wheatley. *Insight and Outlook: An Interview with Meg Wheatley*. Retrieved 6 February 2010 from www.scottlondon.com/interviews/wheatley.html.

Wheatley, M. (1999) *Leadership and the New Science: Discovering Order in a Chaotic World* (second edition). San Francisco, CA: Berrett-Koehler Publishers.

Wikipedia (2009) Macanese People. Retrieved 3 January 2012 from http://en.wikipedia.org/wiki/Macanese_people.

Winsor, B. (2012) Managing Innovation Under Time Pressure: A Practical Perspective. *Technology Innovation Management Review*, August: 5–9.

Wishart, J. (1990) Cognitive Factors Related to Use Involvement with Computers and Their Effects Upon Learning from an Educational Computer Game. *Computers and Education*, 15 (1–3): 145–50.

Wood, D., Underwood, J. and Avis, P. (1999) Integrated Learning Systems in the Classroom. *Computers and Education*, 33, (2/3): 91–108.

Youngblood, M. (1997) *Life at the Edge of Chaos*. Dallas, TX: Perceval Publishing.

Zandvliet, D. B. and Fraser, B. (2004) Learning Environments in Information and Communications Technology Classrooms. *Technology, Pedagogy and Education*, 13 (1): 97–123.

Index

achievement 51, 74, 76, 84, 86, 107–8, 110, 112, 118, 138–9, 143, 149, 153, 175–83
action plans 206–7, 216
active learning 40–51, 54, 79, 85, 93, 106–7, 131, 132, 138, 143, 145, 147, 153–4, 167, 171, 175, 200
assessment 56–60, 94, 113, 123, 131, 132, 138, 144, 147, 175–83, 184
attitudes 6, 8, 18, 30, 32, 46, 53, 56, 74, 75, 77, 81, 87, 104, 113, 133, 137, 138, 139, 140, 145, 147, 157, 165, 174, 186, 193, 196, 197, 198, 202, 212
Automated 7, 83, 139

behaviour 11, 12, 15, 16, 25, 32, 36, 52, 61, 62, 64, 76, 90, 98, 138, 139, 165, 168, 170, 200, 204, 214, 222
blended learning 36, 46–7, 77, 97

Catholic 65–7, 69, 73
change, and complexity theory *see* complexity theory; and ICT *see* ICT; and pedagogy *see* pedagogy; as learning 37, 72, 223; barriers to *see* resistance; climate for *see* climate; commitment in *see* commitment; definition of 3–9; dimensions of *see* dimensions; evaluation of *see* evaluation; facilitation of *see* facilitation; leadership of *see* leadership; levers of 35, 38, 75–6, 82, 98, 109, 204, 215, 216; management of *see* management; nature of 2, 42, 46, 54, 61, 62, 97, 123, 124, 134, 138, 164–8, 184, 192, 195, 200, 204, 209, 220, 231, 232; pedagogic *see* pedagogy; rate of 10, 33, 77, 87, 120, 150, 205, 219, 232; scale of 41, 62, 64, 64, 74; resistance to *see* resistance; staff development in *see* staff development; support for *see* support; *see also* innovation
collaboration 1, 2, 6, 10–11, 38, 40–51, 79, 82, 84, 93, 102, 106–7, 122, 128, 134, 138–9, 143, 145, 147, 148, 149, 153–4, 167, 171, 175, 200
collegiality 15, 23, 79, 80, 98, 121, 131, 134, 140, 211, 214, 216, 219–20, 231, 232
commitment 13, 16, 17, 18, 20, 23, 24, 37, 44, 97, 120, 121, 122, 124, 125, 128, 129, 130, 135, 140, 142, 146, 150, 160, 170, 193, 198, 205, 208, 213, 214, 220–1, 222
communication 4, 7, 8, 14, 22, 24, 26, 28, 29–30, 36, 43, 54, 63, 77, 81, 84, 93, 105, 110, 111, 118, 121, 128, 132, 138, 143, 151, 154, 155, 165, 187, 198, 216, 226–7
complexity theory 23–31, 130, 131, 195–8, 202–3, 207–8, 214, 227–8, 229, 230
computer *see* ICT, tablet
Concerns Based Action Model (CBAM) 19–21, 203
connectedness 26–7, 195–8, 217
constructivism 38–40
cooperation *see* collaboration
culture 2, 41, 68, *see also* organizational culture
curriculum 2, 6, 7, 13, 32, 36, 46, 49, 53, 54, 74, 76, 80, 81, 82, 84, 86, 93, 96, 99, 131, 134, 139, 197

252 Index

Dalin, P. 10, 21, 22, 31, 204, 205, 223
dimensions 2, 4–11, 30, 32, 41, 61, 78, 103, 117, 127, 128, 138–9, 150, 192, 194, 195, 196, 209, 217, 223, 227, 231, 232
Dominicans 69, 73
DyKnow 7, 83, 98, 102, 138, 139

effect size 3, 12, 51, 55, 143, 144–5, 170, 171, 172–3
e-learning 37, 39, 56, 58
email 37, 82, 108, 112, 171, 173, 174
emergence 23, 24, 25, 26, 29–30, 42, 46, 76, 208, 228
empowerment 93, 102, 193
engaged learning 1, 2, 40–5, 49, 93, 97, 106–7, 127, 130, 138–9, 143, 148, 149, 175, 212
English 69–73, 78, 177–9, 187
Escola São Paulo *see* St. Paul's school
evaluation 78, 83–96, 141–2, 144, 148, 149, 151–2, 156–7, 161, 201–2, 206–7, 226
examinations *see* assessment
experiment 87–9, 96, 201

facilitation 13–14, 15, 17, 18, 21, 22–3, 24, 51, 55, 74, 80, 81, 84, 111, 130, 158, 165, 184, 194, 197, 198, 206, 224 5, 232
feedback 28–9, 56–60, 131, 202–3, 208, 212, 226, 227, 232
Fullan, M. 11, 22, 24, 30, 37–8, 61–2, 100, 136, 139, 141, 161, 163, 210

Hall, G. 13, 18, 19–21, 129, 193–4, 198–9, 203, 211, 219, 232
headteacher *see* leadership
higher order thinking 38–9, 47, 51, 56, 74, 93, 107, 132, 138,
homework 71, 75, 77, 81, 82, 98, 101, 108, 122, 133, 138, 149, 151, 170, 183–4, 190
Hord, S. 13, 18, 19–21, 129, 193–4, 198–9, 203, 211, 232

ICT 1, 2, 6, 7, 10, 18–19, 22–3, 36–63, 77, 78–81, 85, 99, 100–4, 109–10, 112, 123–4, 125–6, 127–31, 133–4, 140–1, 150–1, 154–5, 169, 164, 167, 169, 182–3, 184, 187–8, 192, 193, 198, 209, 215–19, 221–3, 232

implementation dip 100, 136–9, 141, 142, 146, 150, 156–7, 169, 210–11, 214
innovation 2, 10, 19–21, 78–83, 85, 99, 100–4, 109–10, 112, 123–4, 125–6, 127–31, 133–4, 140–1, 150–1, 154–5, 159, 164, 167, 169, 182–3, 184, 187–8, 192, 193, 198, 209, 215–19, 221–3, 232; and complexity theory *see* complexity theory; and ICT *see* ICT; and pedagogy *see* pedagogy; barriers to *see* resistance; climate for *see* climate; commitment in *see* commitment; definition of 3–9; dimensions of *see* dimensions; evaluation of *see* evaluation; facilitation of *see* facilitation; leadership of *see* leadership; levers of 35, 38, 75–6, 82, 98, 109, 204, 215, 216; management of *see* management; nature of 2, 42, 46, 54, 61, 62, 97, 123, 124, 134, 138, 164–8, 184, 192, 195, 200, 204, 209, 220, 231, 232; pedagogic *see* pedagogy; rate of 10, 33, 77, 87, 120, 150, 205, 219, 232; scale of 41, 62, 64, 64, 74; resistance to *see* resistance; staff development in *see* staff development; support for *see* support
Interactive learning *see* active learning, collaboration
Internet 73, 82, 101, 144
Interviews 88, 89–90, 91–2, 94, 99, 141, 153
IT *see* ICT

journals 87–8, 89, 90, 91–2

leadership 8, 10, 11–14, 16–17, 25–6, 30, 38, 41, 60–3, 74, 76–7, 83, 97, 109–10, 116–17, 119–35, 142, 145–6, 150–1, 152–5, 158, 163–5, 167, 192–208, 211–12, 213–14, 219–21, 225, 229–30
learning 31, 36–63, 106; *see also* pedagogy, engaged learning
Lenovo 7, 83, 139
Levels of Use 21, 146, 170, 203, 212, 221

Macau 64–75
Management 6, 7, 12, 19, 20, 22, 24, 28, 70, 73, 82, 99, 112

Mathematics 69–73, 78, 177–9, 187
Mediasite 7, 83, 139
Microsoft 7, 83, 139
mission 12, 78, 79, 120, 124, 157
motivation 43–4, 51–3, 74, 76, 79, 93, 105, 106, 107–8, 122, 131, 138–9, 144, 147, 149, 153, 174, 212, 221

needs analysis 9, 99, 109, 215

organizational climate 7, 14–18, 133, 162, 194, 204–5, 219–20
organizational culture 7, 63, 80, 133, 134, 155, 159, 162, 194, 204–5, 219–20, 232
organizational health 7, 14–18, 220

parents 77, 78, 81, 85, 86, 105, 108–9, 11, 115, 117–19, 122–3, 126, 131, 132, 134, 138, 148–9, 151–3, 154, 160, 162, 114, 183, 187
pedagogy 36–63, 74–7, 79, 80, 83, 84, 86, 1–5, 6, 110–11, 113, 114–15, 123–4, 126, 131, 134, 148, 149, 154, 160, 167, 174–5, 184–5, 188, 195, 199, 205; *see also* active learning, collaboration, engaged learning, ICT
perceptions 22, 68, 88, 89, 98, 99, 110, 116, 125, 127, 142, 159, 162, 198, 202, 220–1, 232
performance 5, 17, 32, 36, 48, 53–4, 70–4, 75, 77, 87, 90, 93, 100, 101, 107–8, 112, 115, 118–19, 136–7, 139, 144, 151, 153, 156, 161, 175–6, 178, 180, 182–3, 197; *see also* achievement
PISA 69–73
power 25, 43, 68, 166, 204, 209; *see also* empowerment
PowerPoint 102, 105, 106, 115, 139, 171
principal *see* leadership
problem solving 11, 32, 42, 47, 51, 55, 74
Programme for International Student Assessment (PISA) *see* PISA

questionnaires 87, 89, 91–2, 111, 141, 171, 189

resistance 8, 21–2, 75, 110, 126, 132, 146, 151, 166, 194, 211, 216, 222, 224–5

sampling 94–5
scalability 228–32
self–organization 23–31, 131, 165, 197, 199, 200, 207, 211, 228
senior managers 7, 25, 119–20, 133, 134, 153–6, 163
simplexity 30, 38, 98, 130, 220
St Paul's school vii, 64, 73–82
staff development 121–2, 125, 131, 138, 149, 151, 167, 182, 205, 223–4, 231
Stages of Concern (SoC) 6, 19–21, 129, 174, 203, 212, 221
student-centred learning 28, 35, 40–5, 54–5, 74, 80–1, 124, 138–9, 149, 153, 167, 200
students 81, 104–10, 113, 122, 126, 142–6, 157–8, 159, 174, 180–1
support 11, 12, 15–16, 17, 18, 21, 22, 23, 40, 47, 58, 60, 78–80, 86, 117–18, 126, 142, 147, 158, 192, 205–4, 211–13, 216, 220, 222, 223–4, 229, 230, 232
survey 87, 90, 91–2, 94, 141, 171

tablet 82–3, 86, 98, 101–2, 108, 114, 117, 134, 147, 149, 151, 157, 182, 191
teachers 46–8, 58–9, 81, 85, 102, 108, 110–17, 132, 140, 146–51, 154, 158, 160, 182–3, 203–4, 212
teaching *see* pedagogy

U-curve of innovation 136–7, 142, 146, 150, 156–7, 199, 210–11, 214

video 83, 98, 112, 118, 156, 185–6
vision 14, 16, 17, 60, 120, 124, 129, 155, 158, 161, 192, 193, 200, 213, 214, 230
Vygotsky, L. 38–9, 95

workload 22, 103, 113, 116, 122, 132, 139, 150, 153, 160, 162, 167, 183, 203–4, 216, 224, 228

For Product Safety Concerns and Information please contact our EU
representative GPSR@taylorandfrancis.com
Taylor & Francis Verlag GmbH, Kaufingerstraße 24, 80331 München, Germany

www.ingramcontent.com/pod-product-compliance
Lightning Source LLC
Chambersburg PA
CBHW050628300426
44112CB00012B/1710